Architectural Guide
Phnom Penh

Architectural Guide
Phnom Penh

Moritz Henning/Walter Koditek

DOM
publishers

Contents

Introduction

Moritz Henning / Walter Koditek

When we arrived in Phnom Penh for the first time in 2007, we were struck by the 'otherness' of the urban landscape compared to neighbouring capitals in Southeast Asia. The compact, low-rise city had a rather laid back pace, and it was relatively easy to navigate on foot, by motorbike, or by tuk-tuk. The city, with its authentic charm and its unique architecture and history, had a profound impact on us. So when more than 10 years later, after some pleasant work stays within the country and numerous visits, the opportunity came to write and publish this architectural guide, we couldn't resist.

However, we soon discovered that information on individual buildings was often scarce, if available at all. And so we roamed the streets and back alleys to discover lesser-known historical buildings and hidden places. At the same time, we conducted background research to learn about their stories, which was no less rewarding. Personal conversations often revealed important pieces of information and anecdotes.

In fact, the most rewarding moments of research brought us closer to the city's recent contemporary architecture. We learned about a small but impressive group of local architects who had been able to realise their ambitious projects in an increasingly diversifying market throughout the last years.

This guide presents 141 buildings from all periods of the city's urban history. Phnom

Penh was founded in the 15th century, planned and rebuilt by the French, and then modernised and expanded during the period after Cambodia's independence and prior to Lon Nol's rise to power. As such, the city displays a vast mix of styles and can be seen as a 'layered cake' of urban history. The city has inherited a rich and diverse body of architecture, embodying the last 150 years of the country's urban past. Early religious pagodas and temples, French colonial buildings from the late-nineteenth to mid-nineteenth centuries, and modernist 'New Khmer Architecture' from the 1960s coexist side by side. The city's current built environment is then rounded off by a layer of seemingly unplanned structures that have been built since the 1990s along with mushrooming high-rises and *borey* developments of recent years.

Writing a guide on a city undergoing rapid change inherently comes with a number of risks. Inevitably, some of the information will become out of date, some buildings will disappear, and new ones will arise. The book is intended neither as a complete inventory of the city's architectural heritage, nor as a comprehensive travel guide for the most discerning visitor. But whether you are a resident of Phnom Penh or a tourist with a limited amount of time at hand, we hope you will find this guide an exciting and helpful resource for exploring the intriguing built environment of this fast-changing city.

The Four Faces of Phnom Penh:
A Short History of the City

A. Portail's 'Plan de Phnom Penh', 1920s

The early settlement: Phnom Penh's beginning from the 15th century

It is somewhat uncertain when humans first settled in what is today Phnom Penh. The founding myth of *Daun Penh*, or 'Grandmother Penh', dates back to the late-fourteenth century (see **Wat Phnom 001 A**). This, together with the remaining structures in the surrounding area, among them the ancient *prasat* at Wat Ounalom, makes it seem plausible that an Angkorian or even pre-Angkorian foundation in the Phnom area coexisted with villages on the Mekong riverbank. By the early fifteenth century, the site of modern Phnom Penh was home to a small but growing commercial settlement, stretched along the river. This settlement was likely created as a means for Cambodia to trade with China and thus maintain its prosperity. From Phnom Penh, merchant ships were able to sail down the Mekong to the South China Sea and begin the long journey to China. The location also made it possible to access other parts of the kingdom and present-day Laos by river.

Phnom Penh is situated at a strategic location, at the confluence of the Mekong and its tributary, the Tonle Sap River. The original settlement first became known as Chatomuk (alternatively spelt Chaktomuk), meaning 'Place of the Four Faces', possibly in reference to the four-faced towers of Angkor Thom. The French referred to the conjuncture of the rivers as the Quatre-Bras, meaning the 'Four Arms', a name that recalls the original Cambodian name. The settlement did not acquire its modern name until after the Cambodian court, led by King Ponhea Yat (reign: 1431–1463), left Angkor to settle at the site of modern Phnom Penh. According to the Cambodian Royal Chronicles, Phnom Penh was founded after the sacking of Angkor Thom in 1431, which took place after centuries of attacks from the emerging Siamese (Thai) principalities on Cambodia's western frontier.

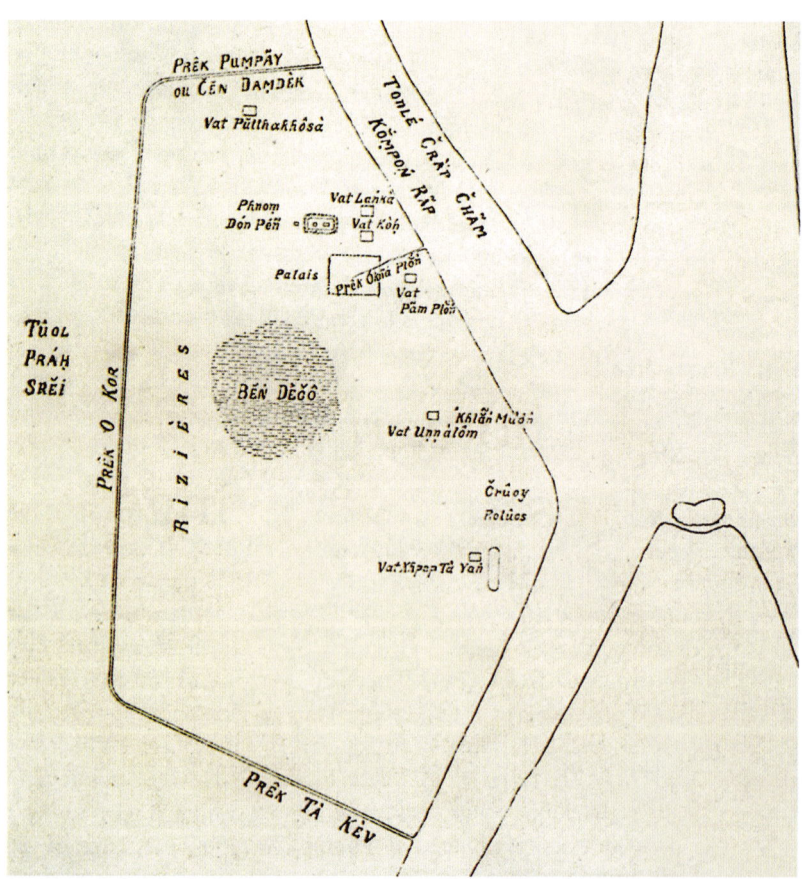

Phnom Penh in the 15th century. Sketch by George Cœdès, 1913

In 1913, the French scholar Georges Cœdès (1886–1969) drew the map *Phnom Penh in the Fifteenth Century* based on the locations named in the Cambodian Royal Chronicles. This map is essentially the only cartographic record of the city as it was before the arrival of the French in the nineteenth century. According to Cœdès, King Ponhea Yat's palace was situated in the upstream section of the city, just southeast of the Phnom. It faced the river and was surrounded by a protective wall. Two temples were located to the north of the palace and one to the east. In the fifteenth century, a covered canal was used to feed the palace moat and provide water to the population. King Ponhea Yat initiated the first programme of drainage works, which proved indispensable for urbanising the plains. This programme entailed filling in the flood-prone areas and organising a drainage system with protective ditches. The whole city was surrounded by an earthen embankment and three straight channels (*prek*). This was based on the traditional Angkorian urban-planning model, which was considered to give a city its ideal surface area by defining its limits. Within the bounded area, almost all buildings were located near the river, while marshy areas were used to cultivate rice. Ponhea Yat's settlement corresponds roughly to today's historic city centre of Phnom Penh, an area confined by the Tonle Sap River, Sihanouk Boulevard to the south, Monivong Boulevard to the west, and the road leading across the Japanese Friendship Bridge in the north. (Interestingly, the contours of modern Phnom Penh's core area were laid down well before the French persuaded King Norodom, in 1865, to move the capital from Oudong to Phnom Penh.) The first period in which Phnom Penh was the country's capital only lasted 30 years. The threat of Siamese or Vietnamese invasion forced the court to move the capital to Longvek (or Lovek), and then to the more defensible site of Oudong, after Longvek was stormed by the Siamese in 1594. Although Phnom Penh was no longer the capital of the country, it further developed into a cosmopolitan trading port in the following centuries, with ethnic

Chinese, Malay, Annamite (Vietnamese), Siamese (Thai), Laotian, and Indian residents. It was also visited by a stream of European missionaries and merchants. According to written accounts of Portuguese and Spanish missionaries, the population of Phnom Penh at the end of the sixteenth century was estimated at 20,000, including 3,000 Chinese and 1,500 Buddhist monks.

Siamese and Vietnamese dominance over the Khmer Empire intensified during the seventeenth and eighteenth centuries, resulting in frequent displacements of the Cambodian court. The capital did not return to Phnom Penh until the early nineteenth century, after Vietnamese and Siamese forces had briefly invaded Cambodia in 1811. In 1813, King Ang Chan (reign: 1806–1934) had a new royal residence built to the south of Wat Ounalom, roughly where today's Royal Palace stands. The Vietnamese predominantly held political influence in the region in the following decades, even holding a garrison opposite the Phnom upstream from the palace, until the Siamese invaded and set fire to Phnom Penh. In 1848, the Cambodian capital was once again relocated to Oudong following a co-suzerainty treaty between Siam and Vietnam. To save Cambodia from being divided and annexed by Vietnam and Siam, King Ang Duong (reign: 1841–1860) agreed to France's offer of colonial protection. This agreement took effect when Ang Duong's son, King Norodom (reign: 1860–1904), signed and officially recognised the French Protectorate on 11 August 1863. This agreement would dominate the subsequent 90 years of Cambodian history. Crowned in Oudong in 1860, King Norodom moved the capital back to Phnom Penh in 1866 at the instigation of the French.

The planned city: Phnom Penh under the French Protectorate (1863–1953)

Under the French Protectorate, Phnom Penh was once again chosen to become the capital and centre of royal power in 1865. And by the end of 1866, the foundation of the new Royal Palace was completed on its present-day site. The young King Norodom (reign: 1860–1904) saw Phnom Penh as an ideal site that could serve as an efficient trading hub and offer protection against Siamese invasions. At the time, Phnom Penh was essentially a small town consisting of thatched huts built on stilts, situated on the dike between the river in the east and the annually flooded plain in the west. A single road, later named Grand Rue, ran from the north to the south. As can be seen in Delaporte's drawing of 1873, travellers arriving in Phnom Penh by boat from Saigon discovered a 'city on water' with the Phnom towering behind. The city had a population of almost 10,000 and was a rather cosmopolitan town with numerous foreign inhabitants. Henri Mouhot tellingly described it as the 'big bazaar of Cambodia' during his visit in 1861.

Until the late 1880s, only a limited amount of land was suitable for construction due to the topographical conditions on the floodplains. Moreover, the royal monopoly on land ownership proved a hindrance to development. Although Norodom granted some land to France as part of concessions, the kingdom lacked the financial resources and technical expertise to carry out systematic town planning. The French were focusing their resources on Cochinchina, and the young and understaffed colonial administration in the new protectorate's capital was not yet ready to commence large-scale construction.

Four distinct spatial divisions, called 'quartiers' by the French and 'villages' (*phum*) by the Cambodians, emerged between 1866 and 1890. In the north, the king granted land to the Catholic Annamite community, thus forming the Catholic Village. The French first settled on higher terrain to the east and south of the Phnom, concentrating their administrative offices and residences inside the areas allocated to them through land concessions. The Khmer communities lived further south, around the Royal Palace and Wat Ounalom, in the Cambodian Village. The sizeable Chinese community occupied the commercial district around the market in the centre of the capital. In response to the rapid population growth, and in order to generate fiscal revenues, King Norodom hired the French contractor Paul Le Faucheur in 1872 to construct 300 Chinese masonry shophouses, known as 'compartiments chinois', thus launching the first wave of shophouse construction. By 1875, the city's population had increased to 30,000, and the urban landscape had completely transformed. The creation of the Phnom Penh municipality in 1884

13 _ Phnom-Penh _ Les bureaux de la Résidence Supérieure .

SEK

CAP SAINT-JACQUES. - PNOM-PENH. - Vue du Canal

Collection Cauvin, Cap Saint-Jacques

provided the administrative framework and financial means for systematic urban management. A new system of land ownership was introduced to Cambodia, which allowed the Protectorate to control the buying, selling, and renting of property in the urban area from this time onwards. This system also introduced to Cambodia the concept of streets as public space and established a cadastre for private property. In 1890, the new French administrator, Huyn de Verneville, initiated major development, sanitation, and beautification projects for the city with the support of the king. De Verneville oversaw the drainage of the plain, which entailed excavating a canal around the French District (completed in 1894) and filling in the various *boeung* (ponds) with earth. He also ordered the widening of the Grand Rue and the building of new roads and bridges. And he continued the expansion of the Grand Dyke and the construction of the docks. He refurbished Wat Phnom, surrounding it with a public garden, and opened today's Norodom Boulevard as a link between the ethnic districts. The early-modern urbanisation of Phnom Penh during that period owes much to the architect and town planner Daniel Fabré (1850–1904), who designed the buildings of the Post Office and Treasury, designed the Naga Bridge, and oversaw the upgrading of the Wat Phnom. Amenities for the general public also gradually improved. A water system,

a sewage disposal system, electric power, and street lighting were introduced between 1895 and 1901. Schools were reformed to meet the French need to train future Cambodian civil servants. Under De Verneville, the population of Phnom Penh increased from between 25,000 and 30,000 to around 50,000 in 1897.

In 1904, King Sisowath (reign: 1904–1927) succeeded King Norodom and introduced a new era of city expansion. The modernisation and transformation of Phnom Penh continued in the early twentieth century, with French engineers drawing plans for roads and buildings based on methods established in France. Between 1890 and 1930, the architectural vocabularies of the major public buildings oscillated between imported neo-classical forms and elements of traditional Khmer architecture. The latter was sometimes reinterpreted, as in the exceptional case of the National Museum. Public buildings were designed with consideration for their adjacent open spaces in attempt to enhance the architectural effects and institutional character of those buildings. This is most obvious in the layout of the Place de la Poste and along the quays of the canal. The standardised streets were designed according to the Haussmann model: the streets were given sidewalks and were lined by trees and candelabra streetlights.

The Protectorate city was still divided into three large districts, based on the

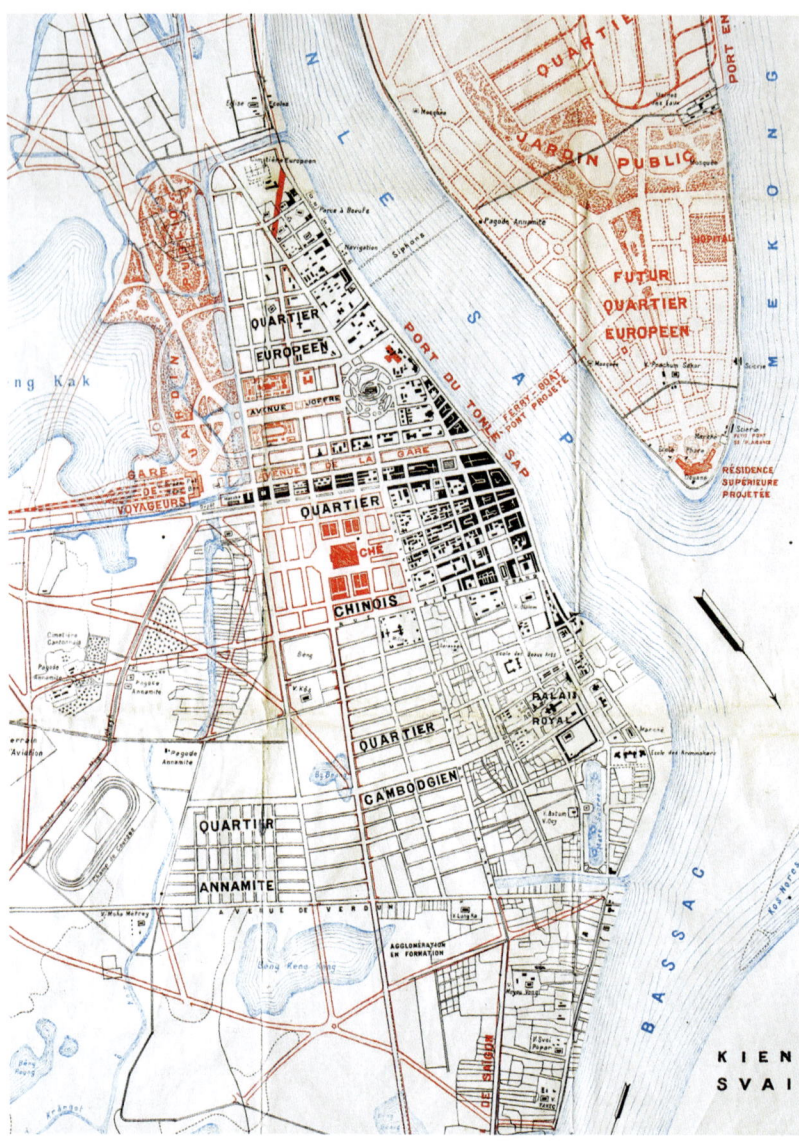

Plan d'Extension de la Ville de Phnom Penh, Ernest Hébrard, 1925

older ethnic divisions, with three different functions as well as populations. The European District, to the north and around the Phnom, was bordered by the canal, and it housed the administrative functions of the Protectorate. Further south, around the central market, was the Chinese District, centred on the commercial activities around the market. It was delimited to the north by the canal and to the south by the royal funeral ground (*veal men*). The Cambodian District lay around the Royal Palace to the south. In addition to this main layout, there was a Vietnamese District to the west of the Cambodian one, and the old Catholic District (mainly occupied by Vietnamese residents) to the north of the European District. Strikingly, this physical segregation in the central part of Phnom Penh would remain almost unchanged until 1975.

France began to pay greater attention to the cities of its colonies and protectorates. In 1921, the architect and urban planner Ernest Hébrard (1875–1933) was sent to Indochina to establish the Indochina Architecture and Town Planning Service (Service d'Architecture et d'Urbanisme en Indochine), with the mission of devising urban development plans for the colonies. The French architects and engineers saw the cities of Indochina as an ideal playground for experimentation. Based on thorough analysis of the terrain, Hébrard designed a comprehensive plan, the Plan d'Extension de la Ville de Phnom Penh, published in 1925. The existing town and the rural areas around it were integrated into a single urban masterplan with a robust road system and defined hierarchy of urban spaces. The buildings and trees were aligned along the roads. The plan envisioned three separate extension projects towards the west, while keeping the physical characteristics of the three existing districts unchanged. A network of new main boulevards and public parks would complete and integrate the existing network, and new concentric dykes west of these districts would link the north of the town to the south.

Phnom Penh underwent significant expansion between the First World War and the late 1930s. Daun Penh Street and Christopher Howes Street (at the time Avenue Maréchal Foch) were created in the 1920s to connect the Phnom to the future cathedral. The esplanade (along with its public gardens), the Hotel le Royal, the Sports Club, and the National Library and Archives were all constructed at once. And these structures together established a new area for culture and recreation. The former interior canal, dug by De Verneville, was completely filled in the early 1930s. The resulting space was used to create another esplanade between the

PNOM-PENH — *Hôtel de la Résidence*

Tonle Sap and the Railway Station, which thus closed the gap between the French and Chinese Districts. Numerous *boeung* (swampy areas that formed lakes during the rainy season) were filled in, among them Boeung Decho, which had to be removed to carry out the extension of the Chinese District. Here, a network of roads, featuring a water supply and drainage system, and an electricity network were built, based on Hébrard's plan, as was the new Central Market, with Chinese shophouses surrounding it. Only Hébrard's plans for the Chrouy Changvar peninsula were never implemented.

Japan controlled the region during the Second World War, before the French reclaimed it again, between 1947 and 1953, during which time they did not have the means to continue their urban programme for Phnom Penh. The city's population fluctuated between more than 100,000 in 1939 and around 360,000 at the end of the Protectorate. Phnom Penh's cityscape remained relatively unchanged between 1940 and 1953.

PNOM-PENH — *Une des rues de Pnom-Penh*

Map of Phnom Penh, 1966

Phnom Penh after 1953: The modern capital of an independent nation

After 90 years of French colonial rule, interrupted only by the brief intermezzo of Japanese occupation in the 1940s, Cambodia finally gained independence in 1953. Two years later, King Norodom Sihanouk, who led the 'Royal crusade for independence', abdicated as king – and was succeeded by his father – in order to launch his political career. He founded the party-like organisation Sangkum Reastr Niyum and won the 1955 general elections with an overwhelming 83 per cent of the votes. The Sangkum, which can be translated only very roughly as 'People's Socialist Community', was tailored specifically to Sihanouk's role as paternal head of state with a royal background. It proclaimed the vague idea of a 'Royal Buddhist Socialism', which combined a rather unique take on socialism with conservative social values, monarchism, nationalism, and the teachings of Theravada Buddhism.

Sihanouk embarked on an unprecedented path towards modernising the country in the following years. Cambodia had too few schools, no universities, no deep-sea port, no international flight connections, no industries, and only a rudimentary railway network at the time of independence. But within a few years, it had built ministry buildings, sport facilities, commercial buildings, market halls, schools, and cultural buildings. A deep-sea port was established in Sihanoukville, and Pochentong Airport was expanded. Cambodia signed economic agreements with China, Russia, the US, and France, which led to a large number of construction projects. The injection of foreign money made it possible to found universities, hospitals, and even industrial companies. These aid funds accounted for over a third of the country's budget at the beginning of the 1960s. Over 50 per cent of the payments came from the US, 23 per cent from China, and 17 per cent from France.

This modernisation drive came hand in hand with a commitment to an architectural language that seemed appropriate for the young emerging country. The new Cambodia was built in a style blending western modernism with Khmer traditions, aptly named by Helen Grant Ross and Darryl Collins as the 'New Khmer Architecture'. A decisive step in this development was the appointment of Vann Molyvann (see p. 280), who had just returned from his studies in Paris, as Chief Architect of the Kingdom in 1957.

Independence Boulevard towards the west, 1960s

Monivong Boulevard towards the south, 1960s

Gradually, other Cambodian students completed their studies abroad. **Lu Ban Hap** (see p. 188) returned from Paris in 1960 as the country's second trained architect, and was immediately entrusted with setting up the Service Municipal de l'Urbanisme et d'Habitat, the urban planning and housing department of the city of Phnom Penh. Mam Sophana, who studied at Miami University, Ohio, returned in 1965, and other graduates followed suit. The phenomenal development of the country and its capital as well as Vann Molyvann's achievements are inextricably tied to the names of a number of foreign experts. Vladimir Bodiansky, a Russian-born engineer who worked with Le Corbusier on the Unité d'Habitation in Marseille and with Candilis and Woods at ATBAT-Afrique in the 1950s, began to work for the UN in Cambodia in 1961. Gérald Hanning, who worked with Le Corbusier on the Modulor, was technical consultant for the UN in Cambodia from 1959 to 1965. There were also a number of French architects and engineers who remained in the country. The Japanese researcher Masaaki Iwamoto has recently described the involvement of Japanese architects, engineers, and construction companies in some of the capital's important constructions. And last but not least, Chinese, Vietnamese, and Soviet architects and engineers carried out planning projects in Cambodia.

The epicentre of these developments was Phnom Penh, which became the scene of a tremendous transformation process. As Christian Goulin wrote in 1965, the city transitioned from 'a colonial warehouse to ... a state capital'. In those early days, the country was still suffering from the legacy of the Protectorate. Until 1953, Cambodia had been administered from Hanoi, but after independence, the former administrative structures disappeared and had to be rebuilt. These initial difficulties were also reflected in the city's population growth, or lack thereof. Phnom Penh barely grew between 1950 and 1958 – increasing from 344,000 to 355,00 inhabitants, according to the official census. But by 1962, the population had reached 400,000, and by the end of 1960s, around 900,000. Major infrastructure programmes, such as the construction of the airport and the road to Sihanoukville, shaped the city's development in the first years after independence. The establishment of banks (such as the Banque Nationale du Cambodge), the growing number of industries tailored to local needs, and the shipyards on the banks of the Tonle Bassac were also important steps in the city's development. Newly created modern amenities included a new factory for purifying drinking water and a hydroelectric power plant.

The 1960s were marked by the construction of state institutions (such as the Ministry of Finance and the Ministry of Defence), hospitals (such as the Khmer-Soviet Friendship Hospital), and market buildings, which became the centres of new districts. New university buildings, in particular the large campus on Russian Federation Boulevard, pushed urbanisation towards the west and became architectural representations of the country's ambitions. The state invested huge sums (around 50 per cent of the total) in its industries, ensuring further growth. The most spectacular development project took place on newly reclaimed land on the banks of the Bassac River. The Front du Bassac, or Cité Sihanouk, planned by an international team under Vann Molyvann, was uncompromisingly modern in a city that till then had consisted almost exclusively of villas and building blocks. The new Cambodia was seeking a new urban form, and the quarter was one of the flagships of Sihanouk's vision of a country rising from its colonial past. In completing the Preah Suramarit Theatre and the Olympic Village Apartments, Vann Molyvann created masterpieces of Khmer Modernism.

The National Bank of Cambodia in the 1950s (destroyed by the Khmer Rouge)

**Housing at the Front du Bassac: Olympic Village Apartments (l, Vann Molyvann),
National Bank Apartments (m, Henry Chatel), Municipal Apartments (r, Lu Ban Hap)**

Lu Ban Hap and Vladimir Bodiansky designed the famous White Building, a low-cost apartment complex modelled after a project by ATBAT for North Africa. Unfortunately, this architectural heritage was destroyed in recent years. As such, the former National Bank Apartments and the small Sangkum Reastr Niyum Exhibition Hall are the only surviving remains of Sihanouk's vision.

The situation changed abruptly in 1970. Sihanouk had already broken relations with the US in 1963, and the subsequent loss of aid payments tore a huge hole in the state's budget. Dissatisfaction spread in the military, which had been beneficiary of a considerable part of those donations. The bloated bureaucracy wasn't able to maintain order among its civil servants, corruption was far from being eradicated, and the many university graduates struggled to find suitable jobs. Last but not least, the effects of the Vietnam War were increasingly felt in the country. Vann Molyvann wrote in 2003: 'By the end of the 1960s, all the structures were in place for Phnom Penh to become the great capital of a clearly developing country.' But the city's successful development had no effect on the political situation. During Sihanouk's stay abroad in March 1970, prime minister Lon Nol seized power. Many, including Vann

Molyvann, left the country soon thereafter. Cambodia gradually descended into chaos. The Vietnam War raged at the borders and in the country itself, as Lon Nol abandoned Sihanouk's policy of neutrality. The emerging civil war drove the rural population into the arms of the Khmer Rouge – and into the capital. By 1975, the city's population had doubled to two million people, most of the newcomers living in straw huts that sprawled across the parks and boulevards. The transport of building materials to Phnom Penh became increasingly impossible due to the civil war, and construction activities virtually came to a standstill. On 17 April 1975, the Khmer Rouge invaded Phnom Penh and forced two million inhabitants to leave the city. Phnom Penh turned into a ghost town for years to come.

The riverbanks with the Royal Floating House, 1960s

Phnom Penh today: A booming metropolis under transformation

In late December 1978, Vietnamese forces launched a full invasion of Cambodia, capturing Phnom Penh on 7 January 1979 and driving the remnants of Pol Pot's Khmer Rouge forces into the jungle towards Thailand. On 10 January 1979, the new People's Republic of Kampuchea (PRK) was established with Heng Samrin as head of state. Following the fall of the Khmer Rouge regime, the city's population rapidly increased. An estimated 100,000 people had settled in Phnom Penh by the end of 1979, and the number dramatically increased to 427,000 in 1985 and 615,000 in 1990. As the majority of the former residents had died under the Khmer Rouge, the new inhabitants mostly came from a rural background and brought their 'provincial' way of life to the city, while taking over empty buildings and abandoned plots. Between 1979 and 1989, the Cambodian–Vietnamese administration focused on the reconstruction of basic infrastructure and services. The city gradually became functional again, despite the economic and political austerity of this decade.

In 1991, the Paris Peace Agreements saw the stationing of a UN peacekeeping mission, the United Nations Transitional Authority in Cambodia (UNTAC), followed by the organisation of a free general election in 1993. Private property ownership was reintroduced in 1989 and public companies began to be privatised, a process that accelerated in the early 1990s. The new constitution adopted in 1993 introduced a market economy, and multiple laws and macroeconomic reforms improved the conditions for local and foreign investors. In 1999, Cambodia joined the ASEAN (Association of Southeast Asian Nations), and in 2004, the WTO (World Trade Organization). These changes had a dramatic effect on the city of Phnom Penh,

Phnom Penh in 1983/1984

as they sparked a massive influx of rural migrants and rapid growth of speculative investment, mostly from foreign sources. The census of 1998 listed the total population of Phnom Penh as 998,804 inhabitants (1,133,430 for present-day territory), while the 2008 census listed 1,501,725 inhabitants (present-day territory).

The last ten years have seen unprecedented growth in Cambodia's capital. Following Cambodia's recovery from the financial crisis of 2008 and subsequent economic development, Phnom Penh has become a real-estate hotspot among Chinese and other Asian investors looking to buy a property without the tedious regulations or instability affecting most neighbouring countries in the region. Consistent economic growth (average annual growth rate of around seven per cent since 1995) and a growing middle class have drawn big international brands in retail, hospitality, and real estate, providing fertile ground for developers looking to tap into

a new wealthier class of urbanites. Recent years have seen much of the money flow into high-end condominium towers in the inner city, which have dramatically changed the city's skyline and put thousands of units on the market, while often adding further strain on already limited infrastructure services and traffic congestion. At the same time, foreign direct investment has led to large-scale private housing and commercial real-estate developments in the peri-urban areas, much of it aimed at the growing middle class and high-end clientele. In 2010, 20 communes from the surrounding Kandal province were integrated into the city, which meant the municipality almost doubled in land area from 376.17 km^2 to 678.47 km^2. This rapid growth, however, has been largely unplanned, resulting in an increasingly sprawling urban landscape as well as growing traffic and congestion. Though various plans related to urban development exist, often promoted by multi- and bilateral donors, the implementation of these plans and enforcement of regulations still remain weak, leaving much room for informality and haphazard development.

As has happened earlier in other countries in the region, rapid urbanisation and modernisation in Cambodia have exerted ever-greater pressure on the built heritage. Speculative land prices have by far outstripped the value of buildings and easily encourage heritage owners to sell their properties and developers to replace them in pursuit of quick returns. Wooden architecture has all but disappeared, French colonial architecture is being demolished to make way for new construction, and architectural masterpieces of the post-independence New Khmer Architecture have been sacrificed. Although an institutional and legal framework for heritage conservation was developed in the early 1990s, and a comprehensive inventory of the city's architectural structures, complexes, and sites is available, an overall heritage policy was never established.

This does not mean that urban heritage is not an issue in Phnom Penh's contemporary development. The authors Adèle Esposito and Gabriel Fauveaud call this phenomenon the 'atomization of heritage politics', referring to the proliferation of conservation practices, driven by specific individual objectives.

With the support of French funding and expertise, the city has carried out rehabilitation projects for public buildings such as the National Museum and the Central Market. Other buildings and objects were targeted by conservation projects entirely sponsored by national funds, including the Royal Palace and iconic public spaces such as the park around Wat Phnom and the esplanade in front of the Independence Monument. Private initiatives rehabilitated numerous historic buildings in the old city centre for use as hotels, restaurants, or retail stores. These 'good practices' set important examples on how to strike a balance between viable economic interests and heritage preservation in times when the destruction of heritages sites is often overlooked or written off as 'collateral damage' of development.

The most recent population projection (conducted for the JICA Urban Transport Master Plan) forecasts that Phnom Penh's population will reach 2.86 million by 2035, growing by an estimated 50,000 people each year. If this trend continues unabated, it is to be dreaded that the landmarks that used to characterise the city's unique historic urban landscape – such as the pagoda towers and *chedey* spires of Wat Phnom or the Royal Palace – will soon be overshadowed by the mushrooming high-rises all over the city. The 'layered cake' of buildings and ensembles dating from major periods in Phnom Penh's history still gives tangible evidence of the diverse cultural, religious, and social activities that took place in the past and which remain an integral part of the nation's history and collective cultural identity. In Phnom Penh, as an urban environment undergoing rapid transformation, maintaining the delicate balance between economic development and heritage preservation will continue to be a major struggle. Short-sighted 'hit and run' investment and 'laissez faire' city planning might be the greatest threat to the architectural heritage and unique character of Phnom Penh.

However, along with the rapid growth of the kingdom's construction industry, the use of architectural services has also increased, and even local architects are currently facing a growing market. With stronger competition in the market, developers also seem to have matured and are coming up with more quality-driven concepts in order to make their projects stand out. Ten years ago, eclectic cookie-cutter designs and generic utilitarian 'boxes' abounded, with exceptional buildings only rarely constructed, mostly in the hospitality sector, and most often by foreign architects. Now, there is a new generation of young Cambodian professionals at work, though still limited in number. Seeing the diversity and ingenuity of some of their recently finished buildings, one can be cautiously optimistic that there might be a 'new wave' of high-quality contemporary Cambodian architecture that references both the local history and context.

Around Wat Phnom

Interview: Ivan Tizianel

The area around Wat Phnom, the founding site of Phnom Penh, bears witness to the early urbanisation of the city. Some of the most well-preserved French colonial buildings can be found surrounding the Post Office Square in the former European District, and the majority of the past administrative and cultural institutions of the French Protectorate still line the wide boulevards nearby. A stroll further north offers an insight into the multicultural (religious) heritage of the city with Chinese temples, early Buddhist pagoda architecture, and the remnants of a Catholic settlement.

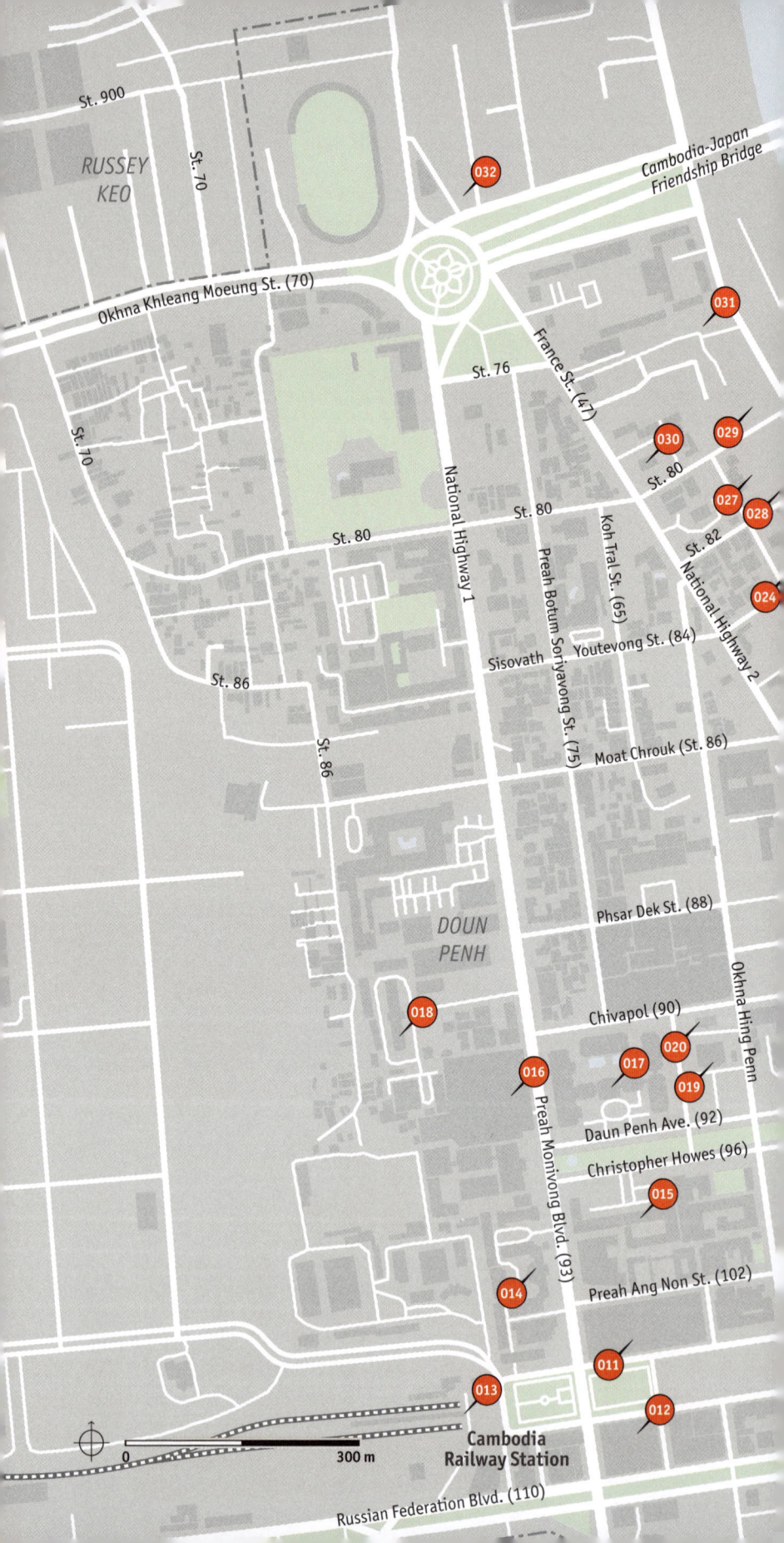

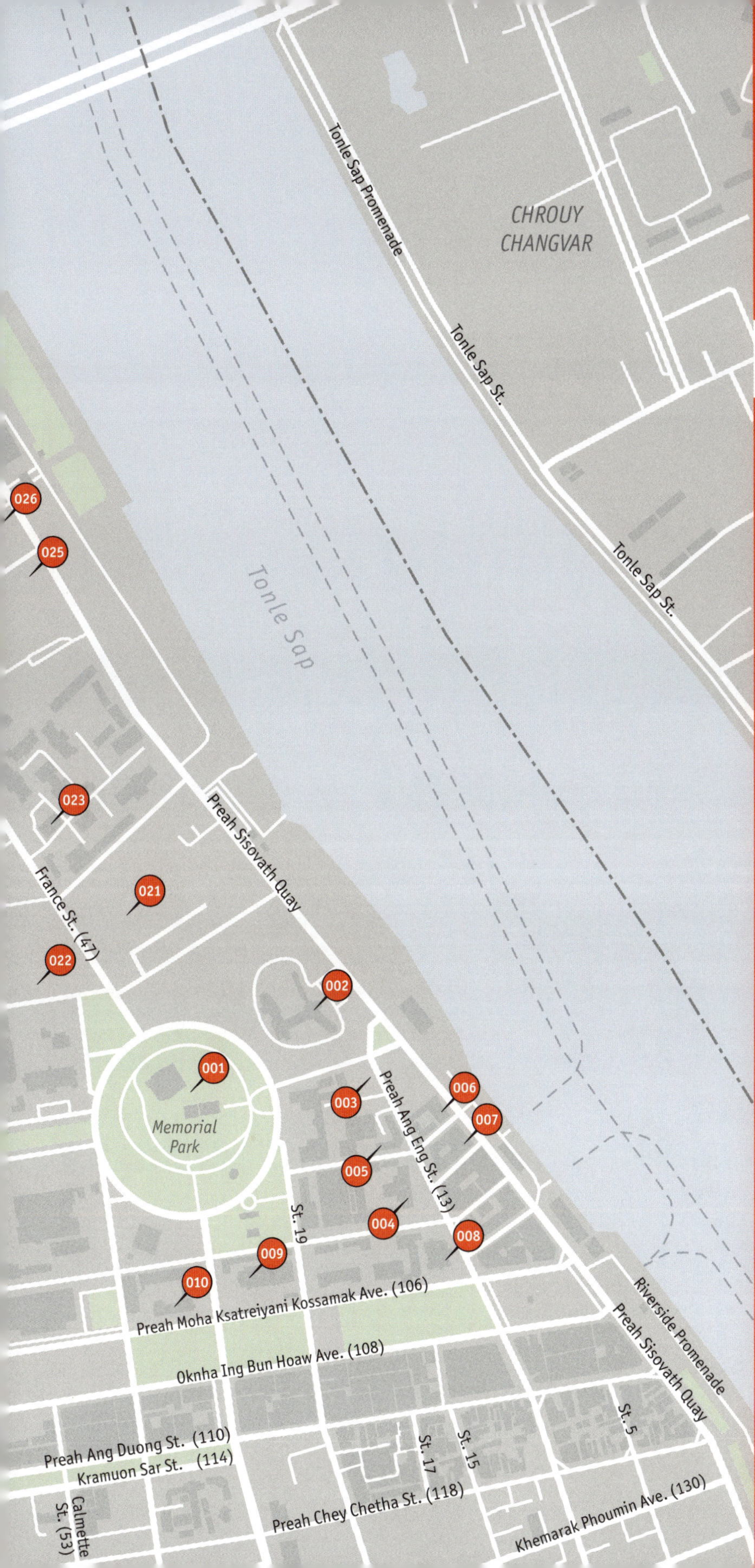

CHROUY CHANGVAR

Tonle Sap Promenade

Tonle Sap St.

Tonle Sap St.

Tonle Sap

026

025

023

France St. (47)

021

022

Preah Sisovath Quay

002

001

Memorial Park

003

006

007

Preah Ang Eng St. (13)

005

004

008

St. 19

009

010

Preah Moha Ksatreiyani Kossamak Ave. (106)

Oknha Ing Bun Hoaw Ave. (108)

Riverside Promenade

Preah Sisovath Quay

St. 5

Preah Ang Duong St. (110)

Kramuon Sar St. (114)

St. 17

St. 15

Calmette St. (53)

Preah Chey Chetha St. (118)

Khemarak Phoumin Ave. (130)

Wat Phnom

Wat Phnom

Architect unknown

1372 (first structure) /
early 1880s

001 A

Wat Phnom, eponym and symbol of the city of Phnom Penh, sits prominently atop a small hill (in Khmer *phnom*) near the Tonle Sap River north of the old city centre. Legend has it that in the season of high waters in 1372, a wealthy widow called Penh (*Daun Penh*, or 'Grandmother Penh' in Khmer), found a large *koki* tree (*Hopea odorata*) floating in the river outside her house. Inside a hollow in the trunk she found four bronze Buddha statues and a stone statue of Vishnu (called *Lok Ta Preah Chao* or 'God of the Kingdom'). In order to protect the sacred statues, Grandmother Penh erected a small shrine on an artificial hill made by the people living in the village. In doing so, she was following the Angkorian royal tradition of raising a hill, sometimes a symbolic one, and constructing a sanctuary on top, a practice that originated from Hindu beliefs in ancient India.

The Cambodian Royal Chronicles mention that King Naray Raja I – son of King Ponhea Yat (reign: 1431–63), who brought the Khmer capital to Phnom Penh in 1432 – raised the height of the hill and rebuilt the wooden pagoda on its peak, adding a *chedey thom* (grand stupa) to enshrine the sacred relics of the Buddha. He then named the pagoda Wat Phnom Penh. There are two principal sacred places on the top of the hill: the *preah vihear*, or sanctuary, and the *chedey thom* located behind it. They are best approached by the main staircase from the east.

A famous sketch by Louis Delaporte from 1873 shows an early vihāra (in Khmer *preah vihear*) that was probably built in 1806 but was unfortunately burned in 1881. The present structure dates back to the early 1880s. In the late 19th century, French town planner Daniel Fabré provided the inspiration for a wholesale renovation of the phnom by constructing this great staircase incorporating Angkorian details, most notably the seven-headed *nagas*, or mythical serpents, at the base of the stairs. The sanctuary was renovated again in 1926 in reinforced concrete. The last comprehensive restoration work took place in 2011.

The sanctuary has an east-west orientation, with the main Buddha statue facing east. The building sits on a rectangular masonry terrace, 1.60 m in height, surrounded by a gallery with a simple plastered balustrade. The *vihear* is built with a symmetrical plan, 11.60 m in width, 22.60 m in length, and 10.70 m in height. The plain outer columns are adorned with figurative eave brackets. These brackets were moulded, with concrete, in the form of sculptures representing *krud* and *kinnor* – mystical, half-human and half-animal creatures. The figures appear to be holding up the edge of the lower roof with their arms.

The traditional roof is divided into an upper section and lower section. The two sections have overlapping slopes and are separated by a gap to form two-tiered pitched roofs. They are decorated with *chovea* finials placed at each end of the two ridge purlins. The triangular pediments (*hocheang*) on the east and west have tympanums (*than hocheang*) moulded from concrete. The east tympanum represents the Hindu/Buddhist god Indra, wearing a royal crown (*mkud reach*) and sitting on the three-headed elephant Airavata. The Indra figure is flanked by parasols (*aphirum*) and a tracery of floral *kbach phni tes* elements, created using an early-modern Khmer plaster-casting technique. The figures of the royal crown and parasols are not mere decoration. They represent the site's direct relation to the king: this is a royal pagoda for celebrating royal rituals, and royal assets were used for its construction.

Inside, the classic sanctuary is divided into three aisles and seven bays. Two rows of six painted concrete columns separate the chief nave (*kroeh*) from the side aisles (*robieng*). The wooden roof structure is hidden by an elaborately painted plank ceiling.

The central altar complex at the western end of the chief nave is dominated by a 2.80-metre-tall bronze Buddha (*Preah Ang Chi*) sitting in meditation on an elevated lotus throne surrounded by other statues and items of devotion and worship. The statue was likely built during the reign of King Norodom or later, while the current vihear was being constructed, in the 1890s. This type of massive gold-stencilled bronze *Preah Ang Chi* is a unique work in Cambodian plastic art. Behind it stands the structure of *Preah Chaktomuk* or the 'Four-Faced Buddha', connected to the Buddha's pedestal in the form of a *prang*, made of stucco, possibly with the original laterite foundation still underneath.

The walls are entirely covered with excellent murals dating back to the mid-1950s. Many depict the *Jataka* tales, revolving around the Buddha's earlier reincarnations before his enlightenment. There are also murals depicting stories from the *Reamker*, the Khmer version of the Hindu epic *Ramayana*. Some of the series of paintings were repainted in the 1990s, though their restoration was conducted only briefly before being stopped. All paintings were meticulously restored

in 2011 by the Ministry of Culture and Fine Arts. For a detailed description of these murals as well as the elaborate ceiling paintings see Chan Vitharong's *Wat Phnom Guide to Art and Architecture*.

The prominent Grand Stupa immediately behind the sanctuary contains the ashes of King Ponhea Yat. The style of the present stupa probably dates back to the 16th or 17th century.

The *chedey thom* has been rebuilt many times, most extensively in 1894, when Phnom Penh's first Resident-Superior Huyn de Vernéville had the pagoda renovated and added the monumental stairway and the newly landscaped gardens surrounding the hill. The landmark building is 33 metres high. Its structure is divided into four major sections: the lower and upper square bases (*kheun* and *tronabb khsach*), the pedestal (*ballang*), the bell-shaped body (*tou ang*), and the conical spire top (*kompul*). The architectural composition of the *chedey*, all built of stucco, laterite, and brick masonry, represents the Buddhist cosmology.

Between the temple and the stupa lies a small but well-frequented shrine dedicated to Grandmother Penh. The *Lok Ta Preah Chao* statue, an imaginative interpretation of the statue found by Grandmother Penh in the tree of legend, is stored in a very popular shrine to the north of the stupa. Inside, there are hundreds of statues of Chinese gods and goddesses. The present *Lok Ta Preah Chao* statue is attired as a high-ranking official sitting on his pedestal and is enormously popular to worshippers of Sino-Khmer and Vietnamese descent.

Sprinkled around the top of the hill are a number of other *chedey* of varying sizes, memorials of forgotten members of the kingdom's royalty, and one mysterious Frenchman. Another monument sits at the foot of Wat Phnom towards Preah Norodom Boulevard. A giant clock is topped by a bas-relief and statue portraying King Norodom Sisowath residing over an important historical event: as a result of the Franco-Siamese treaty of 23 March 1907, Siam ceded the territories today corresponding to the northern provinces of Siem Reap, Sisophon (Banteay Meanchey), and Battambang back to Cambodia.

Council for the Development of Cambodia

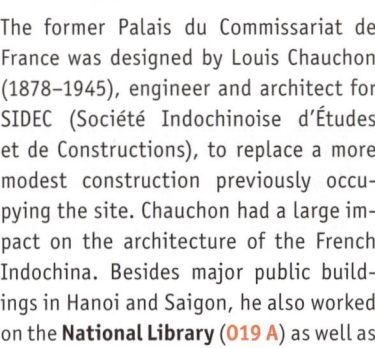

002 A

Preah Sisowath Quay,
entrance opposite Wat Phnom
Louis Chauchon
1938

The former Palais du Commissariat de France was designed by Louis Chauchon (1878–1945), engineer and architect for SIDEC (Société Indochinoise d'Études et de Constructions), to replace a more modest construction previously occupying the site. Chauchon had a large impact on the architecture of the French Indochina. Besides major public buildings in Hanoi and Saigon, he also worked on the **National Library** (**019 A**) as well as the **Central Market** (**033 B**).

The building was built towards the end of the 1930s, during the emergence of the rationalist architectural style that characterises the Central Market and the **Railway Station** (**013 A**). It displays a somewhat 'modernist' style, bare of local influences, and is a wilful expression of colonial grandeur and power, evoking the Trocadéro, site of the Palais de Chaillot in Paris. In fact, the building looks quite strange in this historical context, as it lacks any relation to its urban surroundings. The monumental appearance, despite its Art Deco leanings, awakens unpleasant associations with neoclassical architectures of power that emerged in Paris and in Germany during that time.

The imposing two-storey building reaches out with its wings and colonnades towards the surrounding lush tropical garden. It was called the Résidence Supérieure until 1946, when the French Protectorate ended and Cambodia gained autonomous status within the French Union. This is also when the title of the French colonial administrator changed from Resident Supérieur to Commissaire, and his residence likewise changed its name from the Résidence Supérieure to the Hotel du Commissariat. Governor Jean L. de Raymond, who became the last Commissaire of the Republic of France in Cambodia in March 1949, was assassinated during a lunchtime nap at the Hotel du Commissariat on 29 October 1951. He was killed by a Vietnamese servant, who stole some documents before fleeing to North Vietnam. The assassin had been a member of the Phnom Penh Viet Minh Committee and became a member of the Communist Party shortly thereafter.

The bedroom in which Raymond was assassinated is in the south wing of the building, behind the fourth window from the left on the upper floor. A stupa that was erected in his honour can still be seen next to the entrance of the compound.

Following Cambodia's independence in 1953, the building became a governmental guest house and venue for official state banquets. During the Khmer Rouge era, it was referred to as House No. 1. On 5 January 1979, Pol Pot, also known as 'Brother No. 1', received Sihanouk in

the main reception room. Just two days later, the Vietnamese ousted the Khmer Rouge from Phnom Penh, less than 24 hours after Pol Pot and Sihanouk had fled the city. In 1992–1993, the Hotel du Commissariat became the headquarters of the United Nations Transitional Authority in Cambodia (UNTAC). Today the building houses the Council for the Development of Cambodia (CDC), the government's highest decision-making body for private and public sector investment.

Even though it is a government building, don't hesitate to try your luck (especially on a weekend) and enter the compound, walking in from the main gate opposite Wat Phnom. The interior, with its Art Nouveau and Art Deco decorations, is also worth a visit, if you find someone who generously lets you in. Beautiful frescoes from the French Protectorate and the Independence Period depict life in the Cambodian countryside. Before leaving the property, make sure to look up into the giant Dipterocarpus alatus tree, which is home to a large colony of Lyle's flying foxes.

![building photograph]

Former Cadastral Office
Street 13/Street 94
Architect unknown
1900-1910

003 A

This block, located directly east of Wat Phnom, was the site of the Buddhist pagoda Wat Moha Muntrey until the end of the 19th century. The French colonial villa standing at the corner of Street 13 and Street 94 (Baksei Cham Krong) dates back to that time. It once housed the Cadastral Office. The French administration brought to Cambodia the legal concept of private property as something individual, registered, and recorded in the land registry. The municipality of Phnom Penh was created in 1884, and that year saw the end of the royal monopoly on property and the creation of public and private property in Cambodia. The Protectorate, from this time on, controlled the buying, selling, and renting of property in the urban area. Finally, the Civil Code of 1920 established the system of French land law that fully recognised private property rights. The architect Lu

Ban Hap and his wife Armelle lived in this building for a short period, soon after they had come back from Paris after Lu had finished his studies in late 1959 and before they moved into their own magnificent house on Monivong Boulevard. Lu Ban Hap became the head of the newly founded Service Municipal de l'Urbanisme et de l'Habitat, which was set up in this very building in 1960. In the 1990s, the building, with its striking clock tower, was used by the Service du Port de Phnom Penh. Today it is used by the adjacent national power company Electricité Du Cambodge (EDC). The compound is currently under construction with more buildings to be expected, hopefully respecting their historical neighbour.

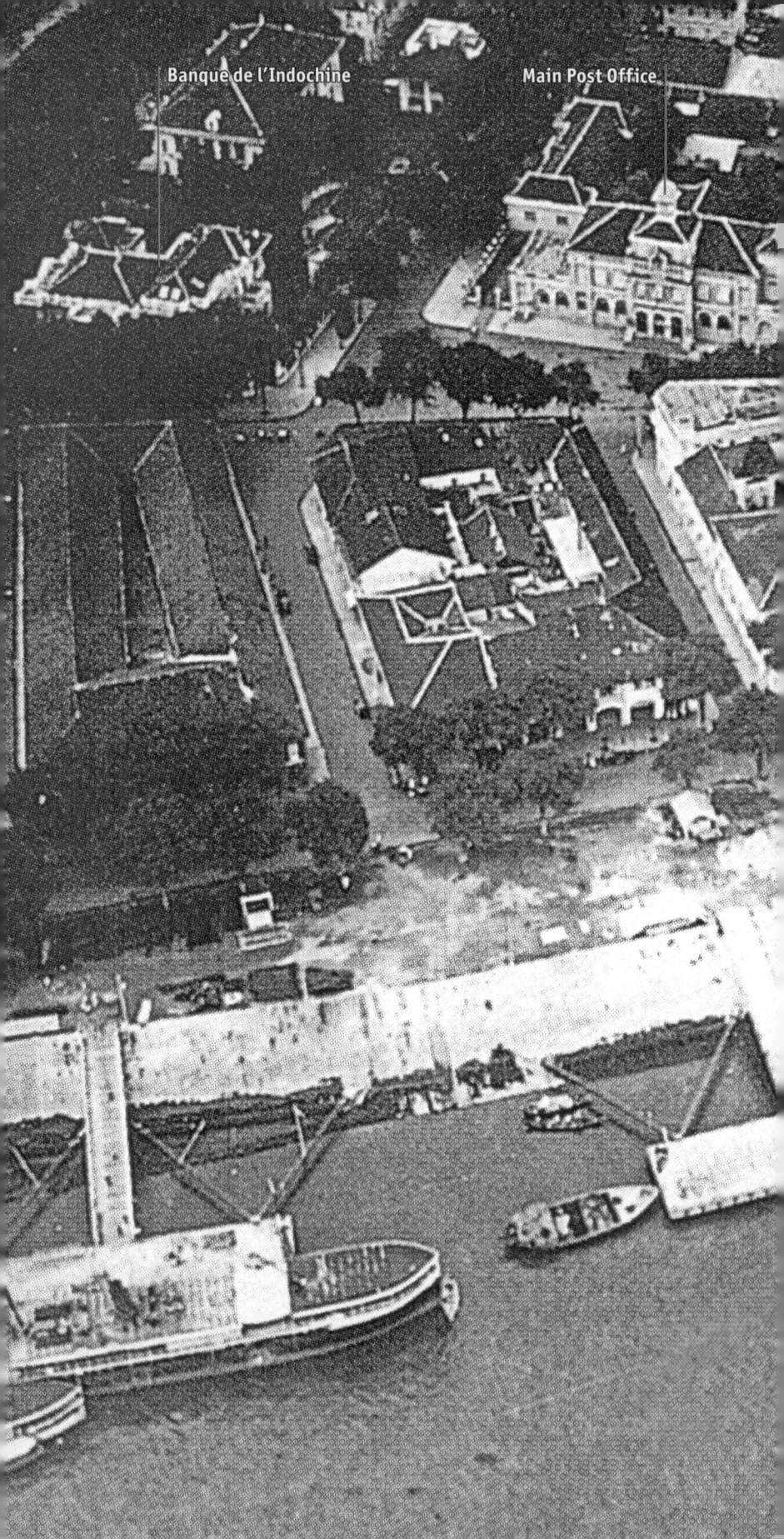

Banque de l'Indochine   Main Post Office

Central Police Station

Bureaux des Messageries Fluviales

Grand Hotel Manolis

Aerial view of the Post Office Square and the river port in 1931

Main Post Office

3 Street 13 (Post Office Square)
Daniel Fabré
1895

004 A

The Bureau des Postes, or Poste Centrale (Main Post Office), looms over the western side of a small square at the heart of the former French administrative district. The former Place de la Poste, with its irregular urban space and changing perspectives, stands out from the standardised and rational urban layout devised by the French engineers elsewhere. Aline Hettreau-Pottier and Christiane Blancot mention in their essay '1863-1953, une ville neuve dans un site d'occupation ancienne' that the ideas of the Austrian architect and urban theorist Camillo Sitte (1845–1903) possibly influenced the design of this space. In Sitte's influential *City Planning According to Artistic Principles* (1889), he formulated an aesthetic criticism of the late 19th century's pragmatic and hygienic urbanism. He instead advocated the human perspective and creation of an irregular urban structure, with spacious plazas enhanced by monuments and other aesthetic elements.

The peaceful square is bordered by a number of once important colonial public buildings. To the north, we see the faded façades of the former **Central Police Station** (**005 A**). Across the street is the former **Grand Hotel Manolis** (**007 A**), which was once the city's only luxury hotel, and towards the south of the square is the former **Banque de l'Indochine** (**008 A**), which was housed in a stately mansion next to some commercial blocks filled with shophouses. Most of the buildings surrounding the square were designed between 1890 and 1930. This largely intact ensemble of outstanding heritage buildings from the French colonial period must be considered exceptional, worthy of being listed as a prime heritage protection zone.

The post office building was designed by Daniel Fabré (1850–1904), an architect and town planner who was responsible for the facelift of Phnom Penh and Wat Phnom in the 1890s and who also designed many other public buildings of the Protectorate. The building is a typical example of late 19th century eclecticism, which the architects and engineers of the French Protectorate used for important administrative buildings. With its symmetrical façade, Roman arched windows, Corinthian columns, balconies with balustrades, pediments, and elaborately sculpted decorations, the building is a fine example of neo-classical architecture in a Southeast Asian context. It lacks, however, any structural adaptation to the tropical climate or local building traditions. The building is in reasonable shape, having been fully restored in 2004. It has been in continual operation since 1895 except for the period when the Khmer Rouge blew up the central bank, banned money, and vacated the city of its inhabitants. Between 1910 and 1920, two one-floor annexes were constructed to the north and south of the main building. The central roof of the original building at that time was still surmounted by a compact tower with a small cupola, which was probably removed in the late 1930s. The second floor of the two side wings was

added in 1991, sustaining the original style. During the extensive renovation, the original windows with their louvred wooden shutters were replaced. While the old windows easily let air in and out, the new windows with tinted glass impede ventilation and block sunlight. The reception hall is open to the public; it still features two rows of the original Corinthian columns made of pre-cast iron that were imported from France. The ornamental and green public garden that was originally in front of the Post Office was replaced in the 1930s with a square. Today this exceptional urban space, despite its tremendous potential for public use, is regrettably mostly used for parking.

PNOM-PENH — L'Hôtel des Postes et Télégraphes

Former Central Police Station 005 A

Street 3/Street 98
Architect unknown
1925–1935

The former Commissariat Central occupies a prominent corner on the Post Office Square. Shuttered and derelict for decades, it was featured in the film *City of Ghosts*, a 2002 drama film co-written and directed by Matt Dillon, about a con artist who must go to Cambodia to collect his share of money from an insurance scam. He checks into the seedy Belleville Hotel, run by a Frenchman named Emile (Gérard Depardieu). In the film, the already abandoned building served as the welcome setting for the Belleville Hotel. The old Commissariat was built in 1892 in the heart of the old French District and served as the colonial police force's headquarters in Phnom Penh. It was originally an unassuming corner building with two floors that could very well be standing in the French countryside, without any architectural features adapted to the tropical climate. The Commissariat was then remodelled in the late 1920s or early 1930s and became the grand three-floor edifice it is today. The triangular building features a central staircase above the main entrance which provides access to screened exterior walkways that were added for cooling and shading purposes. Large Art Deco-influenced windows feature wooden shutters and ornamental screened balustrades.

Today, like many of Phnom Penh's heritage buildings, the Commissariat stands as a shadow of its former glory and faces an uncertain fate. A fence partly surrounds the compound, the exterior walls reveal crumbling plaster, and the wooden staircases are not safe for use anymore. The rear courtyard, however, is quite lively with diverse activities such as a car wash and volleyball tournaments.

A full renovation is what this magnificent building deserves and requires, sooner rather than later. Much of the original fabric remains, which could guide an informed conservation project and conversion into an upmarket boutique hotel or similar uses.

Brown Riverside

Preah Sisowath Quay/
Street 98
Architect unknown/
Hok Kang Architects (renovation)
1890–1900

006 A

Around the corner from the Post Office Square, at No. 98, Sisowath Quay, stands what was once the Bureaux des Messageries Fluviales, the office of a river courier company and ticketing service for the passenger boats to Saigon.

When the period of the French Protectorate began in 1863, Phnom Penh was already 'the great bazaar of Cambodia' (Henri Mohout), the transit point for goods which were transported from Siam to Cholon, the Chinese commercial suburb of Saigon. Here starts the history of the Phnom Penh river port (Port Fluvial), located along the Quay Lagrandiere, where the *appontements*, the docking areas for the ships to and from Saigon, were situated. These wharfs were entrusted to the management of the Compagnies des Messageries Fluviales,

which subsequently ran postal and passenger services to Saigon and on to other destinations in French Indochina, as well as across the Tonle Sap to Angkor and Luang Prabang in Laos. In the 1930s, passengers could spend a comfortable 32 hours on the Jules Rueff, the most modern steamer of the company named after its founder, travelling from Saigon to Phnom Penh. Henri Lamagat describes in his book *Souvenirs d'un vieux Journaliste Indochinois,* published in 1942:

'But the arrival at Phnom Penh, when the first rays of sun appeared, offered the passengers a magical, delightful spectacle which was not, it is true, due to any particular attraction to the Campagnie, but to the nature. The metal domes of the buildings of the Royal Palace, which were already visible a few kilometres before they reached the four arms, glittered as if they were huge and glittering gilded mirrors, while the splendours of the Khmer metropolis were offered upon arrival, as the ship slowly ascended the Tonle Sap to the Fluviales wharf. There, friends, loafers, and the curious crowded on board to

PNOM-PENH — *Bureaux des Messageries Fluviales*

shake hands, to give news. The boss of the Grand Hotel, always present at these arrivals, offered his rooms and his beef steak and came regularly on Saturday, taking delivery of the sheep that the mail brought him from Saigon. This butchery animal, relatively rare in Cambodia, was exclusively reserved for residents and friends of the hotelier ...'

The building's appearance has changed throughout the years, and the original wooden shutters as well as the arched entrance loggia with its plastered anchor decorations are gone. In 2012, the building was renovated by its current occupant, Brown Coffee and Bakery. As with other Brown Coffee branches in the city (see **114 E** and **123 F**), architect and owner Hok Kang opted for a sensitive and unique interior design, exposing the bare brick walls and arches as well as the vaulted ceiling, and creating a warehouse-like atmosphere on the ground floor. Despite the alterations to its original substance, this is an example of successful adaptive re-use of a historic building from French colonial times.

The old wharfs opposite the café are still there, now used as the passenger terminal for boats to Silk Island and Siem Reap as well as to Vietnam. However, this area will soon change its character for good, as a stretch of 1.5 km along the Tonle Sap River is set for a new waterfront development named Phnom Penh Harbour. This will comprise 22 high-rise buildings with a total gross floor space of 1.05 million m² spread along the riverbank.

PNOM-PENH — *Les quais aux basses eaux*

Grand Hotel Manolis

Sisowath Quay and Street 13,
between Streets 98 and 100
Architect unknown
1895–96 (main building)/
1910s–1920s (extensions and
building facing the square)

007 A

The renowned Grand Hotel dates back to the 1890s, though it was not the city's first hotel establishment. It was the brainchild of the then Resident-Superior Huyn de Vernéville, France's highest representative in Cambodia, who assigned a merchant named Borelly to create a hotel-restaurant 'of European standards'. This hotel would be subsidised by the protectorate in return for the permanent reservation of seven rooms for official guests of the French government. In 1918, Monsieur Manolis, a Greek who had initially come to Cambodia to construct the Phnom Penh-Sisophon railway, became the owner of the hotel. The establishment was then referred to as The Grand or The Manolis, or combined, the Grand Hotel Manolis. W. Somerset Maugham expressively described his personal impressions during his short stay in 1922: 'The hotel is large, dirty and pretentious, and there is a terrace outside where merchants and innumerable functionaries may take an apéritif and for a moment forget that they are not in France.' The hotel also deserves a place of its own in literary history for other reasons. In 1923–1924, André Malraux, the celebrated novelist and first Minister of Culture of France, was placed under house arrest in the hotel with his wife Clara for several months following their arrest for the looting of ancient bas-reliefs from the Bantaey Srei temple.

The main building along the river was recently renovated with a heavy hand. The façade has been completely altered, now featuring an insensitive main entrance and tasteless window shutters, and Chez Rina, a petite cocktail bar that once occupied a well-preserved section of the former hotel at Street 98, was sadly shut down just recently. The building opposite the **Main Post Office (004 A)** appeared as the bar run by Gérard Depardieu's character in Matt Dillon's 2002 crime drama *City of Ghosts*. The bar occupied the northern corner of Street 98. The three-floor building makes up the rear side of the hotel, the main entrance of which used to be on the riverfront. By the 1940s, the hotel had expanded from its main building on today's Sisowath Quay to the entire block. The separate building facing the square is marked in a French map of 1925 as the 'Banque Franco-Chinoise', established by Lok Chhaivary, the then owner of **The Mansion** (068 C), and his son Tan Pa (see former **Tan Pa Residence** (035 B) and **Tan Pa Building** (051 B)). It is also said to have housed the city's Chamber of Commerce at a certain time, and, after the Khmer Rouge period, post office employees were lodged here. By the 1990s this part of the Grand Hotel had been divided entirely into small apartments and, today, is occupied by some 30 families. Although large parts of it are rather run down, recently, some private apartments have been nicely refurbished. A construction fence was blocking the northwestern corner at the time of research, hopefully indicating a proper renovation in the near future. Catch a glimpse of the former splendour by climbing one of the original wooden staircases to admire the beautiful floor tiles on the first floor.

HOTEL MANOLIS

(Ex. Grand Hôtel), quai de Lanessan — PNOMPENH

Entre l'autocar et le bateau

L'Hôtel le plus connu et le plus renommé du Cambodge

Confort — Cuisine saine — Accueil sympathique

PRIX MODÉRÉS

ARRANGEMENTS SPÉCIAUX POUR FAMILLES

A good and comfortable Hotel where you will return when coming back to Pnompenh.
A first class cuisine, old wines and moderate terms make it the Hotel where people like to stay.

Entrance of the former main hall of the Banque de l'Indochine at Street 13

Former Banque de l'Indochine   008 A

5 Street 102, Street 13
Architect unknown
1890s–1910s / 1920s–1930s

Few buildings evoke the 'old world charm' of Phnom Penh quite like the former Banque de l'Indochine (Indochina Bank), now housing the Palais La Poste restaurant (towards the Post Office Square) and offices of the Agence Française de Développement and Asia Insurance (towards Street 13). Thanks to its excellent restoration between 2003 and 2004, this imposing mansion is in superb condition and retains the grandeur of its early days. The two-storey edifice occupies a plot south of the **Main Post Office** (004 A). It completes the rich ensemble of colonial-era architecture around the Post Office Square. The eclectic architecture is characteristic of early 19th century France. The cream yellow façade features imposing porches, decorative balustrades, arched doors and windows, elaborate pediments, and sculpted ornaments inspired by a fusion of classical architecture and Italian Renaissance palaces.

Both the main wrought iron gate at the corner, at the main entrance (today Asia Insurance offices), and the mosaic-terrazzo floor in the main dining hall still carry the monogram 'BIC' of the Banque de l'Indochine. The bank was established in Paris on 21 January 1875 to help the French government manage its colonial properties in Southeast Asia, and later shifted operations to China and the Pacific. The present stately mansion was built between the 1890s and 1910s and then comprehensively remodelled between 1920 and the 1930s to replace the first, more humble façades. It originally consisted of three parts, each with its own entrance: the main hall of the bank, open for customers (on Street 13); the bank vaults, offices, and archives, open to bank staff only (on Street 102); and the private residence of the bank director (on Street 106). Upon entering the restaurant, you can still see on the right the three original vaults that once housed the kingdom's gold reserves, now used as the restaurant's administrative offices. Their reinforced steel doors were made by the Parisian firm Fichet, and the company's insignia remains intact on all of them.

In 1960, the property was purchased by one of Cambodia's earliest industrialists, Van Thuan, who had managed to amass a small fortune as an owner of the Chip Tong sandal factory. The Van family lived in the house until they were forced to flee the country at the outbreak of the civil war in 1970. After 1980, the building served as the headquarters of the State Rural Development Bank. In 2003, with the country's economy opening up, the Van family procured their former house from the Cambodian government and the youngest daughter Porleng was given the task of restoring it to its former grandeur. With great attention to detail, she conducted research at the Archives Nationales d'Outre-mer in Aix-en-Provence, France, the branch of the National Archives of France documenting the French colonies. She thus obtained accurate historical accounts of the building. The restoration took place between August 2003 and April 2004 with most of the genuine tiles, coloured windows, and original woodwork being preserved. In 2007 the family decided to open the building to the public and started the Van's French fine-dining restaurant. In late 2018, the restaurant changed owners and now operates under the name Palais la Poste.

The magnificent building is a prime example of a successfully restored colonial-era property in Phnom Penh. It showcases the economic feasibility of adaptive re-use combined with thoughtful heritage preservation.

240　　CAMBODGE — PNOM-PENH — Avenue de la Poste

National Treasury

19 Street 106
Daniel Fabré
1891–92

If you stand in the public gardens between Streets 106 and 108, you are on the site of the city's former grand canal that was built in 1894, under the supervision of Hyun de Verneville, the then Resident-Superior of Cambodia. The semi-circular **De Verneville Canal** was about 3 km long and surrounded the European District. Its southern section was formerly known as the Quai de Verneville (now Street 106) and Quai Piquet (now Street 108). It extended from the Chinese District and was met, at today's Norodom Boulevard, by the **Naga Bridge**, also dubbed Treasury Bridge, in reference to the administrative edifice at its northeastern end. The original bridge was designed in 1892 by Daniel Fabré (1850–1904), who later also designed the Treasury building the same year. The bridge became redundant when the canal was filled in between 1928 and 1935 to become a public park linking the **Railway Station (013 A)** and the Tonle Sap River. A modern reconstruction of the bridge was inaugurated in 2007. Seven-headed *nagas* – mythical serpents – face outwards at both ends of the sculpted stone balustrades.

The building of the Treasury still stands today and is used as the General Department of National Treasury under the Ministry of Finance. Its function is written in Khmer letters on the historic parapet wall above the main entrance decorated with Angkorian and religious motifs. In its early stages, the Protectorate made attempts to create a unique 'Cambodian style' as a blend of French neo-classical architecture and

CAMBODGE. - 521. - PNOM-PENH. - Le Trésor

local traditional features. Similar to the later **National Museum** (073 C) by George Groslier (1887–1945), Daniel Fabré here designed a solid-looking building bare of French embellishments. The heavy base of the building evokes the image of Angkorian temples, and the traditional Khmer roof is flanked by a pair of pediments derived from traditional Buddhist pagoda architecture. Unfortunately, during recent renovations, the original wooden window shutters were replaced by the metal grilles that make so many Cambodian houses look like prisons, and the light iron fence surrounding the compound was upgraded to a solid concrete wall. The main gate with its guarding pair of Angkorian lions seems historic though.

A smaller building located on the eastern side of the compound was recently levelled to make space for the construction of a four-storey building in a retro French-colonial style.

Around the corner...

Further to the east at No. 16, Street 106, there is the French **Hotel de Ville**, which housed the former Bureau de la Residence (city hall offices) during the times of the Protectorate. The stately edifice was recently renovated with a heavy hand and painted somewhat silverish grey. It will be converted into the Icanavarman Museum, showcasing the kingdom's economic and financial evolution from the first century to the present day.

(176) CAMBODGE : Pnom-Penh - Le Pont du Rajah.

Ministry of Public Works and Transport

Preah Norodom Boulevard,
between Streets 102 and 106
Architect unknown /
Grimeret (1950s building)
1900–1910 / 1925–1935 / 1958

The Ministry of Public Works occupies an entire block along Street 106 (Preah Mohaksat Treiyani Kossamak). It is housed in a building ensemble with an architectural history spanning almost 120 years. The oldest remaining building is the modest two-storey edifice facing the public gardens. It was initially built to house the Bureaux de la Direction des Travaux Publics (Office of the Directorate of Public Works) at the end of the 19th century. With its eclectic style, it is a well-preserved example of a French administrative building from the first phase of the Protectorate. It features a nice medallion displaying civil engineering tools on its central parapet wall above the former main entrance. Another early office building from the French period was located on Street 51 (Rue Pasteur), though it has since been demolished and replaced by a new building. Added probably in the late 1920s, the initially three-storey building, oriented towards Street 102 (Preah Ang Non), was used by the Ecole des Conducteurs de Travaux Publics, founded in 1945, and transformed into L'Ecole Nationale des Travaux Publics, du Batiment et des

Mines (National School of Public Works, Building and Mines) in 1961. With its large classroom windows facing the street, the building is a fine example of the more rational architectural style used for public buildings in the later colonial phase after 1925. The building was originally connected to its older neighbour by a covered walkway. In 1966, it was extended by one floor in the same architectural style, and became part of the expanded Faculté du Genie Civil (Faculty of Civil Engineering). With the completion of the former Institut Technique Supérieur de l'Amitié Khméro-Soviétique, today the **Institute of Technology of Cambodia** (119 F), and the foundation of the **Royal University of Fine Arts** (074 C), a large part of the teaching was probably transferred there. The modernist building tract towards Norodom Boulevard was designed by the French architect Grimeret and probably built in 1958 as a second addition to the ensemble. Scant information is available about Grimeret, who also worked together with Vann Molyvann on the Council of Ministers building (demolished) in the 1960s. The front façade of the building is structured by vertical brise-soleils that are angled towards the south, thus sheltering the offices from the direct morning sun. The building is attached to the former faculty building, and originally exceeded it by one floor. The ground floor used to be open and served as a main entrance to the site.

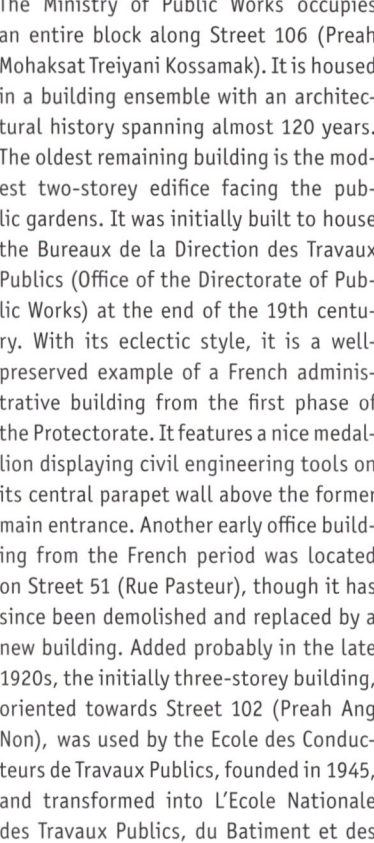

Regrettably, the year 2017 saw the latest addition to the striking building ensemble, with the construction of an ordinary but massive office building inexplicably squeezed in between the old buildings in the block interior and towering behind the humble but elegant former Bureaux de la Direction des Travaux Publics.

Further to the west across Street 51, on the site of today's Landmark Tower, used to stand the Magasins de la Voirie (road warehouses) and the Salle de la Philharmonique of Phnom Penh, a more humble version of the magnificent French opera buildings in Saigon and Hanoi. Both were destroyed years ago.

1603. CAMBODGE-PHNOM-PENH — Hôtel des Travaux Publics

P. Dieulefils. - Hanoi

Vattanac Capital Tower
66 Preah Monivong Boulevard
TFP Farrells
2018

011 A

After years of construction, the Vattanac Tower opened its doors in 2014, but large parts of the building remained empty for several years. The building was then officially inaugurated on 26 May 2018 by Prime Minister Hun Sen. At the time of its completion, the 187.3-metre-high tower was Cambodia's tallest building. The size and design of the tower obviously focus on the needs of a global real-estate market that has to meet similar requirements across national borders. The vast amount of glass and steel, the luxury design, and the somewhat iconic appearance were seemingly intended to establish the Vattanc Group, owner of the $250 million building, as a player on the global market. The architects describe their design as inspired by traditional *naga* motifs and a 'memorable form responsive to local conditions and detailing grounded in the region's rich culture'.

In the middle of Phnom Penh, opposite the historic **Railway Station** (013 A), the complex rises above a comparatively low building development and marks a huge leap in scale. The complex consists of a lower structure facing the Monivong Boulevard and the tower behind. The 39-storey tower houses Grade A offices, luxury retail space, and on the 14 upper floors, the Rosewood Hotel, an 'ultra-luxury hospitality experience' with a total of 175 rooms, a 20-metre swimming pool, a fitness centre, and a sky bar. In the slightly lower Lifestyle Cube, you will find a cinema floor, a fitness floor, and a medical floor among other attractions. According to the corporate website, the building is 'a symbol of social and environmental responsibility', and it has indeed managed to obtain the city's first Gold LEED certification for the fully glazed office, hotel, and commercial space under Cambodia's tropical sun.

Canadia Tower

315 Street 110
PBL Group
2009

012 A

Canadia Tower, named after its owner Canadia Bank PLC, stands 118 metres tall. Inaugurated in 2009, it was the very first skyscraper ever built in Phnom Penh, a fact that is hard to believe when you consider the multitude of high-rises that came to dominate the city's skyline just a decade later. Construction work on the foundations of the building started in 2005 and required extensive work due to Phnom Penh's infamously soft riverside terrain. With 30 storeys of office and retail space and additional underground parking, the tower has a floor space of about 45,000 m². The building combines a number of different architectural elements. The enormous base has about the same height as the surrounding buildings. It is clad in natural stone and features a mix of historicist elements. A completely glazed square tower, crowned by a cylindrical section with a helipad on top, rises above it. Canadia Bank, whose head office is located here, was established in 1991, as part of a joint venture between overseas Cambodians and the National Bank of Cambodia. Today it is the largest local bank in Cambodia and was involved in some of the largest real-estate developments in Phnom Penh, among them the **Diamond Island Development City** (098 D), **Olympia City** (105 E), and the **Apartment Building –The Sixties** (024 A).

Around the corner …
Just behind Canadia Tower, at No. 299, Street 110, you will find **Raintree**, another interesting development by Urbanland Asia and Hok Kang Architects. The office building with its lush green façade is intended for temporary use until another high-rise building will claim the space.

Royal Railway Station

013 A

Street 108
Jean Desbois
1932

The Royal Railway Station is located at the western end of a large green corridor starting from the Tonle Sap River, formerly the location of the **De Verneville Canal (009 A)**, which surrounded the European District. The canal was filled between 1928 and 1935 to create the public park and enable the development of the wetlands west of today's Monivong Boulevard. On 5 July 1929, King Sisowath Monivong, Pierre Marie Antoine Pasquier (the then Governor General of Indochina), and Fernand Marie Joseph Antoine Lavit (the then Resident-Superior of France in Cambodia) attended the groundbreaking ceremony for the construction of the railway, at the very location of Phnom Penh's current main railway station.

Construction was hampered by the rainy season, but the station was finally completed in 1932 and began to service the railway line to Battambang.

Built in reinforced concrete, the station was the first of two major projects that brought the architectural language of early European modernism to Phnom Penh. Stripped of references to vernacular architectural styles and traditional decor, 'the internal space of the station is a dynamic expression of the potential offered by reinforced concrete used in an imaginative way,' as Ross and Collins once wrote. The Phnom Penh Railway Station has much in common with the **Central Market (033 B)**, which was the follow-up to the railway station in terms of its approach to modernising tropical architecture. Both buildings were designed by the French architect Jean Desbois (1891–1971). Desbois studied at the Regional School of Architecture of Rennes and at the Ecole

A peek inside the Phnom Penh railway depot

Nationale Supérieure des Beaux-Arts in Paris. In 1922, he sought a job in the Public Works Department of the General Government of Indochina. While working in Phnom Penh between 1931 and 1937, he collaborated with Ernest Hébrard for the design of the **Hotel Le Royal** (017 A), and together with Louis Chauchon designed the new Central Market of Phnom Penh between 1934 and 1937.

The high ceiling inside the main hall is supported by six parabolic arches. Large screen walls with elegant Art Deco patterns allow indirect lighting and ventilation. An additional floor with offices is arranged above the main hall, with the staircases located in the towers on the short sides of the building. As his biographer Marie-Laure Crosnier Leconte describes, Jean Desbois was inspired at the time by recent structures such as the Centennial Hall (Jahrhunderthalle) built in 1913 by architect Max Berg in Wrocław, and the public market (Grossmarkthalle)

of Leipzig, built between 1927 and 1929 by Hubert Ritter and Franz Dischinger. Desbois might also have known about the Wrocław Market Hall, designed with similar parabolic reinforced-concrete arches by Richard Plüddemann and built between 1906 and 1908 as the Breslauer Markthalle Nr. 1.

The Cambodian railway was one of the last to be built in French Indochina, during a decade which historian Henri Locard characterises as 'the climax of the French achievements in the colonial age'. Paid for by German war reparations and originally operated as a franchise, the North Line opened in 1933 as a 330 km route from Phnom Penh to Monkolborey. It was returned three years later to the colonial government and operated as a branch of Chemins de Fer de l'Indochine (CFI). In 1938, works began to connect Battambang with Thailand via Poipet, but the track was used only sporadically until 1970. Following independence, in 1954, the port of Sihanoukville (Kampong Som) was developed, and in 1960 works began with French, West German, and Chinese assistance to build the new South Line to connect Sihanoukville with the capital. The line was opened in 1969 but ceased operation just a few years later as the country descended into war. The railway station in Phnom Penh has a peculiar political history as well. Between 28 and 30 September 1960, the Kampuchean People's Revolutionary Party (KPRP) held a secret congress at the station, during which the party was renamed the Workers Party of Kampuchea (WPK). In Democratic Kampuchea, this pivotal meeting would later be seen as the founding date of the party. Following the fall of Phnom Penh in April 1975, the first important meeting of the Khmer Rouge leadership, including Pol Pot, was held at the railway station, during which the decision was taken to evacuate the cities. Put into operation by the Khmer Rouge five months after the initial evacuation of Phnom Penh in April 1975, railroads were a crucial means of transport during the 'second evacuation', which forcefully relocated Cambodians to different work camps across the country. Rail services on the North Line resumed in the early 1980s, but war and

neglect had left the network in a dilapidated state, and guerrilla activities by marauding Khmer Rouge militias continued to disrupt the service in the early 1990s. In 2009, the Royal Government of Cambodia outsourced its railway operations to Australian Toll Holdings under a 30-year exclusive concession. Since that time, operating under the name Royal Railway and with funding from ADB and AusAID, the company has embarked on an ambitious $143 million project to rehabilitate the entire 641 km of Cambodian rail network. The South Line from Phnom Penh to Sihanoukville was reopened in January 2013, with the Phnom Penh to Sisophon line following suit in July 2018. The envisaged link from Poipet to Sisophon will eventually serve as a means of cross-border transport to and from Thailand. For a shorter railroad experience, a passenger train now runs from the Phnom Penh station to Pochentong Airport.

Around the corner...
Located about 1 km west of the station is another built vestige of Cambodia's railway history. For steam locomotive enthusiasts, the somewhat adventurous path following the railway tracks from Street 221 is well worth the effort. Here, an entire section of the **Phnom Penh Railway Depot** is occupied by rusting ex-CFI Mikados, Pacifics, and Moguls, and the Royal Railway has restored one of these to full working order for steam charters.

Train station and depot in the 1960s, the former Council of Ministers to the right

University of Health Sciences 014 A

73 Preah Monivong Boulevard
Leroy & Mondet
1955

In 1930, French engineers began to introduce architectural rationalism for important public buildings such as the **Railway Station (013 A)** and the **Central Market (033 B)**. This newer style marked a contrast to the great eclecticism imported from Paris starting in 1890. For the Faculty of Medicine of the University of Health Sciences (1955), the architects Leroy & Mondet still used a somewhat neo-classical layout, with a colonnaded entrance portico at the centre of the symmetrical façade. However, they completely renounced any elaborate decorative details, and introduced horizontal bands of windows on the first two floors, thus giving the building an overall rather modernist appearance. A central semi-circular annex and two wings extend from the main building on Monivong Boulevard, thereby forming a large courtyard. The three-floor building

perpendicular to the street directly south of the university originally contained the faculty's boarding school. The main building remains more or less in its original condition, with the wooden window profiles still present along the first floor on the right side of the building. For their later Centre Universitaire du Sangkum Reastr Niyum, today the **Royal University of Phnom Penh (120 F)**, Leroy & Monet then fully committed to the tropical modern design vocabulary inspired by Le Corbusier.

The University of Health Sciences was first established in June 1946 as the School for Medical Officers, after which it became the Cambodian Royal School for Medicine in 1953 and the Faculty of Medicine and Pharmacy in 1962. When the Khmer Rouge took control of Phnom Penh on 17 April 1975, it did not spare the Cambodian medical community and completely destroyed the healthcare system. The faculties were abandoned and severely damaged throughout Pol Pot's rule. The professors and students were treated the same as the rest of the population of Phnom Penh. Many were massacred at the very beginning, others were chased from the city, forced to work in the countryside, murdered, or eventually died from disease, exhaustion, and starvation. When Phnom Penh was liberated by the Vietnamese on 7 January 1979, the healthcare system of Cambodia was non-existent, and only a few healthcare professionals remained. Not a single professor survived the genocide. Medical and surgical education had to be completely rebuilt from scratch, when the combined Faculty of Medicine, Pharmacy and Dentistry was reopened in 1980. Today the University of Health Sciences (UHS) is the only state-owned medical university in Cambodia.

FACULTÉ DE MÉDECINE À PHNOM-PENH

Phnom Penh Capital Hall (former Catholic Diocese)

015 **A**

69 Preah Monivong Boulevard
Architect unknown
1925–1935

The imposing cream-coloured building directly opposite Hotel Le Royal on Monivong Boulevard is currently the **Phnom Penh Capital Hall**. It was once the seat of the **Catholic Diocese** and residence of the bishop. The surrounding enclosure, with its cross-shaped patterns and *fleur-de-lys* ornaments, recalls the former function of the site.

The three-storey building is a representative example of French-colonial administrative edifices. It was built between 1925 and 1935 on the site of the former canal surrounding the French District in the west. The newly added high-rise building behind and to the left attempts in vain to respect the historical context of the compound. Ironically, it houses the Municipal Town Planning Department.

A few steps further to the south on Monivong Boulevard, we find the enormous headquarters of the **Ministry of Posts and Telecommunications**. The monumental office building in a

The Catholic Cathedral in the 1960s, with the Lycée René Descartes to the left, and the Hotel le Royal and the Catholic Diocese (in the background) to the right

retro French-colonial style is less than four years old. It is the result of a clumsy attempt to replicate the elegant style of the historic **Main Post Office** (**004 A**). The massive edifice occupies the western end of a principal axis along the historic promenade (former Avenue Daun Penh, today Street 92) from Wat Phnom to the west as can be seen in the historical photograph. This used to be the site of the **Catholic 'Notre Dame' Cathedral**, financed by the French government as reparation to the Catholic Church after the war. Designed by Maurice Masson and supervised by Henri Chatel, the cathedral was inaugurated in 1955 and destroyed during the Khmer Rouge era. Henri Chatel, who did the site work with the building contractor Société Indochinoise d'Études et de Constructions (SIDEC) between

1952 and 1955, told Helen Grant-Ross of ARK Research 50 years later that he thought the cathedral was 'hideous' and that he was not sorry to learn that the Khmer Rouge had destroyed it. The Khmer Rouge's systematic destruction of all but three of the 72 churches in pre-1975 Cambodia was probably driven by their contempt for western colonialism, but even more for their Vietnamese enemies, as most Catholics in the country were ethnic Vietnamese. By 1979, only three churches had survived: the **Chapel of the Sisters of Providence Hospice** (**031 A**) in the French District of Phnom Penh; the St. Michel Church in Sihanoukville; and the **Church of the Carmelite Convent** (**132 G**), on the Chrouy Changvar peninsula, which was sadly and incomprehensibly demolished just recently.

Lycée Francais René Descartes and National University of Management `016` A

1132 Street 96, between Preah Monivong Boulevard and Street 61
Leroy & Mondet / ADA Adrien Desport
1951 / 2015

The **Lycée Francais René Descartes** is the oldest international school in Phnom Penh. It was built in 1951 by the French government in the late days of the Protectorate to a design by French partnership Leroy & Mondet. The same architect duo stayed in Cambodia after France's withdrawal from Cambodia and later designed the **Royal University of Phnom Penh** (118 F). The school was closed in 1975, and the Khmer Rouge used parts of it to lodge the army's troupe of dancers, singers, and musicians. More notoriously, they also used it as a base for their security police, the *Santebal*, giving it the code name K-33. After years of war and neglect, the school opened again in 1989 at the initiative of a group of parents. At that time, only 13 students were enrolled and the premises were dilapidated. The economic and political future of Cambodia was uncertain, so most of the

The Petit Lycee (front) and the main building (back) in the 1960s

premises were retroceded to Cambodia. Only the small high school (Petit Lycee) was kept for its original purpose, while the main building became the National University of Management. Since then, school enrolment has steadily increased, with the number of students rising to more than 1,000 as of September 2016. The exclusive school soon needed an expansion and new facilities. In 2012, the school launched a design competition, inviting three architecture firms to take part. The brief was to renovate the existing school, provide additional classrooms and a library, and design a masterplan along with three new buildings. The winning entry by ADA Adrien Desport Architects included designs for a new kindergarten, a canteen, and a gymnasium-cum-theatre building. These new constructions were completed in 2015.

The historical aerial photo on the previous double-spread illustrates the original urban design concept. Both school buildings are set back from the boulevard of the former Avenue Joffre. The building is a mirror reflection, in terms of position and massing, of **Hotel Le Royal** (017 A) across it, and the two buildings together emphasise the monumental green axis between **Wat Phnom** (001 A) and the former site of the **Catholic Cathedral** (015 A). In the 1930s, various styles began to emerge in Phnom Penh in parallel to the architectural rationalism characterising the Central Market and Railway Station. Leroy &

Mondet gave the Lycée a utilitarian design, opting for a modern building, but added traditional design elements that clearly refer to the Hotel Le Royal, such as an arcaded ground floor and a traditional roof. The classical arched ground floor arcades are even accentuated by a small clay-tiled canopy. Above them are two modernist floors with open corridors giving access to the former classrooms. The strikingly horizontal structure is interrupted by two protruding staircases with vertical concrete screens that block the sun and provide ventilation. Like the Hotel Le Royal, the central part of the building is emphasised by an additional floor, and the building is rounded off by a traditional Khmer-style (*roong duong*) roof. Unfortunately, between 2000 and 2003, the main building was extended with two massive five-storey wings that counteract the historic building line along the boulevard. The smaller building of the Petit Lycée to the left is still used by the French school. The two-floor construction is more discreet but features similar modern design details, such as the horizontal layout with continuous windows, the screened stairways, and the traditional roof shape. The recently added nursery and canteen buildings have a pleasantly restrained formal language and embody the idea of climate-adapted architecture, with their covered walkways and open spaces. A new sports hall lies at the rear of the compound.

Hotel Raffles Le Royal 017 A

Street 92/Preah
Monivong Boulevard
Ernest Hébrard and Jean Desbois/
Henri Chatel, Koh Say Wee (renovations)
1927–1929/1958, 1996 (renovations)

Le Royal Hotel first opened its doors to the public on the evening of 20 November 1929, during an event that was attended by both King Sisowath Monivong and the then Resident-Superior of the Protectorate. The prestigious hotel, featuring 54 rooms, was designed by French architect, archaeologist, and urban planner Ernest Hébrard (1875–1933) together with architect Jean Ernest Louis Desbois (1891–1971). Situated on the scenic park boulevard towards Wat Phnom (formerly Avenue du Maréchal Joffre), Hotel Le Royal was built in a modernist French colonial style with elements of traditional architecture. Unlike George Groslier, the founder and architect of the **National Museum** (073 C), Ernest Hébrard refused to use classical Khmer architecture as a model, referring to it as a 'mimicry of Angkor Wat'. He instead conceived a unique 'Indochinese style'. For this style, he came up with a modern reinterpretation of local design elements found in vernacular Cambodian houses: large sloping tiled roofs, shuttered windows, and open galleries and covered walkways for better shading and air circulation. **Hotel Cambodiana** (066 C), built in the 1960s,

bears obvious similarities to Le Royal Hotel, although the former's architect, Lu Ban Hap, denies drawing any inspiration from the earlier hotel. In both hotels, guest rooms are located in lower side wings, which are connected by a corridor to a large central building. The triangular dormer windows, which once adorned the sloped roof of Hotel Le Royal, can also be found at Hotel Cambodiana.

Its glamour and convenient location made Hotel Le Royal the hotel of choice for affluent visitors to the city throughout the 1930s and into the 1960s, attracting celebrities such as Charlie Chaplin, W. Somerset Maugham, actress Paulette Goddard, and American first lady Jacqueline Kennedy. The US Legation operated from the hotel for a brief period when diplomatic relations were established in November 1950. The building remained essentially unchanged until architect Henri Chatel added extensions and improvements between 1957 and 1958. These included 30 new studios separated from the main building, an outdoor restaurant, and a swimming pool. He also transformed the entrance hall and revamped the furnishings.

The hotel was simply known as Le Phnom during the Lon Nol period (1970–1975). Prior to the fall of Phnom Penh to the Khmer Rouge on 17 April 1975, it was declared a neutral zone by the Red Cross and converted into a refugee camp and hospital. The hotel was used as a residence

for reporters during the Vietnam War and the Khmer Rouge era. The Washington Post's Elizabeth Becker, one of the few westerners to have met dictator Pol Pot, stayed at the hotel and called it a 'historic treasure'. She lived in room No. 27 on the top floor, with a fan and cold water, for around $100 a month. In 1979, the hotel was reopened as the Hotel Samaki (Solidarity Hotel) and taken over by international aid agencies. The UNTAC (United Nations Transitional Authority in Cambodia) occupied the premises in the early 1990s.

When Singapore-based Raffles International Ltd got involved in the hotel's renovation in 1996, they demolished the surrounding bungalows and replaced them with three new, more sizeable wings, while leaving the main building intact and restoring it to its previous grandeur. Under the supervision of architect Koh Say Wee, the elegant arched lobby known as The Conservatory was meticulously reinstated. Likewise, two symmetrical octagonal light wells to the east and west of the lobby were restored to their original understated splendour. The art historian Darryl Collins reports that the architect Koh Say Wee used terms such as 'architectural layering' to describe the methodical process of slowly stripping away later modifications to the building. Following this extensive makeover, the luxurious hotel now boasts a total of 175 guest rooms and suites. The venue

and its surrounding gardens are a sanctuary of quiet and luxury.

Following the faithfully copied and arranged black-and-white floor tiles along the ground floor corridor towards the east wing, an unpretentious door leads directly into the former dining area, now accommodating the famous Elephant Bar (happy hour 4–9 pm). The bar was completely refurbished in 2015, and the ceiling frescoes were repainted by the master painter of the Royal Palace. When a monkey from the nearby Wat Phnom gardens sneaked into the bar, the artist decided to immortalise this little creature by adding it into his paintings.

Ministry of Information

018 A

62 Preah Monivong Boulevard
Architect unknown
1920s

The building of the former Service des Eaux et Forêts (Water and Forest Administration), today the Ministry of Information, is strangely located behind some characterless commercial buildings, set back from Monivong Boulevard by about 150 metres. A look at a map from the late 1920s reveals that the administrative edifice was actually constructed on a narrow peninsula, completed in 1894, in the wetlands west of the semicircular canal surrounding the French District. Huyn de Verneville, the then Resident-Superior of Cambodia, had ordered the excavation of the peninusla. He had wanted to use the extracted soil to fill in the *beung* (small water channels and ponds) and drain the western plain for future development. The peripheral canal to the west was called Prek O Kor and followed Boulevard Miche (today Monivong Boulevard), while the Service des Eaux et Forêts was connected by a narrow causeway crossing the waterway. In the early 1930s, the canal was filled in, and roadside construction along the west of the boulevard commenced. A map from 1966 shows the then Direction des Eaux, Forêts et Chasses (Directorate of Water, Forests and Hunting) on a now continuous stretch of land, with the former **Catholic Diocese** (**015 A**) along the boulevard, and a large water-supply station further south, just behind the former **Cathedral** (**015 A**).

The stately building is divided into three main parts: the heavy base on the ground floor, which evokes the image of an Angkorian temple; the colonnaded gallery on the first floor spanning the entire 100 metres of the building; and the enormous traditional wooden roof structure adorned by three pediments derived from traditional pagoda architecture. Some alterations have been made over time. For example, two timber columns supporting the central pediment alongside the enlargement of the central stairway were removed. The façade on the ground floor used to be structured by horizontal mouldings, and a historical photo seems to show dark wooden wall panelling all along the first floor, perhaps a reference to the building's function as the Water and Forest Administration. Just like the entrance verandah of the **National Museum** (073 C), the gallery used to be completely open without any balustrade. The *kbach* decorations on the pediments where added later. Christiane Blancot and Aline Hetreau-Pottier describe in their essay '1863–1953, une ville neuve dans un site d'occupation ancienne' a probable connection between the building and the work of George Groslier:

'The Khmer architecture reserved for pagodas, Cambodian institutions and the Royal Palace will be used by Georges Groslier for the construction of the Cambodian School of Arts and the Albert Sarraut Museum ... The outer spaces composed around courtyards surrounded by raised galleries, the roofs, and the decoration are inspired by Angkorian monuments and religious buildings. This experience will not be followed. The Department of Archeology and Urbanism of Indochina, created by Ernest Hebrard, will move from the end of the 1920s towards a more rational architecture.'

Since the 1990s, the building has been used by the Ministry of Information. Established in January 1996, it is responsible for public information and for 'guiding and monitoring' the activities of the Cambodian media. The current minister (since 2004) is Khieu Kanharith, who started his career in 1982 as editor-in-chief of *Kampuchea*, the first Cambodian newspaper to be established after the Khmer Rouge period.

Entrance of the Water and Forest Administration building, 1960s

National Library of Cambodia 019 A

Street 92/Street 61
Louis Chauchon
1924

Next to **Hotel Raffles Le Royal** (017 A), a group of cultural and administrative public buildings line the north side of the well-planned Street 92 (Rukhak Vitei Daun Penh). The National Library, with is neo-classical style, resembles a Greek temple. It was designed by the architect Louis Chauchon and opened to the public on 24 December 1924, with an initial collection of just 2,879 books, mainly in French. The library was managed by French staff until the appointment of the first Khmer director in 1951. After independence in 1954, there was a steady growth in Cambodian publishing, which was reflected in the increased number of Khmer-language books.

Similar to its sister building, the **National Archives of Cambodia** (020 A), situated immediately behind it, the building's appearance today largely remains the same as during colonial times. Only

the surrounding manicured French gardens have unfortunately been replaced by parking, and a solid boundary wall separates the compound from its urban context. The existing library building is situated in the centre of the site with its prominent front façade and main entrance facing south towards the park. The building has a symmetrical floor plan of about 38 by 30 metres, with smaller administrative and reading rooms lined up on both sides of the grand central hall. The building's main elevation is structured by double columns in front of the vast entrance porch and smaller side wings, which follow the division of the building façade into a seven-metre grid.

Despite its neo-classical style, the building features a number of Cambodian design elements. On the right-hand side of the building stands a statue of Vishnu, who symbolises knowledge and intelligence in Cambodia. The decoration on the wall on the left side is inspired by ancient temples in Cambodia, as it features the *kbach phkar phñi* floral style. On the wall next to the main door are bas-reliefs similar to those on ancient temple walls. On the right-hand wall of the library's entrance porch, a sign above the door reads 'Force binds for a time, ideas join forever,' words attributed to François-Marius Baudoin, France's Resident-Superior in Cambodia from 1914 to 1927.

A national library's role is to preserve the country's knowledge and culture, which are precisely what the Khmer Rouge were trying to eradicate. The library's collection was largely destroyed in the brutal years of Pol Pot's regime. The grounds of the library and the archives were used to keep chickens and pigs for the neighbouring hotel, while the buildings were used to house the pig keepers. Inside, many bookshelves were cleared of books to store food and cooking utensils, and the books were evidently used to light cooking fires and as cigarette papers. It has been reported that 35 of the 41 employees of the National Library were killed during the Khmer Rouge period; only two returned to their jobs.

In 1980, the National Library was re-established with the assistance of various overseas governments and agencies. Today the National Library holds some 103,635 copies in various languages (Khmer, French, English, German). Special collections comprise 8,327 national documents, including documents published in French between 1925 and 1970, plus some books and documents published in the Khmer language dating from the years 1955–1975. There is also a special collection of *sastra*, or palm leaf manuscripts, which are available on microfilm. Managed by the Ministry of Culture and Fine Arts, the National Library also functions as the only public lending library in the country.

Regrettably, the current facilities seem no longer appropriate for the needs of modern day library functions and users. The building does not provide suitable conditions for the protection of books. There is no climate control or air-conditioning, which are vital in a country with such humid conditions.

Around the corner...

Further east along Street 92, across Street 61 (Oknha Hing Penn), there is an imposing three-storey building set back from the street. This used to be the former Bureaux de la Résidence Supérieure (photo on p. 12) and the Haute Commissariat de France during the time of the Protectorate. It was recently renovated and now houses the Ministry of Economy and Finance. The building dates back to 1925–35, while the side wings were raised by one floor later on.

A

A

National Archives of Cambodia 020 A

Street 61, behind the
National Library
Architect unknown
1926

Facing the rather unattractive rear side of its prominent sister building, the **National Library (019 A)**, is the National Archives of Cambodia (NAC) building. This edifice was built in 1926 and inaugurated just two years after the National Library. To the west of the archives building is a four-storey annex which was built after 2007 with financial support from the Vietnamese government and styled to match the existing archives building.

The NAC building has a rather unassuming façade, decorated with large panels resembling Angkorian ornamentation. But behind this façade is a delightful interior that in fact lends the building most of its character. It features a central three-floor atrium with chequered cement floor tiles, and this atrium is traversed by concrete bridges. The space is brightly lit with diffused light. The 1,800 linear metres of wooden shelves, symmetrically arranged over three floors on both sides of the central axis, are filled with brown cardboard boxes. They recall movie sets, for example the one used for *Brazil* (1985), directed and co-written by Terry Gilliam. The reinforced-concrete structure displays elements that somewhat recall the Art Deco style, as does the ceiling, which is adorned by a rectangular skylight, just like the central hall of the National Library.

As with the National Library, the National Archives were used during the Khmer Rouge period as barracks for the people working in the piggery on the compound. Although newspapers stored on the ground floor were destroyed, fortunately there was no systematic effort to attack the thousands of archival dossiers held on the upper floors.

The NAC was reopened in 1979 and renovated in 1995 with support from various international donors. In 1986, responsibility for operating the National Archives was transferred to the Presidency of the Council of Ministers. The NAC is responsible for preserving documents, created by the Government of Cambodia, that possess enduring legal and historic value and making them available for future generations. It holds documents produced or collected by the French colonial government and by the Cambodian government since independence, covering almost any imaginable subject over a period of one and a half centuries. Tens of thousands of records are stored within the premises. Most records comprise files, but the archive also has significant holdings of newspapers and magazines, photographs, posters, maps, architectural drawings, and a comprehensive reference library.

The National Archives building is a peaceful and old-fashioned place, worth visiting to conduct research, study, or just take in the nostalgic ambience. The helpful staff will kindly assist you in French, English, or Khmer; however, do make sure to bring plenty of time in case you are looking for something particular.

Caserne Beylié

Street 90/Street 47
Architect unknown
1880–1890

021 A

The former Quartier Beylié was the main military base of the French Protectorate in Phnom Penh. Two entire blocks in the European District north of Wat Phnom used to be occupied by the French military garrison. The western part, the former Camp des Tirailleurs, is now used by the **Kantha Bopha Children's Hospital** (**022 A**). The eastern part of the former military compound was also the site of the first Tribunal de France (or Palais de justice), the French colonial court. It is now completely covered with an informal maze of tiny dwellings, most of them constructed since the late 1990s. You can access the interior of the block through a small alley off Street 90, about 25 metres from the intersection with Street 47 (France Street). Some 50 metres down the alley, if you look up to the right, you will see the corner and roof of a two-storey building in masonry and faded ochre lime plaster, which clearly dates back to the time of the French Protectorate. This is one of very few buildings left in the city that testifies to the military presence of the French rulers in Cambodia. It was a part of the Caserne d'Infanterie, as we can read on a French military map from 1920. The colonial military forces in Cambodia, tasked with quelling potential insurrections, consisted of a light infantry battalion (Bataillon Tirailleurs Cambodgiens) and a national constabulary (Garde Nationale, also called Garde Indigène). Today, the massive building is entirely subdivided into private flats, and most of the ground-floor façade is covered with added make-shift constructions. With a bit of luck, you might even be able to see the odd monkey from the nearby Wat Phnom gardens frolicking about the zinc roofs.

Around the corner...

When back on Rue France (Street 47), look for the muddled mixed-use building just opposite the Kantha Bopha Hospital. The four–storey linear **apartment block** was designed by Henri Chatel with 24 apartments for military personnel and dates back to 1957. The design originally included V-shaped columns to raise the building, and deep recesses provided each apartment with a loggia and protected the façade from the sun. Today the ground floor is completely taken over by small-scale businesses, and substantial extensions and other adaptations have been carried out by the private owners of the units over the years. However, the vertical screen walls in front of the three staircases with their weathered, dark-brown granite finish as well as the expressive concrete canopies marking the entrances are still recognisable. The original roof was formed by two shallow ventilated slopes shading the last floor from direct sunlight.

A

1810 — CAMBODGE — Pnom-Penh — Caserne de l'Infanterie Coloniale

Kantha Bopha Children's Hospital

022 A

Street 90/Street 47
Atelier G+S (Kantha Bopha IV + V),
Dr. Denis Laurent (Kantha Bopha I
redevelopment)
2005–2019

In December 1991, Dr. Beat Richner (1947–2018) was asked by King Norodom Sihanouk and the Cambodian government to rebuild and manage the Kantha Bopha Children's Hospital, which had been destroyed during the civil war. Kantha Bopha had been the name of King Sihanouk's beloved daughter, who died of leukaemia in 1952 at the age of three. In 1992, Dr. Richner created the Kantha Bopha Foundation in Zurich, moved to Phnom Penh, and brought the Kantha Bopha Children's Hospital back into operation. In the following 25 years, he opened four more hospitals, which today treat around 80 per cent of the sick children in Cambodia. The Swiss Kantha Bopha foundation finances and administers the hospitals. In 1994, the Health Ministry assumed responsibility for the Kantha Bopha hospitals to ensure that their 2,500 Cambodian employees receive decent salaries, that the hospitals remain sustainable, and that their policy of corruption-free, cost-free treatment for everyone is maintained.

The extensive hospital complex along Street 47 (France Street) is integrated into two city blocks. It comprises Kantha Bopha I (under redevelopment) as well as Kantha Bopha IV and V. The construction of Kantha Bopha IV started in 2004 after the purchase of a plot adjacent to Wat Phnom, formerly the site of the French Camp du Tirailleurs, and the new hospital was inaugurated on 29 December 2005. Swiss architecture firm Atelier G+S designed the building complex, addressing first and foremost the country's harsh climate conditions, since extreme heat and heavy rainfalls are a constant issue in Cambodia. The local climatic realities led to some recurring design elements throughout the complex, for example the covered walkways and exterior-facing corridors. A series of courtyards

A

and open staircases create an airy atmosphere inside and between the various buildings. Perforated brick walls perform a similar function, allowing ventilation and offering protection from direct sunlight. This climate-adapted approach to architecture is environmentally friendly and energy efficient, since there are very few air-conditioned spaces throughout the complex (only the laboratories and operating theatres have air conditioning). The hospital's arrangement and structure correspond to the shape of the site and to the flow of patients from consultation to hospitalisation. The first courtyard, located behind the entrance for outpatients on Street 90 (Chivapol Street), features a large tensile roof structure and serves both as a waiting area and a space for initial consultations. The internal north-south corridor connects to Kantha Bopha V, thereby crossing a street that has been partially closed for public use. At Street 88 (Phsar Dek Street), make sure to have a look at the neighbourhood market: you will be rewarded by the striking signature brick façades of Kantha Bopha V, divided by leafy courtyards and towering above the market stalls. Regrettably, the original U-shaped building of Kantha Bopha I, an early and rather conservative work of Vann Molyvann from 1959, had to be demolished in 2018 to make way for another hospital extension along Street 61. Kantha Bopha Children's Hospital is not open to public visitors. However, at the northern end of the hospital, set back from Street 47, stands a meticulously restored French-colonial building, which today houses the hospital's visitor centre and a permanent exhibition on the history of the Kantha Bopha Children's Hospital and Foundation. The building is the only remainder of the former Maternité Roume, constructed in the 1920s.

Dr. Beat Richner passed away after a serious illness on 9 September 2018. His vast legacy includes not only his achievements in children's healthcare but also the creation of a remarkable contemporary building ensemble that could serve as a future model for efficient and sustainable hospital architecture in the tropics.

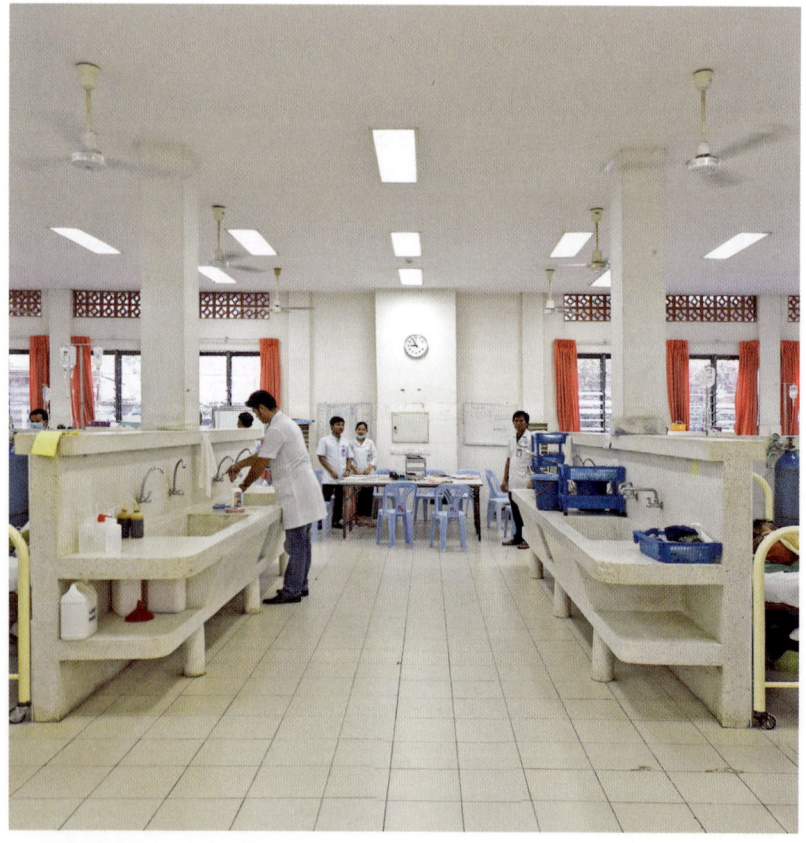

Preah Ket Mealea Hospital (former Hôpital Mixte)

48 Street 47 (Rue France)
Architect unknown
1880s–1960s

023 A

The Preah Ket Mealea Hospital occupies an entire block between Rue France and Sisowath Quay. It was formerly Hôpital Mixte, whose fate was deeply intertwined with Cambodia's colonial history. Hôpital Mixte was originally built to fulfil a promise, made by Commander Doudart de Lagrée and Dr. Honnorat to King Norodom in 1886, to build a palace and hospital. At the end of the 19th century, several hectares of land in the European District near the Tonle Sap River were handed over to the French as part of a concession. And

on this land, a straw-hut hospital called La Paillote was constructed in 1891. This was used as a mobile ambulance for the care of soldiers. Until 1885, there had only been two hospital structures in the capital: the barracks infirmary for French soldiers, and the hospital of the **Sisters of Providence of Portieux** (031 A), reserved for indigenous people. The need for hospital care increased as the city expanded. From 1889, new masonry buildings were erected, and existing pavilions were raised with additional floors to treat European soldiers and civilians. The first pavilions for non-Europeans were built on the east of the hospital compound until 1910. And in the 1930s, large utilitarian buildings further increased the hospital compound's capacity. By 1953, Hôpital

Mixte had become a mixed civilian and military hospital comprising eight buildings and a total of 500 beds. The period of the Sangkum Reastr Niyum and then of the Khmer Republic saw a sharp increase in the number of Cambodian doctors and in the construction of new large hospitals, such as the Calmette Hospital in 1959 and the **Khmer-Soviet Friendship Hospital** (117 E) in 1960. The **Faculty of Medicine** (014 A) was established in 1963, and as a result, there were 530 accredited doctors in the capital in April 1975. In 1963, Hôpital Mixte became Preah Ket Mealea Hospital, named after the legendary king, whose father, god Indra, is said to have built Angkor Wat. After the Khmer Rouge entered Phnom Penh on 17 April 1975, the hospital saw very limited activity, and a large number of doctors disappeared, either killed or exiled under the Khmer Rouge. The hospital's reorganisation commenced, slowly, on 7 January 1979, and the hospital became an exclusively military hospital caring for wounded soldiers and mine victims. In 1998, the hospital once again became a mixed hospital focusing on surgery and specialty medicine. Although it has undergone multiple transformations, the complex is still representative of the administrative colonial architecture at the turn of the century. To the right of the main entrance on Rue France is a nicely renovated administrative

A

building, with two floors, dating back to 1900–1910. Flanking a courtyard on the northern end of the north-south axis are two three-floor buildings. These are the Pavillon Civil and the Pavillon Militaire, each accommodating 120 in-patients. They were both built with a utilitarian design, between 1927 and 1930, to replace the early hospital buildings. The building bordering the courtyard to the north dates from the same time, but was modified in the 1950s. In 1959, a large operating theatre and a radiology department were added to the southern end of this ensemble, connecting the older wings with open filigree walkways made from reinforced concrete. The former operating theatre (Pavilion Européen de Chirurgie) from the 1930s can be seen on Sisowath Quay. It is surrounded by a verandah and sheltered by beautiful plastered screens.

Hôpital Mixte in the 1920s/1930s

Apartment Building – The Sixties

Street 84 / Street 39

Jamshed Phirosza Petigura /
Yvon Chalm (renovation and extension)
1950s / 2017

024 **A**

It is almost a miracle that the apartment building built by the architect Jamshed Phirosza Petigura in the 1950s still exists. Instead of demolishing the structure to replace it with yet another condominium tower, as is usual in Phnom Penh today, the current owner, Canadia Bank, decided to preserve and modernise it. The building's architect Jamshed Petigura was born in Fuzhou, China, to Indian and Chinese parents and died in 1970 in Phnom Penh. Petigura, who had a French diploma, worked in Saigon Before coming to Cambodia. Lu Ban Hap, head of the Service Municipal de l'Urbanisme et de l'Habitat in the 1960s, remembers Petigura as one of the few architects working in Phnom Penh at the time. According to him, Petigura regularly submitted building applications to him, including a number of villas that have not yet been identified. However, we do know that he was involved in a number of other buildings, such as the **Apartments for the National Bank of Cambodia** (**101 D**), the **Hotel Monorom** (**057 B**), and the **Paradise Hotel** (**054 B**), which also features port-hole windows that where not common in Phnom Penh at that time.

In the 1950s and 1960s, not many of such grand freestanding apartment buildings were built in Phnom Penh. Housing was almost exclusively designed in a form

resembling Chinese shophouses or detached villas. The originally five-storey, almost austere building has an axially symmetrical structure and a well-proportioned, plastered façade, which is, like on many other buildings in Phnom Penh from the time, structured by joint lines. Unlike most of the buildings of the Modern Movement, the façade was – and still remains – painted beige and covered with a coating made of chippings (*thmo lieng*) very commonly used in Southeast Asia. During the remodelling by French architect Yvon Chalm, some later extensions to the building were removed in order to regain the original shape. Two additional floors, which clearly stand out from the existing building, were added during the modernisation, which led to 24 new contemporary apartments on the upper floors. The ground floor is used as office space and was given a single-storey extension on the right side. Before the conversion, Yvon Chalm compiled an extensive inventory and conducted material research, since many of the original components and materials had survived. Although the conversion preserved the original structure, including the stairwells and lifts, some of the details were regrettably lost, such as the green metal window grilles, which were sold at a price per kilo shortly before the start of the conversion. Moreover, the colour of the windows was changed from green to black without the architect's intervention. The newly installed serviced apartments are run under the name The Sixties by Dara, a Cambodian hospitality group.

A

The Chinese House

45 Preah Sisowath Quay/
Street 84
Architect unknown
1903–1905

025 A

The so-called Chinese House is a unique masterpiece of restoration thanks mainly to the art historian and author Darryl Collins, who lived there from 1994 to 2007. It sits on a block that was originally the site of the palace of the Vice Roi or *Upayuvarech*, a son of King Ponhea Yat, founder of Phnom Penh. In 1903, the land was bought by Tan Bunpa (1871–1952), a Hokkien Chinese who amassed a fortune through the import and export of food products. Tan Bunpa also financed the nearby **Wat Pipoat Riangsey** (030 A), sometimes known today as Wat Preah Put Khousacha. He held the position of Honorary Mandarin at the Royal Court.

The house was most probably built between 1903 and 1905. It is amongst a very few in Phnom Penh that have remained in their original state, with few alterations or additions. The building represents an interesting blend of styles. Its symmetric layout and traditional roof shape were inspired by Chinese architecture; it has a French-style arched main façade with a verandah facing the Tonle Sap River; and it features attached outhouses for the kitchen and bathroom that resemble the structure of vernacular Khmer houses. The ground floor features a patchwork of stunning Belle Époque-era tiles that must have been imported from France, based on the manufacturers' names engraved on them.

Tan Bunpa's family occupied the house until the 1970s. It stood abandoned when the Khmer Rouge emptied the city of its population in April 1975. In the 1980s, several families working at the nearby **Preah Ket Mealea Hospital** (023 A) occupied the house. It was then purchased from them by the family of Kith Meng in the early 1990s. It was finally bought by a reputable Oknha, known for preserving historical buildings in Phnom Penh, such as **The Pavilion Hotel** (094 C), who happens to be a granddaughter of Tan Bunpa. Until recently, the Chinese House was used as a stylish bar and restaurant, though a new public establishment is expected to open in the second half of 2019. The renovation and décor of the building are nothing short of breathtaking, and its structure and historic surfaces remain remarkably untouched. All exposed walls, bare hardwood beams, and faded colours, along with elaborate Chinese ornamental furnishings and artworks throughout, create a Bohemian mix of vintage decay and opulence.

![Decorative circular carved and painted medallion featuring dragons, framed in a square panel]

Hokkien Temple and School

026 **A**

39 Sisowath Quay,
near Street 82
Architect unknown
1890s (original building)/
1964 (current building)

The **Hokkien Temple** (Chinese name Xie Tian Gong) is the most beautiful and authentic Chinese temple in Phnom Penh. Hokkien is a fluid ethnic label designating the descendants of Chinese immigrants from the Fujian province in southeast China. The Hokkien's presence in Cambodia is a very early one. Hokkien people often emigrated to become merchants – you will note the temple is near the port. The current building is made of concrete and dates back to 1964. It was preceded by a wooden structure that was built in the 1890s at the same location. According to art historian Darryl Collins, in 1887, King Norodom prayed at the former Hokkien temple near Psar Chas to the gods, asking to be relieved of his health problems. His prayers were answered, and the grateful king offered the land at the current location for a new temple to be built. After passing the school buildings located on both sides of the courtyard, you can enter the temple from either the left or right of the massive red doors – the central one is reserved for the gods. The layout of the temple follows traditional Chinese design principles, with a two-hall, three-bay building divided by a courtyard (now partly covered). The small patio to the left features a fresco of a tiger and a plant container, symbolising the earth element. The one to the right features a dragon and a fish tank, symbolising the water element. The curved main roof ridge is adorned with playful dragons and other figurines made of broken china mosaic portraying Chinese folk stories. Unlike Chinese temples in Vietnam, which display features of Buddhism, Confucianism, and Taoism, Phnom Penh's Chinese temples are places of worship only for Taoist divinities. The statue of the main god is displayed at the centre of the rear wall, topped by an inscription defining him as the 'Emperor of Divine Beings'.

Former Cantonese Congregation and School

Alley off Preah Sisowath Quay, between Streets 80 and 82
Architect unknown
1930

027 A

Hidden in a small alleyway off Preah Sisowath Quay lies another historic treasure trove of Chinese history in Phnom Penh. The former Cantonese Congregation and School has played an important role in organising the cultural and social lives of the Cantonese community, above all during the time of the French Protectorate.

There are five Chinese congregations in Cambodia, which are based on ethno-linguistic divisions: Teochew, Cantonese, Hakka, Hokkien, and Hainanese. The Cantonese and Hokkien communities are the oldest in Phnom Penh. The arrival of Cantonese people began in the 15th century but accelerated after 1679, when pro-Ming Cantonese generals gave up the struggle against the Qing dynasty and began to emigrate with their troops from the regions south and east of Canton. Before the Khmer Rouge, the Cantonese formed the second largest Chinese community after the Teochew.

The ensemble of two-storey buildings with an ochre limewash façade and large French-style windows featuring louvred shutters probably dates back to 1930, as this year is inscribed on a pediment on the first building to the left of the alley. If we continue straight ahead, the Chinese inscription hidden behind power cables inside the arched passageway says 'No. 2, physical education / sports ground', so we can imagine the voices of children's laughter on the courtyard. Today, the three-sided courtyard complex is completely embedded in informal miniature dwellings, and various families also use the subdivided original buildings. The main building shows a strange mixture of French-colonial architecture, vaguely modern elements such as perforated screen walls, and traditional Khmer design features such as Angkor-style decorative columns inside the air vents. Note also the elaborately moulded concrete corbels supporting the widely cantilevering roof, and the colourful tile patterns high up on the rear façade of the main building.

Former Société Khmère de Montage Automobile (SKMA)
Street 82, near Sisowath Quay
Architect unknown
1930s

028 A

A

Around the corner, on Street 82, you will notice a long low-rise building. The inscriptions on the curved pediments above the ground floor have mostly faded away. Try to decipher 'CITROEN' on one of them. The building used to be a Citroen warehouse and a primary school for the children of the company's Cambodian employees. In the early 1960s, it housed the Société Khmère de Montage Automobile (SKMA), a venture started by Citroen's agent in Cambodia, Georges Desrues, in order to locally assemble a box-van version of the 2CV. Operations were launched in Sihanoukville in 1958, but seem to have been unsuccessful, as the company was closed in 1962. The photo shows the Laquemant-Laquemant team and its DS19, winner of the third Rally of Cambodia in front of the SKMA garage in 1960.

Former Cantonese Temple

 029 A

Alley off Preah Sisowath Quay,
between Streets 78 and 80
Architect unknown
Second half of 18th century

At the end of a nameless alley off Preah Sisowath Quay lies a hidden architectural gem. A grandiose Chinese roof sticks out of a neighbourhood packed with small informal dwellings. This is the Temple of the Cantonese Congregation. Its Chinese name Di Shan Gong (literally 'lush/green (jade) mountain temple') is written on an inscription above the central entrance. According to research by Khmer Architecture Tours, this is the oldest Chinese temple in Phnom Penh and its most ancient part dates back to the second half of the 18th century. The Chen Damdek block has been a Chinese neighbourhood since even before the 20th century. Most of the Chinese residents worked as blacksmiths, and the name of the block actually translates to 'Chinese blacksmith'.

The temple, like the **Chapel of the Sisters of Providence Hospice (031 A)** or the **Caserne Beylie (021 A)**, is one of the last surviving testimonies to the conversion of existing building structures after the Khmer Rouge era. Tens of thousands of people returned to Phnom Penh at that time or arrived here for the first time, seeking a better future in the city. In the 1990s, the whole pagoda compound was gradually taken over by informal settlers. Look out for some original architectural elements among all the parasitic constructions. The stone bases and frame of the main entrance gate can still be seen, and if you peek into an apartment on the left or right you might discover the original giant timber columns and tiled floors. Further historic column bases made of solid granite are neatly lined up in the alley behind.

The temple roof, however, is remarkably intact. Three superb wooden panels with golden Chinese calligraphy are attached to the massive timber roof structure high above. The main roof ridge features intricate figurative ornaments made of colourful glazed earthenware, displaying a picturesque ensemble of traditional Chinese buildings. Sadly, the original Chinese figurines that once stood in the front, with their imperial robes and impressive beards, have not survived the times. The five elements of *feng shui* are traditionally sculpted on gable ends of temples (and sometimes shophouses); here, the impressive curved gable decorations symbolise the water element. Unfortunately, their full splendour can only be appreciated from higher up, so we suggest you intrepidly go and find an accessible balcony or rooftop nearby.

Visiting this place is something for the more curious, but those who do will be rewarded with discovering one of Phnom Penh's most interesting and unique historic and spatial situations.

Wat Pipoat Riangsey

Street 47 / Street 80
Architect unknown
1887 / 1910s–1930s

Wat Pipoat Riangsey (Piphup Raingsi), located north of the old European District not far from the famous Phnom, is one of the oldest pagodas in the city. The compound already existed in the 15th century, as shown in the 15th century map drawn by George Coédes in 1923 based on the royal chronicles. It has a pretty slender main *vihàra* (in Khmer *vihear*), whose core consists of timber columns supporting the wooden roof. It is closed on all sides by self-supporting brick walls built in 1887, as indicated by a stone plaque on its eastern wall. The exterior is clearly divided into three distinct parts: the slightly raised basement, the body, and the roof. The basement, 21 m in length and 12 m in width, is decorated by *kbach* motifs inspired by Angkor Wat. Its gallery is typical of the ones built during King Norodom's reign: it is narrow, with massive rectangular pillars, and opened only on the short sides by two little sets of steps. The traditional two-tiered roof has a tympanum on each side, and '1937' is cast in concrete on each tympanum, probably indicating the date of renovation. The roof is supported by eave brackets resembling *garuda* and *kinnari* (mythical creatures) and decorated by four *chovea* elements in the form of *nagas* (mythical serpents). The interior has three aisles and seven bays, formed by two rows of six columns each. The wooden columns have granite bases with deep mouldings. Surprisingly, the wooden parts have been painted with Chinese dragons and heavenly *devatas*, but, according to research by Khmer Architecture Tours, have the old stencil-work in black-gold patterns from 1887 underneath. The floor is covered by colourful encaustic (inlaid) cement tiles arranged according to the functional division of the interior space. We can surmise that the sanctuary's oldest painted decoration was probably executed around 1887, since the roof and ceiling of this building are original. The vertical planks of the ceiling framework depict episodes from the *Vessantara Jataka* and the *Vidhurapandita Jataka* as well as scenes from the life of the Buddha. The paintings of the décor are now among the oldest still existing in situ in Phnom Penh. But the main interest of this wat lies in the presence of a superb mural painted on the eastern interior wall of its vihàra. The vast painting depicts the stay of the Buddha in the sky of Indra, home of the 33 gods, and his descent to earth. In this

episode of the life of the Buddha, the Master goes to the heaven of Indra to preach *Abhidharma*, the 'higher teachings'. On his right is Indra, with the green face, and on his left, well detached, the mother of Buddha, sitting with her knees bent. Placed above him is the stupa in which the hair of Prince Siddhartha, the historical Buddha, is buried. The Buddha is seated, with his hands calling the earth to witness (*bhumisparsa mudra*). Below, we see the descent of the Enlightened on earth, where he is received by animals and men. On the left are the terrestrial animals and the fish on the right, illustrated with a very delicate palette of colours. The background, influenced by Western art, represents trees and foliage, with a perspective effect. The whole mural, probably dating from the construction of the vihâra 100 years ago, is a superb work of art, with a finesse of details and a rare beauty, worthy of the frescoes of the **Silver Pagoda** (060 C). The artist was anonymous, but it could have been the famous official painter and architect of the time, Oknha Tep Nimith Mak, or a member of his workshop.

Unfortunately, the monks of the pagoda have 'restored' the brick walls of the sanctuary by covering it simply with cement-based plaster instead of the original lime-based plaster, before remaking a clumsy modern fresco of little interest. The disastrous work was done between 1993 and 1995, shortly after the return of King Norodom Sihanouk to Cambodia and the restoration of the monarchy. The concrete cover led to erosion of the brick walls behind the plaster, as the humidity caused by rising groundwater and annual flooding was trapped inside the walls. The mural paintings were spoiled in their lower part, where the illustration of the infernal worlds used to be. A recent systematic restoration initiative by the Heritage Department of the Ministry of Fine Arts and Culture tried to preserve what was left as a national heritage. To the north of the pagoda compound, we can find a rather peculiar Art Deco-style building with curved brick walls and a traditional pagoda roof built by a wealthy Chinese merchant named Tan Bunpa (see **Chinese House** 025 A) probably in the 1920s or 1930s. The building used to be a primary school for monks; today it is sadly used as a storeroom. To the east of the vihâra lies another monastery building in similar style and the refectory (*sala chhan*), both built in the 1910s, as well as a 19th century brick stupa.

Around the corner...

Have a look at the adjacent pagoda to the south, across Street 80. It is known to locals as **Wat Chen Dâmdek** or 'Chinese Blacksmith Pagoda', due to the former use of the surrounding neigbourhood. The main vihâra was built between 1955 and 1965, but the foundation of this pagoda also dates back to the 15th century.

Chapel of the Sisters of Providence Hospice

031 A

Street 78
Architect unknown
1900–1910

A small passageway leads into a crowded residential area off Preah Sisowath Quay, with informal constructions arranged anarchically along nameless alleys. This formerly exclusive area used to mark the northern end of the French District. It was named Providence after the title of the congregation, and it kept this name during the time of the French Protectorate and the Sangkum Reastr Niyum.

The Chapel of the Sisters of Providence Hospice is the last remaining pre-war church building in Phnom Penh. It is unknown why the chapel wasn't destroyed by the Khmer Rouge like all the others. The Mission des Soeures de Providence Hospice was built at the end of the nineteenth century by the Sisters of Providence of Portieux, who settled in Cambodia in 1881. The architect remains unknown, though was likely a French priest. The ensemble comprised an orphanage, a hospice, and a school for young girls, called École de Providence. A three-floor building with the sleeping quarters of the orphans and the sisters was situated next to the church, but has since been demolished. The French cemetery was located north of the church, between the northern end of today's Street 47 and Preah Sisowath Quay, with Street 70 (Oknha Khleang Moeung) bordering it to the north. Unlike the chapel, the cemetery was largely destroyed under the Khmer Rouge.

The chapel's neo-gothic structure is almost intact, although it has some parasitic micro-dwellings latching onto it. It has a cross-shaped basilica layout, with the former main entrance to the west now blocked. The gable end on top of the western façade is adorned by a stone cross and a medallion. The three windows underneath have been filled in with masonry. All main windows and doors have lancet arches and feature louvred shutters. Rose windows above the main windows on the longitudinal façades let further light and air into the building.

The interior still presents an imposing gothic rib-vault ceiling with small decorative rosettes. The rest of the interior however, is more secular: it has been completely taken over and transformed into partitioned rooms where around 20 families have settled since the 1990s. Entering through the side entrance, we can still recognise the beautiful tiled floor. On both sides of the now walled-in central nave, the aisles for the seat benches used to be accentuated by a different pattern of encaustic (inlaid) floor tiles. With nothing remaining of its original function, the chapel symbolises the fate of Phnom Penh after the war, just like the **Cantonese Temple** (**029 A**) and the **Cantonese Congregation and School** (**027 A**).

PNOM-PENH — *L'Orphelinat des Sœurs de la Providence*

House for Lon Non

1 Col de Monteiro Street
Chhim Sun Fong
1970

032 A

Little is known about the Cambodian architect of this villa. Born in 1941, Chhim Sun Fong left for Australia in 1963, where he graduated from the Faculty of Architecture at the University of Adelaide in 1968 before returning to Phnom Penh. He worked for Lu Ban Hap both in his private office and in the Urban Planning Department. Lu acknowledges him as a contributer to his **Hotel Cambodiana** (**066 C**) and **Chenla State Cinema** (**116 E**). In 1971, he was an employee of the Faculty of Architecture at the Royal University of Fine Arts. Chhim Sun Fong is presumed to have died under the Khmer Rouge.

Lon Non was the brother of Lon Nol, who led the 1970 military coup against Norodom Sihanouk. He was an officer of the military police under Sihanouk and was quickly promoted after his fall. He first became a colonel, then general, and commanded the US-trained Khmer militia of the Khmer Serei and Khmer Kampuchea Krom. He is believed to have been responsible for the massacres of Vietnamese civilians in Phnom Penh, carried out by the military in the period following the coup d'état. He was also linked to international heroin trafficking in collaboration with the CIA, and he made around $90 million by selling arms from military stocks on a large scale. Lon Non's house is a typical 1960s villa. It bears major similarities to the houses built by Chhim Sun Fong's former boss Lu Ban Hap at that time. The roof especially recalls the roof of Lu's own home on Norodom Boulevard (destroyed), and the house overall resembles Lu's residence for the Indian Ambassador (today, only a ruin is left of this villa on Norodom Boulevard). Shortly before the construction of Lon Non's residence, Lu had ordered a redesign of the traffic circle on which Lon Non's Villa is located. In the middle of the roundabout, he erected an imposing dome, several metres high. The layout was chosen due to the fact that Lu's employees at the Horticultural Office were complaining that they had nowhere to store their equipment in this part of the city. The 'knotted gun' memorial now located there was inaugurated in 1999 to symbolise government efforts to eliminate illegal weapons.

Ivan Tizianel
Asma Architects
Phnom Penh

Ivan Tizianel is one of the founders of Asma Architects, a French-Cambodian collaboration, which made its first appearance in Cambodia with the completion of the Kantha Bopha Hospital's conference centre in Siem Reap in 2001. Asma Architects design with attention to detail and context, striving to create architecture that harnesses and responds to the climate and which is relevant to the local context.

What is it that makes Phnom Penh special among cities in Southeast Asia?
Phnom Penh had two main phases of development: the time of the French Protectorate, and the time after the country gained independence. Development during these periods was planned, and the result was a beautiful city with even proportions, white and light-yellow buildings, lots of trees, and low-rise constructions with a height limitation respecting the Royal Palace. We are now seeing a third and very intense phase with high and chaotic constructions all over, but the feeling of the former city remains in the historical areas.

What are the key elements for a 'local' and sustainable/climate-adapted architecture in Cambodia?
In tropical countries, one must above all provide shade and good ventilation to avoid heat. Whatever technology is used, exposing glass surfaces to the sun is the worst thing you can do. It was not smart to build fully glazed towers in northern

countries in the 1970s and 80s, and doing so now in tropical countries is senseless.

Where do we find good examples?
Any building designed before the introduction of affordable air conditioning is a good example. All buildings from the 1960s have large balconies, loggias, and concrete awnings that provide outdoor space and shade. New designs often omit these features to increase indoor space. The result is large spaces without any character, and very high energy costs.

Can you tell us a bit about the state of contemporary architecture in Phnom Penh? What are the challenges for its future development?
The most difficult challenge is the city's growth. During the first two phases of development, the city was planned before construction started. The city grew with a network of public streets and roads, and buildings were built along this urban fabric, connecting all parts of the city. Now, the main issue is the proliferation of *borey* (gated communities), which occupy huge plots of land without any connecting street. They produce private pockets, blocking circulation and increasing traffic congestion all over the city.

What should architects visiting the city pay particular attention to?
The **Olympic Stadium** (105 E) is a masterpiece of 20th century modern architecture, as well as the **Central Market** (033 B). The **University Compound** (118 F) has a very interesting ensemble of buildings, along Russian Boulevard. I would also recommend a visit to the State Palace in the Chamkarmon compound.

What are your favourite buildings or places in the city, and why?
I like the **Royal Palace** (060 C), the riverside, and the old Chinese District areas. Also the pagodas in the centre, where you can find old buildings and feel the spirit of Phnom Penh. I hope the **Renakse Hotel** (061 C) will be renovated to preserve the ambience along the river. In the same area, the **National Museum** (073 C) and the **Royal University of Fine Arts** (074 C) behind are the most quiet places to visit.

Around the Central Market

Interview: Ester van der Laan

The high-density commercial district surrounding the architectural masterpiece that is the Central Market (Phsar Thmey) used to be the Chinese District during the French Protectorate. East of Norodom Boulevard near the riverfront lies the oldest part, while the areas west of Norodom and finally west of Monivong Boulevard (Orussey Quarter) were developed successively. It is still a rather homogeneous area with regular blocks of Chinese shophouses and countless modernist apartment buildings from the 1950s and 1960s, as well as a cluster of (former) hotels from that period along Monivong Boulevard. The streets and pavements lining the small-scale shopfronts are buzzing with all kinds of commercial activities, so keep an eye on the traffic while wandering the area.

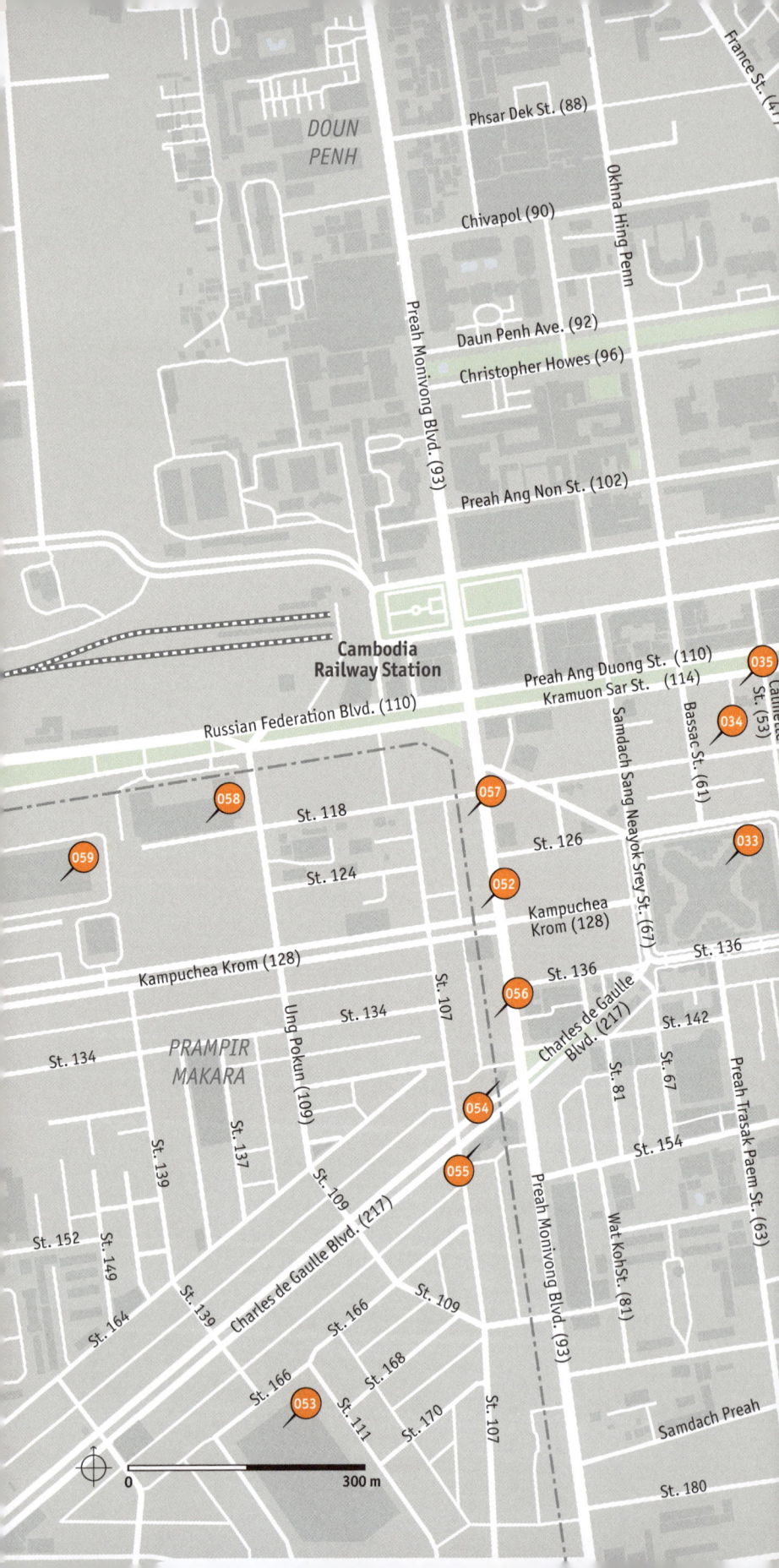

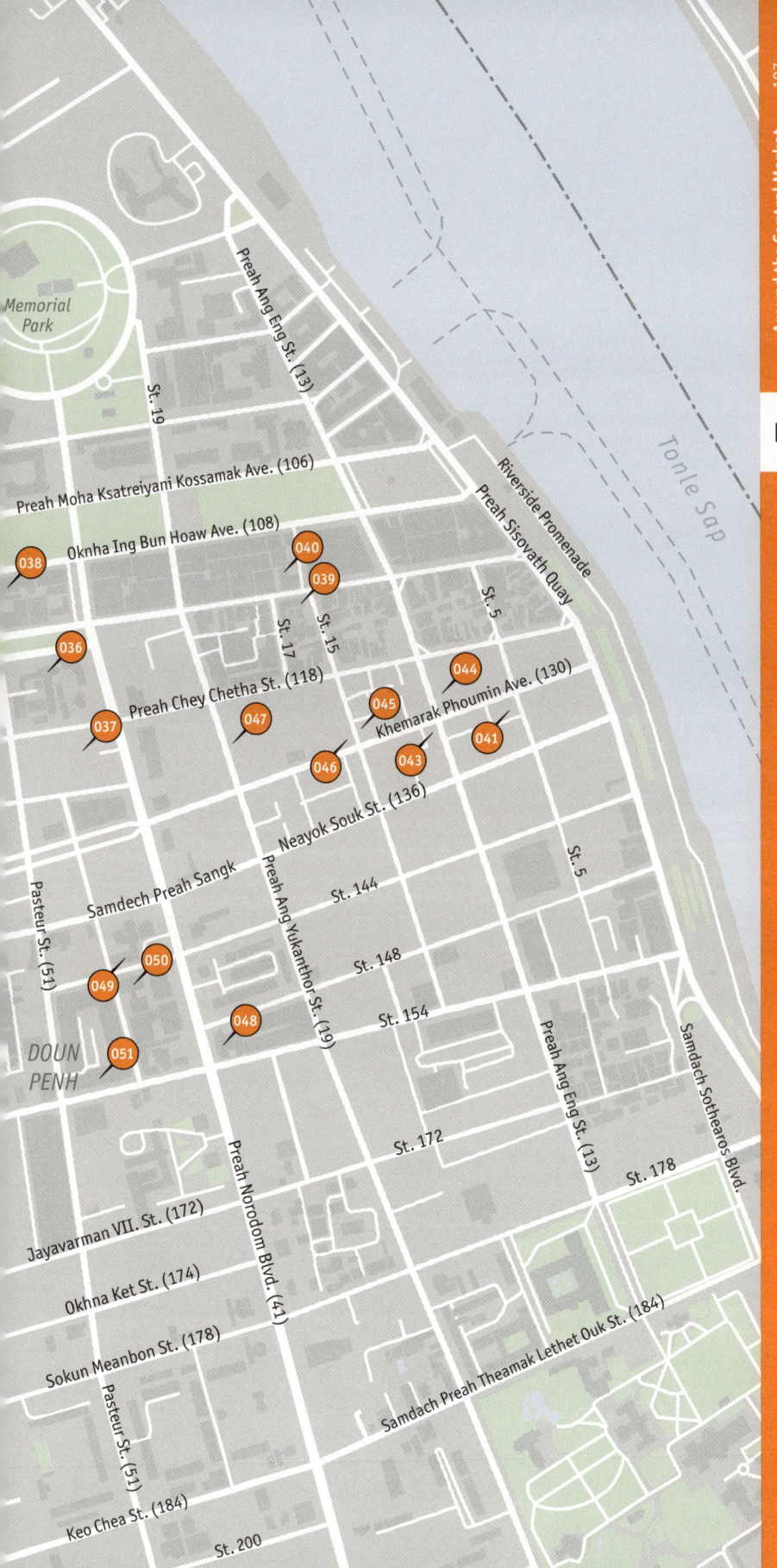

Memorial
Park

St. 19

Preah Ang Eng St. (13)

Riverside Promenade

Preah Sisovath Quay

Tonle Sap

Preah Moha Ksatreiyani Kossamak Ave. (106)

Oknha Ing Bun Hoaw Ave. (108)

038

040

039

St. 5

036

St. 17

St. 15

044

Preah Chey Chetha St. (118)

037

047

045

Khemarak Phoumin Ave. (130)

046

043

041

Neayok Souk St. (136)

Pasteur St. (51)

Samdech Preah Sangk

Preah Ang Yukanthor St. (19)

St. 144

St. 5

St. 148

049

050

St. 154

DOUN
PENH

051

048

St. 172

Preah Ang Eng St. (13)

St. 178

Samdach Sothearos Blvd.

Jayavarman VII. St. (172)

Okhna Ket St. (174)

Preah Norodom Blvd. (41)

Sokun Meanbon St. (178)

Pasteur St. (51)

Samdach Preah Theamak Lethet Ouk St. (184)

Keo Chea St. (184)

St. 200

B

View of the Central Market at the end of Charles de Gaulle Boulevard

Central Market (Phsar Thmey) 033 B

Intersection of Street 63
and Street 130
Jean Desbois, Louis Chauchon /
Arte Charpentier with
Vann Molyvann (renovation)
1937 / 2011 (renovation)

The Central Market is without a doubt one of the city's most impressive structures. It was built on the site of a former lake that in 1434, when King Ponhea Yat first moved the capital to Phnom Penh, was created so that the excavated earth could be used to raise the hill at Wat Phnom. The French in turn brought 651,000 m³ of earth to drain the lake and build a masterpiece of Art Deco design. Around this time, in the early 1930s, Phnom Penh's population had grown to over 90,000, and the old market (Phsar Chas) was no longer considered sufficient. The then city architect Jean Desbois (1891–1971) was thus commissioned to design a new market. The engineer Wladimir Kandaouroff carried out the calculations required for the state-of-the-art structure, which was then realised on site by architect Louis Chauchon (1878–1945), who was also the architect in charge of the **National Library (019 A)**. The market was built by the Société Indochinoise d'Études et de Construction (SIDEC) and inaugurated by King Sisowath Monivong in September 1937.

With its groundbreaking use of building materials and its renunciation of historicist decorations, the market can be considered, along with the **Railway Station (013 A)**, as one of the first and most radical modernist buildings in Phnom Penh. The enormous construction of the dome, 26 m in height and 30 m in diameter, and its four wings, each 44 m long and 12 m high, push the possibilities of reinforced concrete to its very limits. According to the aforementioned authors Ross and Collins, part of France's legacy in Cambodia was the establishment of a construction industry with workers capable of using reinforced concrete. The authors argue that the skills acquired in this way would later to play an important role in architectural developments during the post-independence building boom.

The four wings of the market radiate cruciformly from the massive dome on a square plot. There were once small public parks between the arms. The four wings originally stood on columns, which, in combination with the high ceiling vaults and the large number of ventilation openings in the walls and roofs, ensured good temperature control.

In 2011, the market was completely overhauled, and the improvised stalls, which in the meantime had completely filled the formerly open spaces, were replaced by fixed stands with concrete roofs. However, this cannot be seen as a successful intervention: the massive new roofs obscure the contours of the historic building and dominate the view. The rearrangement of the stalls carried out as part of the modernisation also detracts from the pleasantly chaotic flair of the market.

The Central Market in the late 1930s

Chey Cheta Street Apartments 034 B

Street 118 (Preah Chey Chetha
Street), between Street 61 and
Street 53
René Nguyen Khac Scheou
1960s

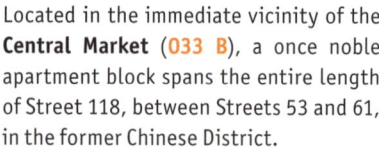

Located in the immediate vicinity of the
Central Market (033 B), a once noble
apartment block spans the entire length
of Street 118, between Streets 53 and 61,
in the former Chinese District.

The complex is arranged around one
of the narrow backyards typical of this
time. It has a stylish front building facing the street and a less elaborately designed rear building. The front and rear
buildings are connected by open bridges
that cross the backyard. At the centre of
the building on Street 118, a generous
main staircase leads to open galleries
in the inner courtyard. Two more modest
entrances are located on Street 61 and
Street 53.

It is worth crossing the small shop that
has settled in the foyer of the central
staircase and ascending to the second
or third floor. The former lift, a luxurious and rather unusual feature for this
time, can still be clearly seen, indicating that this building was once built to
meet high standards. Swiss architect
Martin Aerne established his office on
the second floor some time ago. From the

outside, one can clearly see the façade
module of his office, which has been restored to its original state with Swiss attention to detail. It clearly differs from
the other chaotic conversions, additions, and superstructures – including
the rooftop extensions – which take little account of design aspects. A closer
look, however, reveals a number of beautiful original details, such as the carefully crafted metal railings.

Vietnamese architect René Nguyen Khac
Scheou came to Phnom Penh in 1957. Born

in Saigon in 1908, Scheou went to Lyon, France, in 1927 and studied architecture there, at the studio of Tony Garnier among others. In 1935, he returned to his hometown, where he began his career as an architect at the Public Works Office. From 1947 onwards, he worked as a freelance architect with his own architectural firm and ran a furniture factory.

In Phnom Penh, René Nguyen Khac Scheou realised, besides the apartment building on Street 118, the huge **Tan Pa Building** (**051 B**). Thierry Delfosse, author of *Saigon – Phnom Penh – Saigon: The Itinerary of Rene Nguyen Khac Scheou, a Modern Architect*, suspects that some buildings in the vicinity were also created by the Vietnamese architect, due to the stylistic similarities they display. These include the **Office for Land Managment Daun Penh District** (**039 B**) and the **Norton University City Campus** (**047 B**) on Street 130. However, it has not been possible so far to unequivocally attribute them to Scheou. In 1964, Scheou returned to Saigon, where he died in 1985.

Foreign Trade Bank (former Tan Pa Residence)

035 B

Street 114/Street 53
Architect unknown
1923

Today's Street 114 (Kramuon Sar) was called Avenue Boulloche during the time of the Protectorate. This beautiful avenue stands out due to its magnificent old African mahogany trees (*Khaya senegalensis*), which line a public garden that extends from the Russian Federation Boulevard in the west all the way to Norodom Boulevard. At the corner, where Street 114 intersects with Street 53, stands a splendid villa. This villa was built in 1923 as a residential mansion for Tan Pa, a wealthy Sino-Khmer entrepreneur who founded the Cambodian branch of the Banque Franco-Chinoise with his father Lok Chhaivary, a civil servant at the Royal court (see **The Mansion 068 C**). In 1993, Maybank Malaysia moved into this building, and today the Foreign Trade Bank of Cambodia occupies its premises. Until the early 1990s, such villas formed ensembles that were quite homogeneous. They were surrounded by gardens and displayed eclectic architectural styles inspired by classical temples, Italian Renaissance palaces, and French seaside resorts. These ensembles characterised the residential neighbourhoods in the European District north of Wat Phnom and in the Cambodian District southwest of the Royal Palace. But all but a few of them have been demolished, due to rapid development and excessive land prices. And few have been preserved in such a pristine condition as this magnificent complex.

Around the corner...

Just across the boulevard to the north, at No. 5, Street 53, is the tiny **Hainan Chinese Temple** tucked in between shophouses. From the late 17th century, Chinese migrants came from Hainan Island and settled in Kampot province to grow pepper. From the 1920s onwards, many moved to Phnom Penh and built this Taoist temple. The building is another vestige of ethnic Chinese heritage in the city.

Department of Oral Maxillo-facial Surgery and Dentistry (former Institut Ophtalmologique)

036 B

Street 114/Street 53
Architect unknown
1920s

Further to the east, along Street 114, there is an interesting pavilion with an entrance canopy influenced by the early Art Déco style, similar to the **General Department of Customs and Excise** (**037 B**) around the corner. The building used to be the French Institut Ophtal-mologique, dedicated to the diagnosis and treatment of eye disorders. Today, it houses the Department of Oral Maxillo-facial Surgery and Dentistry. It is part of the Preah Ang Duong Hospital, on the former site of the French Dispensaire Municipale (Municipal Dispensary). The elegant corner building still looks almost the same as it did during the French colonial years, except that the wood-en shutters and air vents have been covered by glass windows, air conditioning units have been added, and the entrance doors have been inconsiderately altered. In the block interior behind the build-ing, another historical hospital building still survives. The three-storey building follows the design of the former Hopital Mixte, now **Preah Ket Mealea Hopital** (**023 A**). Originally, Phnom Penh had a number of healthcare buildings recall-ing the European Art Déco style, such as the Municipal Dispensary and the Health Service Office. Besides the small hospital building and the Department of Customs and Excise, only the **Railway Station** (**013 A**) and the **Central Market** (**033 B**) still testify to the presence of this archi-tectural style in the French colonies.

Around the corner...
Just across the wonderful tree-lined av-enue, where the street intersects with Norodom Boulevard, the **Ministry of Women's Affairs** occupies another French colonial building, which used to be the office of the Service d'Hygiene. A map from the 1960s marks the building as the Embassy of Japan.

General Department of Customs and Excise

037 B

6–8 Preah Norodom Boulevard
Architect unknown
Early 1920s

The former Direction des Douanes & Regies building on Norodom Boulevard is a fine, well-preserved and colonial administrative building. It is, however, connected to a perhaps less distinguished history of French colonial presence in Indochina. The building was originally constructed as the Chambre Mixte de Commerce et d'Agriculture. The original Hotel des Douanes et Régies used to be located on Sisowath Quay, east of the **Former Cadastral Office (003 A)**.

According to Pierre Brocheux and Daniel Hémery, the principal income of the French Gouvernement Général de l'Indochine came from customs returns and state-controlled companies. In the colonies, salt, alcohol, and opium was each controlled by a dedicated state-run company, or *régie*. In essence, the French regime had a monopoly on each of these products and levied a tax on them

on three levels: for the purchase, manufacture, and sale to consumers. These *régies*, combined with the official licences and large-scale wholesalers, constituted a global mechanism for extracting money from the peasant economy. The alcohol monopoly was operated differently across the four regions of Tonkin, Cochinchina, Annam, and Cambodia. But by 1907, the Société des distilleries de l'Indochine (SFDIC) had an effective monopoly of production, and the state's Department of Customs and Excise had systems of surveillance and repression in place across all four regions. Between its creation in 1897 and its end in 1945, the alcohol monopoly was described as one of the three 'beasts of burden' ('bêtes de somme'), along with the salt and opium monopolies, of the colonial budget, providing the regime with the tax revenue necessary for its survival. The opium monopoly was maintained until 1950 and only disappeared with France's ratification of the Drug Convention of the United Nations. The Cambodia Customs Administration was established in 1951, before the country's independence. After

the Khmer Rouge, the customs operations were resumed again in August 1979. Today, the General Department of Customs and Excise of Cambodia (GDCE) is a public administration under the Ministry of Economy and Finance.

The one-storey edifice has a strict axially symmetric layout, arranged around a majestic entrance portico. A large circular canopy with Art Nouveaux influences cantilevers elegantly over the central main stairs. On both sides, the façade, with its arched windows and louvred shutters, is structured by pilasters and ornamental eave brackets. These elements support a large cornice that provides shading to the rooms. As you approach the historical edifice, you will notice behind it an enormous high-rise building, which was under construction at the time of writing. The rendering of the building on the webpage of the Cambodian construction company depicts a 33-storey monolithic tower under the project title 'General Department of Customs and Excise of Cambodia'. When finished, this new office building will completely dwarf its historic namesake.

Around the corner...

One block further south along Norodom Boulevard, you will find the massive building of a Chinese bank with rounded corners and obnoxious brown stone pilasters. This used to be the **Garage Peugeot**, an elegant white Art Deco building with stylish horizontal windows built in the late 1930s or early 1940s. Regrettably, due to unsympathetic renovations, only the overall volume and rooflines of this building remain today. The National Bank of Cambodia used to stand on the opposite side of Norodom Boulevard. Built in 1953 by Henri Chatel as the currency issuing authority for French Indochina, the expressive building later became the National Bank of Cambodia. The building was then destroyed by the Khmer Rouge. It was rebuilt in a somewhat eclectic faux French-colonial style, and then destroyed again in 2019 to make way for the new headquarters of the bank. The new building will be a pyramidal high-rise, intended to resemble the Prasat Phnom or ancient Khmer mountain temple structure.

Row of Shophouses, Street 108 `038` B

Street 108/Street 51
Architect unknown
1915–1925

The shophouse is a very popular mixed-use typology present all over historic commercial centres in Southeast Asia. It is a long terraced building with a narrow roadside façade, divided from its neighbours by party walls. It combines trade on the ground floor towards the street, often preceded by arcades, with living quarters on the first floor and sometimes a second floor. Due to its functionality and efficiency, the basic shophouse typology was used more or less unchanged from the 1890s to 1960s in urban areas across Cambodia. However, different eclectic or modern architectural styles were applied to the front façades, according to the prevailing taste of the time. For further information on Chinese shophouses see **Row of Shophouses, Street 240** (091 C).

Perhaps the most elaborate and lavishly decorated façade of all shophouses in the city can be found at this coherent group of six at the northern border of the former Chinese District, along the former **De Verneville Canal** (009 A) (Quai Piquet, now Street 108). The original owners, who were probably rich businesspeople, once commissioned the intricate lime plaster decorations resembling neoclassical French villas to show off their wealth. Note the arched windows with their moulded pilasters behind balustraded balconies on the first floor, and the elaborate plasterwork on the parapet walls above, resembling classical floral motifs and stating '1931'. However, the buildings probably date a bit earlier, as they are already included in a map from the late 1920s. Unfortunately, during recent renovations, the original louvred wooden shutters were replaced by soulless glass frames, and the façades on the ground floor were altered and obstructed by billboards. The setback pitched roof with another added floor was changed later as well. The buildings used to comprise single-family units, each with a private courtyard, but the system has become more complex. The courtyards are now semi-private, accessible from Street 51 (Pasteur). This change allowed the creation of a second row of apartments, at the rear of the plots, where outhouses for kitchens and bathrooms used to be.

Do also take a look at the ochre-coloured building directly to the left. It is a distinct semi-detached shophouse on a slightly wider plot. Note the original condition of the clay-tiled roof, and the main façade with its nice wooden folding door, ornamental window grilles, and louvred wooden shutters.

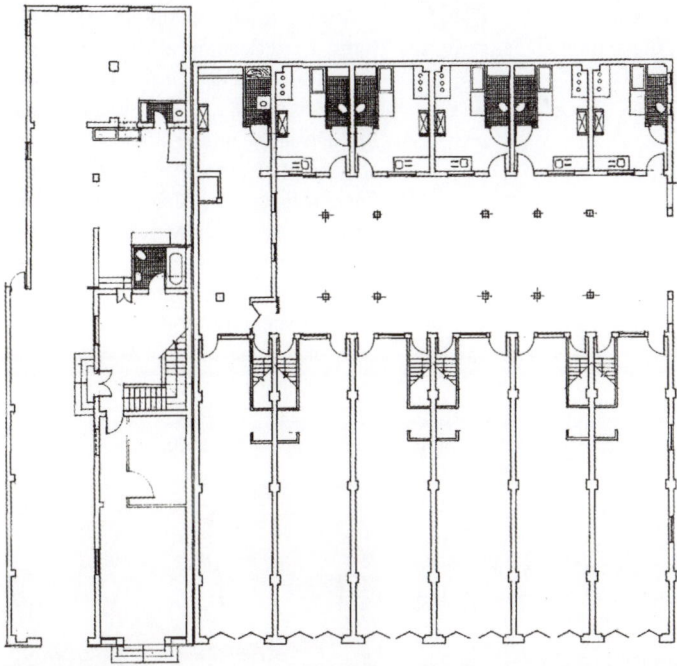

Ground floor

Offices for the Land Management Department, Daun Penh District

039 B

Street 115, between Street 15 and Street 17
Architect unknown
1950s–1960s

In a bustling environment, in the former Chinese District, not far from the banks of the Tonle Sap and directly opposite the Old Market (Psar Chas), stands a regularly overlooked architectural gem. Almost a third of the entire block along Street 115 is occupied by a three-storey residential and commercial building. The design of the balconies, loggias, and canopies, which create a strong sense of horizontality, deviates significantly from the shophouse typology of the 1950s and 1960s that otherwise characterises this quarter. At the intersection of Streets 15 and 115, there is a striking, beautifully detailed portal, recalling the late Art Deco style. It leads to offices now occupied by the Land Management Department of the Daun Penh District. Presumably, these offices were originally used in a different way, as the staircase landing on the first floor features a large mosaic with a cargo ship on it, suggesting a maritime purpose. A map from 1966 shows a branch of Tan Pa & Fils at the intersection of Street 115 and Street 15. The loggia on the second floor, resembling a ship's bridge, could also be read as a reference to this former use affiliated with the nearby river. The flooring made of small green tiles and the wonderful green terrazzo staircase with three flights are remarkable. Another, much simpler staircase is located at Street 17, giving access to the residential part of the building.

Apartment Building near Phsar Chas

040 B

Street 115 / Street 15
Architect unknown
1950s–1960s

This impressive building is one of the constructions about which no information could be found during the research for this book. Although it is a four-storey building and therefore would have needed a building permit at the time of construction, no documents seem to exist. Nor did we find any historical photographs or any other information. This is a situation we encountered repeatedly, especially while researching buildings from the 1950s and 1960s, which still make up a large part of the city. To us, this has shown once again that the city's turbulent history has left a kind of vacuum, not only in terms of documentation, but also in terms of research on urbanisation and architectural development, which has still not really been dealt with to this day. Although the French have carried out much research, this has dealt predominantly with the legacy of the French Protectorate. The current wave of rampant

demolition makes it seem probable that buildings like this one will simply disappear before they can be documented more thoroughly. Nevertheless, or precisely for this reason, we have decided to include the building here.

The building features a number of unusual details if we compare it with the conventional shophouse typology with commercial units on the ground floor and apartments on the upper floors. The corner, at a 45-degree angle, orients the building towards the intersection, which is not exactly common. The dominantly protruding façade grid and the deeply recessed balconies give the building a strict, reduced appearance, contrasting with the elegant lines of the building opposite. The minimalist design is continued in the façade, for example in the railings. The are several old wooden French doors, which add a slightly Parisian touch to the explicitly modern building. Breeze blocks are embedded below the balconies for better ventilation. The brise-soleil was dispensed with to accentuate the clarity of the concrete grid, and there is hardly anything else that could be omitted.

B

French Apartment Building `041 B`

30–32 Street 130 /
Street 5
Architect unknown/
Heritage Mission (renovation)
1910–1920 / 2008–09 (renovation)

Standing at the heart of the expat bar district, near the riverfront, is one of the rare examples of well-preserved mundane residential buildings from the French colonial era. The three-floor corner building follows the basic shophouse typology and plot layout, with commercial use on the ground floor and residential uses upstairs. However, the building has an independent entrance on Street 5 that leads to a central staircase giving access to the separate apartments on the upper floors. The building stands out from its neighbours due to its original façade, decorated by moulded pilasters and protruding balconies with wrought iron railings. The windows and doors, with their wooden shutters, are topped by semi-circular fanlights and arched geometric plaster ornamentations.

The Heritage Mission (Mission du Patrimoine) meticulously surveyed the building and devised a restoration proposal. The building's private owner then took up the proposal and carried out a comprehensive restoration project between 2008 and 2009. The outcome is a fine example of a successfully restored colonial-era building in Phnom Penh, and its success is all the more remarkable since the building is secular and privately owned. The Heritage Mission was created in 2005 as a cooperative project by the Kingdom of Cambodia and the French Embassy in Cambodia. It is now attached to the Heritage Center (Centre du Patrimoine), a public institution under the supervision of the Ministry of Culture and Fine Arts. The Heritage Mission team focuses on 'remarkable architectural styles' among the most threatened heritage, of which the non-Angkorian heritage includes urban, vernacular, and religious sites. Its Regional Training Center has trained several batches of Cambodian students and young architects in heritage conservation practices since 2007.

Former Établissement Dumarest d'Indochine

042 B

Preah Sisowath Quay/
Street 148
Architect unknown
1905

The remaining three- and four-storey shophouses along Sisowath Quay today mainly cater to the needs of tourists. Most of them have been converted into hotels, cafés, restaurants, and expat bars. They served a different purpose for around 100 years until the 1970s: they were linked to Phnom Penh's status as a river port, which could receive vessels carrying up to 6,000 tonnes of freight in the high water season. Maritime commerce here comprised ship chandlers, provision stores, and the offices of shipping agents, occasionally interrupted by a few cheap restaurants. The corner building, with its turquoise French-style shuttered windows, dates back to around 1905 when it was owned by French trading company Établissement Dumarest d'Indochine and the Cambodian trading offices of Dumarest & Fils. Upscale apartments were situated upstairs. Établissement Dumarest d'Indochine traded in fabrics, glassware, ceramics, furniture, perfumes, electric refrigerators, umbrellas, and French cigars, among other commodities, and was involved in rubber plantations across French Indochina.

The Riverside Bistro on the ground floor sports a decently long history, having opened in April 1996. Walking inside is like returning to the past – arches reach high above the spacious halls, and the recently renovated upstairs extension offers magnificent views over the Tonle Sap River and Chrouy Changvar peninsula. The river promenade below is especially entertaining in the early morning hours and during sunset, when it attracts a lively and mainly local crowd strolling along, power walking, or doing all kinds of exercises, while street hawkers offer their fares, tourists try to cross the neverending stream of tuk tuks, motorbikes and cars, and elderly expats watch the world go by from behind their glass of beer on the streetside tables.

Former Hotel International

Street 13/Street 130
Architect unknown
1900–1910

043 B

Walking along Street 13 (Rue Ohier during the time of the French Protectorate), it is hard to imagine that this was once considered to be the Champs Elysées of Phnom Penh and the most exclusive shopping street of the city. The former Hotel International stands on the corner of the street, where it intersects with Street 130. The tired and loveable building lies in a sorry state today. It has been altered many times, and its façade is now a hotchpotch of countless window formats, caged-in balconies, and billboards. Recently, a monstrous billboard for a phone shop was applied to the corner of the building. This billboard sadly also obstructs the original sign reading 'Hotel International' just below the louvred French windows on the second floor. Today, the guilty phone shop occupies what was once the lobby of the hotel. Meanwhile, the building itself was divided into tiny flats years ago, and its roof is completely covered with informal, makeshift shelters.

PNOM-PENH — *La rue Ohier*

Corner Building, Street 13

Street 13/Street 130
Architect unknown
1950s–1960s

044 B

This corner building is another beautiful example of the many variations of the multi-storey apartment-type shophouses built in the 1950s and 1960s. It comprises two layers of commercial space on the ground and first floors and apartments on the second and third floors. The first floor, above the commercial units on the ground floor, has an open layout and a separate entrance on Street 13, indicating that it once served as a multi-purpose space or perhaps as a restaurant. The apartments on the second and third floors are accessed by a separate entrance on Street 130 and are served by an open rear passageway on the backside of the building. The main façade of the building mirrors the division of commercial and residential functions inside: the ten apartments along Street 13 are emphasised by vertical concrete slats separating the balconies, while the commercial first floor and the rounded corner of the building are structured by horizontal brise-soleils and railings.

B

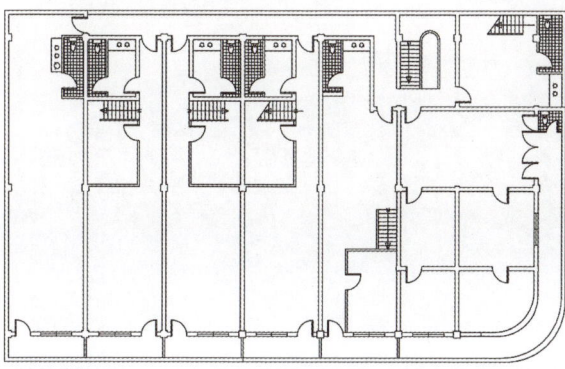

Second floor

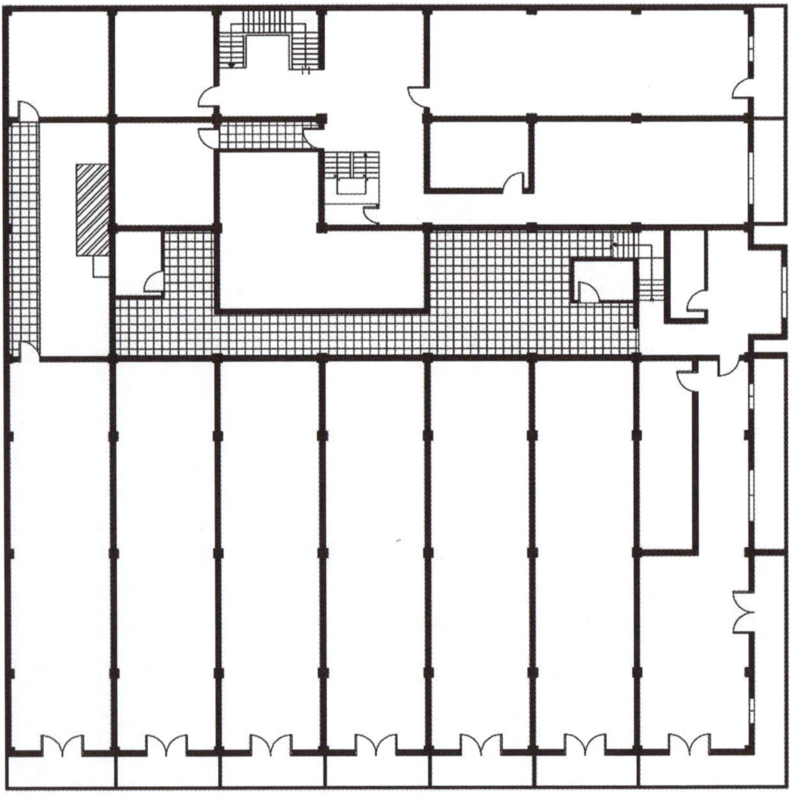

First floor

Four Corner Buildings

Street 130 / Street 15
Architects unknown
1910s–1960s

045 B

In the old commercial quarter, at the intersection of Street 15 and Street 130, we can find a remarkable quartet of corner buildings that give some insight into the evolution of multi-family residential buildings in the historic city centre through a time span of 50 years. We will start with the oldest building on the southeast corner (p. 128) and go in a clockwise direction, ending with the youngest of the four (p. 131).

The three-storey building on the southeast corner is unique, as it is one of the last preserved early apartment buildings built in Phnom Penh in the 1910s. The building was constructed on the formal grid typically used for Chinese shophouse plots. The building layout is arranged around an inner courtyard, which functions as a source of light and ventilation and provides access to the upper-floor apartments via open walkways. The

section facing Street 130 contains seven 4 m x 15 m units. Its façade shows some alterations in the door, window, and balustrade designs, which express the individual preferences of the apartment owners. The façade facing Street 15 has a more original feel. It features lovely balcony railings made from cement and wrought iron as well as an oriel window accentuating the entrance to the common staircase. A small inscription on the first floor indicates that the building was partly used as a hotel for some time. The building still features a timber roof structure, covered with clay tiles and supported by wooden corbels.

The comparatively nondescript building on the southwest corner perhaps dates back to the 1930s, as it originally had only three floors, with the last floor obviously added later on. The building seems to have no internal courtyard or circulation core, as all rooms are accessed by the exterior corridors, with the common staircase located behind louvred air vents facing Street 130. The doors and windows are still fitted with wooden

louvred shutters and topped by horizontal air vents. Note also the nice geometric pattern of the balcony railings realised in cement and limewash.

The elegant four-storey building on the northwestern corner, with its filigree façade detailing, was probably constructed in the 1950s. The name 'Kim Seng Sar' (White Kim Seng) is displayed in Khmer letters on the corner, which suggests that the building formerly might have been (partly) used as a hotel. The building is structured around a curved corner. Long horizontal strips of plaster extend over the southern and eastern façades and thus visually lengthen the corner. The open staircase protrudes behind an elegant concrete screen wall on Street 130. It is further accentuated by square concrete blocks that recur on the façade as a decorative motif. Large well-structured windows complement the façade, allowing most rooms to overlook the street. The commercial ground floor is protected by a cantilevered balcony. The building has partly been renovated for its current use as an upscale residential building and mostly remains in its original condition, apart from the fancy penthouse on the top floor and the disgusting aluminium façade panels bordering the former **Hemakcheat Cinema (046 B)**, both added later.

The slender five-storey building that fully occupies a narrow plot on the northeastern corner is the youngest of the four buildings and probably dates back to the 1960s. It has a double façade, which decreases the impact of the high-density massing. Recessed floor plans reduce the impact of the harsh sunlight and permit a formal expressiveness that is further enhanced by the rounded corner and vertical concrete columns. The rooms are accessed via exterior corridors, with the staircase hidden behind a louvred concrete screen in the north of the building, facing Street 130. Horizontal brise-soleils and large air vents with angled slats above the doors and windows further add to the climate-adapted design.

Similar buildings, with a pleasantly reduced, almost minimalist vocabulary of architectural components, materials, and colours, form the basic structure of the urban expansion areas of the 1950s and 1960s. An illustrative example is in the the **Orussey Quarter** (**053 B**), situated to the west of Monivong Boulevard. If you walk the streets and manage to blend out the countless alterations, advertising panels, and cables, you will see that this remarkable building typology still dominates large tracts of the urban fabric in the inner city of Phnom Penh.

Former Hemakcheat Cinema and apartments

Former Hemakcheat Cinema and Apartments

046 B

93 Street 130
Architect unknown
1960s

Based on what is typically shown in Phnom Penh's multiplex cinemas today, it is hard to believe that Cambodia once had a vibrant and creative film scene. Its history probably began in 1909 with a small open-air cinema on Phnom Penh's riverfront. At first, French and American films were mainly shown to Europeans, but soon Cambodians joined the audience. It wasn't until the late 1940s that Cambodia began to produce its own films. A notable participant was King Norodom Sihanouk, who is considered to be Cambodia's first filmmaker. In the 1950s, the United States Information Service (USIS) produced a series of documentary films about the country to promote film as a medium of education, development, and anticommunist propaganda. In the process, they also trained camera operators, editors, and sound technicians. Another group of filmmakers emerged under the influence of Norodom Sihanouk, who had already sent Cambodians to France for training in the 1940s. Cambodia's first full-length feature film in colour was shown at the Capitol Cinema in 1960. Between 1960 and 1975, nearly 400 films were produced in the small country and more than 30 cinemas operated in Phnom Penh. Most of the films that were made in the following years were based on Cambodian legends, but occasionally also on contemporary subjects. But this 'Golden Age of Khmer Cinema' ended abruptly when the Khmer Rouge came to power in 1975. Almost all actors were killed under the Khmer Rouge regime and only a few of the directors were able to flee the country. Only around 30 original films remain today, and this paucity is also reflected in the architectural testimonies of that time. Not a single one of the old cinemas is still in operation, and most have been demolished or converted into massage parlours, offices, or restaurants. Davy Chou, a French Cambodian filmmaker and grandson of Van Chann, one of the greatest producers in Cambodia in the 1960s, has documented this 'Golden Age' as well as the Hemakcheat (Golden Sin) Cinema in his film *Golden Slumbers* (2013). **Bophana Center** (084 C), co-founded in 2006 by film director Rithy Panh, collects archive images and sounds on Cambodia and offers free public access to this unique heritage. Bophana Center also trains young Cambodians for careers in filmmaking, broadcasting, and new media.

Some of the largest cinemas were located along Street 130 at the time, and the Hemakcheat was one of the most outstanding. It seems to be the last historic cinema standing today, although only the façade indicates its former purpose. The box-shaped building's ground floor was originally intended as a restaurant but is now used as a motorcycle parking space. The cinema hall was arranged above, topped by another two storeys with apartments, which are accessed via an open staircase located on the adjacent side street. In the meantime, another layer of makeshift shelters has been added to the building. After the fall of the Khmer Rouge and the return of the population to Phnom Penh, hundreds of inhabitants took informal residence in the cinema, which once offered space for 1,000 spectators. The cinema equipment has completely disappeared, and the residents have divided the shell into dozens of small chambers.

Norton University City Campus 047 B (former École Miche)

152 Street 118 (entrance), Street 19/Street 130

Architects unknown

1960s

The downtown campus of Norton University used to house the Miche Catholic School (École Miche). It was opened in 1911 as a private Catholic primary school run by the Christian Brothers of Jean-Baptiste de la Salle and was named after the 19th century bishop Jean-Claude Miche, who had been instrumental in securing the French Protectorate over Cambodia. During the 1930s and 1940s, many Hokkien and Hakka Chinese attended the Miche School to receive an education that would enable them to hold commercial and administrative positions at the time of the French Protectorate. According to historian David Chandler, Saloth Sâr, later known as Pol Pot, attended the elite Catholic primary school between 1935 and 1942. Its teachers were French and Vietnamese, and lessons were given in French. École Miche had a good reputation, and it offered the same curriculum as was taught at the other main primary school in Phnom Penh, the **Lycée Preah Sisowath** (**081 C**), which was run by protectorate authorities and catered exclusively to Europeans and a handful of Khmers from aristocratic families. Most ordinary Cambodians in the 1930s received no primary education at all. Across the country, no more than a few thousand from half a million school-age children had access to even rudimentary modern education. In March 1970, the new Lon Nol government closed École Miche along with other non-Khmer language schools, notably Chinese schools, as part of Lon Nol's racist policies. As the war against the Khmer Rouge progressed and refugees from the countryside filled Phnom Penh, the former École Miche was used as a refugee camp. The northern part of the school compound included the Catholic Eglise du Sacré-Coeur (Church of the Sacred Heart) that was built in 1906 by bishop Jean-Claude Bouchut and destroyed by the Khmer Rouge in 1976. The modern school building on the southwest corner dates back to the 1960s. It features an elegant white double façade with repetitive vertical cement sunshades protecting the classrooms from direct sunlight. The building was possibly the work of Rene Nguyen Khac Scheou, a Vietnamese architect who designed a number of apartment buildings in Phnom Penh between 1957 and 1964.

Ciné Lux and Apartments

048 B

Preah Norodom Boulevard
Architect unknown/
Roger Colne (renovation)
1938/1950s (renovation)

The demolition of Ciné Lux had started shortly before this book went to print, which means that soon, another precious work of the city's built heritage will be lost forever. We nonetheless decided to keep this unique building in our pages as a reminder of the heydays of Cambodian cinema, which lasted from the 1950s to the early 1970s. The city at that time boasted at least 33 cinemas, and Ciné Lux, originally built in 1938 and completely refurbished to plans by French architect Roger Colne in the 1950s, was the last one standing that still performed its original function. All the other cinemas in Phnom Penh, such as the **Hemakcheat Cinema (046 B)**, the Bokkor, and the Kirirom, which thrived in the 1960s, have either been demolished or converted into shelters, restaurants, snooker halls, or KTVs.

The Lux was built in a striking *Streamline Moderne* Art Deco style and formed a coherent ensemble with the adjacent apartment buildings on Streets 148 and

154. It was one of the most famous cinemas of Phnom Penh. With a capacity of 800 seats, the building was used until the early 1990s for a variety of activities including film screenings and theatre performances. Between 1984 and 1995, the building's façade was heavily altered for the first time. This is when the balconies on the elegantly curved northwestern corner, housing the Lux Parfumerie on the ground floor, were closed with dark glass façades. Changes continued, until the corner was covered entirely by an enormous billboard. In 2001, the cinema re-opened after extensive renovations, before closing its doors for good in 2016. Fortunately, the two neighbouring residential buildings at Streets 148 and 154 remain more or less untouched, and their curved stairway halls and horizontal balconies offer a glimpse of the once splendid architecture of the ensemble.

The **Roung Kon Project** (see p. 268) was launched by an interdisciplinary group of young architects and students in 2016. The group has located, documented, and partially surveyed 33 former cinemas in Phnom Penh. In June 2017, the group organised a public exhibition entitled 'Phka Riek Phka Riouy' at Ciné Lux.

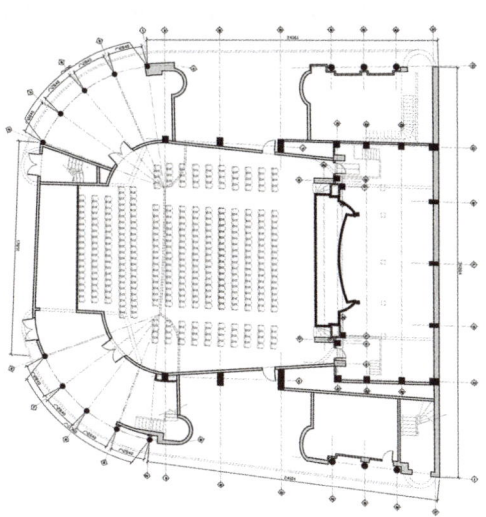

Ground floor

Office Building for General Ngo Hou

049 B

Street 144 / Street 49
Vann Molyvann
1958

The humble three-storey corner building, attributed to Vann Molyvann, must have been one of the first works the architect completed after returning from his studies in Paris. It is believed to have been designed for General Ngo Hou, a high-ranking military member and advisor to Norodom Sihanouk. Today, it belongs to the Ministry of Industry and Trade, but in the 1960s, it was rented out to the United States Information Services (USIS) and the United States Agency for International Development (USAID). USIS's tasks included promoting the acceptance and awareness of US policies, promoting dialogue between American organisations and their counterparts abroad, and informing the US government of how its policies were being received abroad. For this purpose, the Voice of America agency produced broadcasts in many languages for many parts of the world. USAID established libraries and promoted cultural exchange through scholarships such as the Fulbright Program. It also provided press services and ran a feature film service. US aid was used to train teachers and support the construction and equipping of schools. Other US-funded projects included the construction of health centres and the extension and improvement of infrastructure. One of the highlights of such infrastructure projects was the Khmer-American Friendship Highway. This road, which cost 25 million dollars to build, was designed to connect Phnom Penh with the newly built port of Sihanoukville. Another major undertaking was the construction of the **Université Technique Royale, Faculté des Arts et Métiers (134 G)**. The building shows all the features that characterise the 1950s and 1960s urban buildings in Phnom Penh: deeply recessed windows, brises-soleils, and perforated screens made of concrete blocks. On the ground floor, the building once had display windows in which the achievements of American civilisation were presented to the Cambodian people. This site, at the intersection of Street 144 and Street 49, was once the stage for the 'troubled relations' (Kenton Klyner) between the US and Cambodia (see following page).

B

Former American Embassy

Street 144/Street 49
Architect unknown
Early 1950s

050 B

Not much is known about this building, which once housed the United States Embassy. The US and Cambodia didn't establish direct diplomatic relations until 1950. On 7 February, the French National Assembly granted autonomy to the Indochinese countries Cambodia, Laos, and Vietnam within the French Union, and shortly thereafter, the United States recognised the new Cambodian government with the young King Norodom Sihanouk as its head. At the beginning, the US Legation operated from the **Hotel Le Royal** (**017 A**). In 1954, the embassy moved into this former apartment building. In the mid-1960s, the embassy became the scene of violent anti-American demonstrations. A telegram sent from the besieged embassy on 11 March 1964 describes the situation:

'Just before demonstration began, men carrying red paint tins and brushes painted sign "US go home" on Embassy and USIS buildings. Police who were standing by in numbers made no effort to interfere with them ... After about twenty minutes of peaceful procession past Embassy, violence started with rock throwing. Within twenty minutes, there was almost every window in Embassy and USIS broken, and at least one official vehicle completely destroyed.'

One year later, on 26 April, the embassy was stormed by a mob of Cambodian students. They hurled rocks, ink bottles, and other projectiles at the building and ripped down the American flag. On 3 May 1965, Cambodia broke off diplomatic relations with the United States, and the embassy was closed. In 1970, diplomatic relations where resumed.

Today, the US Embassy is located opposite Wat Phnom. The 60-million-dollar building was constructed in 2006 on the location of the former Cercle Sportif. The club, which opened in 1929, had served as the heart of leisure-time activities for Cambodia's French colonial elite. It is reported that a large number of Cambodian officials, who had allegedly escaped to safety at the French embassy before the Khmer Rouge invasion, were taken to the Cercle Sportif a few days later and executed there, with their bodies thrown into the half-empty pool.

Tan Pa Building

Tan Pa Building

Block between Street 51, Street 144, Street 49, and Street 154

René Nguyen Khac Scheou
1960s

051 B

This rather dilapidated urban block was once a luxurious apartment building for higher-income groups and, in the 1960s, a popular residence for high-ranking Khmer and foreign officials stationed in Cambodia. The building is commonly referred to as the Tan Pa Building, after its former owner, the entrepreneur Tan Pa. It used to feature basketball and volleyball courts in the courtyard, guarded parking lots, and a garage. Each floor was provided with mail and laundry services, and each of the four stairwells came with a lift for greater convenience. Residents could end the day watching the sunset in a panorama bar or exercise in the sports club, located on the rooftop above the fourth floor. The building's architect, René Nguyen Khac Scheou, seems to already have had experience with upscale residential complexes when he began this project. His **Chey Cheta Street Apartments** (034 B) was obviously also planned for a more affluent clientele.

Today, it is hard to imagine that the building was once such a luxury residence, as it is in an advanced state of decay. Now, it houses around 400 resident families, who are significantly less well off than

the former occupants. The conceptually coherent architecture of the apartment block, however, is still unique and definitely makes the building worth a visit. The stairwells are open towards the street and provide access to the interior walkways that wrap around the entire inner courtyard. The four rounded corners of the block are accentuated with vertical concrete slats. The same slats also give the long façades along the streets a regular structure. The apartments facing the street feature deep balconies, some of which still have the beautiful original metal railings. On the south side, along Street 154, an elaborately designed portal leads to the block interior, which today is informally subdivided and filled with houses. An interesting tower-like structure along Street 51 contains a former water tank.

Until 2002, one of Phnom Penh's numerous informal settlements was located on the roof of this building. Over 1,000 inhabitants had gradually settled there, after the Vietnamese-backed government had called on the population to return to the city following its victory over the Khmer Rouge. However, most land registers had been destroyed, and many of the original property owners had been murdered. Buildings were awarded on a first-come, first-serve basis, but there were far too few dwellings to accommodate everyone. As such, people sought shelter anywhere they could – in pagodas, in churches, in squatter camps, and on rooftops. The history of the rooftop squatters in the Tan Pa Building illustrates how the city as a whole was re-occupied after the expulsion of its inhabitants by the Khmer Rouge. Here, the story begins in 1981. At that time, the lower part of the building was occupied by employees of the Ministry of Hydrology, but six families decided to sell their apartments and move to the roof. Gradually, other families followed this example, and people from outside the building also moved in. In 2002, a large fire on the roof destroyed the homes of almost 250 families, and the residents were resettled elsewhere.

Round Corner Building

052 B

Preah Monivong Bvld (Street 93)/
Kampuchea Krom Bvld
(Street 128)
Architect unknown
1960s

This massive tired corner building forms a monumental prelude to the western urban expansion area following Kampuchea Krom Boulevard. It was built based on the typology of the modernised Chinese shophouse at the time of the Sangkum Reastr Niyum. Nearby, along the western side of Monivong Boulevard, you can find further residential buildings with the same design features.

The building displays a number of elements, often found in buildings of the 1960s, designed to deal with the country's tropical climate. Its generous floor heights ensure a good indoor climate, ventilation openings provide good air circulation, and protruding balconies shade the façade from the harsh sunlight. Awnings are fitted above the balcony doors to provide additional shading and complement the horizontal structuring of the façade. The building is accessed via open walkways at the rear, which are connected to a stairwell on Kampuchea Krom Boulevard. The roof is covered by informal dwellings, many of which were constructed as makeshift shelters when Phnom Penh was being repopulated in the 1980s after the terror of the Khmer Rouge. The fact that the building has a lift (regrettably now out of order) indicates that the building was once intended for a rather wealthy clientele. The metal doors of the lift still bear the logo of the German exporter C. Illies & Co., based in Hamburg, which all the more points to the building's once luxurious past.

B

The coherent cityscape of Orussey Quarter

Orussey Quarter, Street 139

Orussey Quarter

Area between Charles de Gaulle
Bvld, Preah Monivong Bvld, and
Street 182 (Oknha Tep Phan
Street)
*Lu Ban Hap with the Service Municipal
de l'Urbanisme et de l'Habitat*
Early 1960s

Many quarters in Phnom Penh have retained the urban structure they acquired
during the city's great expansion in the
1960s. But the Orussey Quarter (sometimes spelt O'Russey), part of the Khan 7
Makara (7 February District), is perhaps the one that has most tenaciously
held onto its original use and appearance. Thus, it is worthwhile to take a walk
through the streets around the Orussey
Market, in the area between Oknha Tep
Phan Street, Charles de Gaulle Boulevard, and Preah Monivong Boulevard.

Under French rule, the city expanded primarily through new developments in a
north-south direction along the river. In
contrast, the rapid population growth in
the 1960s led to the city's expansion further westwards, beyond the north-south
axis of Monivong Boulevard.

Charles de Gaulle Boulevard, one of the
many boulevards named after heads of
state – such as Mao Zedong, Josip Broz
Tito, and Jawaharlal Nehru – forms a

suitable north-western border for the
walk. But those prepared for a longer trek
can stroll further north to Kampuchea
Krom Boulevard, or further south to
Boulevard Josip Broz Tito. The quarter
around the market lies in a morpholog-
ically complex situation, which leads to
a number of interesting plot geometries
and building layouts.

In the early twentieth century, the lake
Beng Dechor (or *Boeung Decho*) was filled
in based on French plans from the early

1920s. The **Central Market** (033 B) was built in its place in 1937. In the 1960s, a plan was designed to further develop the area around the Central Market towards the south and west. The plan marked out a triangular area, bounded on one side by a radial road axis (today Boulevard Charles de Gaulle) running southwest from the Central Market and on the other side by the north-south axis of Boulevard Monivong. This triangular plot of land was then developed in the 1960s and became the heart of the Orussey Quarter, with the Orussey Market at its centre. The Service Municipal de l'Urbanisme et de l'Habitat, directed by Lu Ban Hap, carried out the urban planning for the quarter. With his private office, Lu also planned the individual Chinese shophouses (*Comptoires Chinois*) surrounding the market square and developed the area around the Olympic Market. He also carried out several other construction projects with his office. In addition, Lu

Ban Hap designed the original Orussey Market, as a light metal construction, but it had to give way to the present, unappealing hall, which was developed by Taiwanese investors. The northern part of the quarter, up to Kampuchea Krom Boulevard, remains one of the most densely populated urban areas in the city. It is also the second largest former Chinese district and a busy commercial centre. Here, shops and small workshops can be found, and entire street sections are filled with clusters of stores selling all kinds of hardware, along with sewing shops, pharmacies, and dental practices. Restaurants that offer authentic Chinese dishes lie hidden in small alleyways, and workshops repairing unidentifiable items with archaic tools open onto the streets. A visit to the market hall is worthwhile at the end of your stroll for the overwhelming range of goods on offer alone, which reflect the needs of the surrounding Sino-Khmer communities.

Asia Palace Hotel and Paradise Hotel on a postcard from 1985

Paradise Hotel 054 B

Intersection of Preah Monivong
Bvld and Charles des Gaulle Bvld
Jamshed Phirozsha Petigura
Early 1960s

The Paradise Hotel also underwent
some changes, but the façade at least
was not subjected to the historicist alterations – such as the addition of columns, cornices, arches, and sundry other decorations – otherwise rampant in
the city. Like the Asia Palace Hotel, the
Paradise Hotel was originally painted
white, as you can see in photographs
from the 1980s. None of the original details have been preserved, other than the generously curved façade
protruding into the intersection. As in
his other buildings, the architect Jamshed Petigura used some interesting details here, for example the circular port-
hole windows, which are sadly bricked
up today. A restaurant is located on the
uppermost floor, which was added later, and offers a view over the busy traffic on the intersection of the two boulevards and up to the Central Market.

Asia Palace Hotel

Intersection of Preah Monivong
Bvld and Charles des Gaulle Bvld
Architect unknown
1963

The impressive Asia Palace Hotel is one of the many hotels from the 1960s that used to line Monivong Boulevard. Scarce information is available about the building, and it has unfortunately lost some of its clarity of design due to stylistic changes that have been made since the date of construction: the terrace overlooking the busy intersection was raised by one floor, as was in fact the rest of the building. The altered sections were given a historicist décor, which, together with the new yellow paint and green-tinted windows, gives the building a rather unfortunate appearance. The building was originally painted white (and was appropriately referred to as the White Hotel). Its once elegant façade used to captivate with its filigree detailing. The Asia Palace Hotel, together with the Paradise Hotel across the street, forms the gateway to Charles de Gaulle Boulevard.

![Asia Palace Hotel building photograph]

Apartment Building (former Hotel Mondial)

193 Preah Monivong Boulevard
Roger Colne
1960s

Hotel Mondial was one of the many hotels built in the 1960s along Preah Monivong Boulevard. It was once one of the more comfortable, air-conditioned establishments. The architect Roger Colne was born in Paris in 1921 and studied at the École National Supérieure des Arts Décoratifs. In 1947, he moved to Saigon and worked for Atelier d'Arts Francais, a company specialising in interior design and artisan production. In 1955, he came to Phnom Penh and worked as a manager at Arts et Decorations, a company specialising in interior design, decoration, furnishings, and forged iron. Colne was also commissioned as municipal architect for other cities such as Kep, Kampot, Kirirom, Siem Reap, and Sihanoukville and worked for the Société des Auberges Royales, the Ministry of Information, the National Tourism Organisation, and the Department of Urbanism at the Ministry of Public Works. At the end of the 1960s, Colne became a war reporter. In 1992, human remains were discovered in a riverbed to the south of Phnom Penh during a US-Cambodian excavation. They were identified as the remains of the NBC cameraman Colne and two other journalists, who had disappeared on 31 May 1970. Today the former hotel, which surrounds a narrow inner courtyard, is used as a residential building. The former hotel rooms have been converted into apartments. Visitors should not hesitate to cross the small shop in the entrance area on the left side of the building and take the stairs to the upper floors. The foyer on the first floor is dark and cluttered, but the higher you ascend the once prestigious staircase, the brighter it becomes, and the better your view of the courtyard, which is traversed by bridges.

Hotel Holiday Villa (former Hotel Monorom)

89 Preah Monivong Boulevard
Jamshed Phirozsha Petigura
Early 1960s

Souvenir card of Hotel Monorom, 1960s

Hotel Monorom was one of the first large hotels in Phnom Penh. When it first opened, it stood next to **Hotel Le Royal** (**017 A**), the most luxurious hotel of the city at the time. Both hotels were run by the Société Cambodgienne de l'Hôtellerie et du Tourisme. Like Hotel Le Royal, Hotel Monorom served as the headquarters for international journalists and correspondents in the early 1970s before the Khmer Rouge entered the city and Cambodia's darkest hours began. The hotel mainly catered to European and American businesspeople and tourists. It had 70 rooms, which, like the bar and restaurant, were air-conditioned and equipped with the latest furniture and decorations.

At its prominent location not far from the Central Market and the train station, it marks the start of a series of hotels along Monivong Boulevard that were built as part of the city's westward expansion until the end of the 1960s. But despite the constant growth of tourism, the number of hotel rooms remained comparatively small over the years. By the end of 1969, Phnom Penh, then a city with almost one million residents, only had seven hotels, with a total of 340 rooms, that the Department of Tourism classified as 'international class'. This would change when the construction of **Hotel Cambodiana** (**066 C**) began in the late 1960s. Development took a different path from 1970 onwards, after the head of state Norodom Sihanouk was deposed. The owner of the hotel changed several times over the years. The building, originally all white, also went through changes and has lost some of its original appearance. Its current dark-grey colour is poorly suited for the filigree façade structure as it is for the oversized entrance portal, the pseudo-historical columns, and the balustrade on the roof. The top floor, elegantly set back in the original design, has been filled with additional rooms. This might make sense from a commercial point of view, but from a design perspective it is at best questionable.

Office of the Prime Minster

38 Russian Federation Boulevard
Chea Bunseang
2010

The Office of the Prime Minister, also known as the Peace Palace, was inaugurated in 2010. It is a building that, along with the **New Norton University (128 G)** and the **Ministry of Environment (096 D)**, represents Cambodia's attempt to define a new Khmer architectural style by combining Angkorian decorative elements with modern architecture.

In the 1960s, architects alluded to local cultures and vernacular building traditions by engaging with the surrounding landscape, considering the climatic conditions, and using vernacular spatial configurations. In contrast, architects today seek to create a national architectural identity primarily by using traditional decorations, which are therefore given prominence in the design. The building for the Office of the Prime Minister reflects this more recent trend. It features cantilevered cornices, and the area above the main entrance displays a modernised version of traditional *Bang Klaeng* ornaments. These ornaments date back to the ninth century and can be found in various temples around Angkor such as Preah Ko and Banteay Srei. The young Cambodian architect Chea Bunseang, hired by the construction firm Ly Chhoung Company, was responsible for the design. According to Prime Minister Hun Sen, the Peace Palace is a symbol of Cambodia's great achievements, since all the engineers, architects, builders, and designers involved in the construction were Khmer. The 50,000 m² building was planned and constructed within a period of just 17 months. It cost 50 million dollars and was fully financed with the national budget.

Council of Ministers

41 Russian Federation Boulevard
Architect unknown
2009

The Office of the Council of Ministers, also called Friendship Building (*Mittapheap*), was one of the many gifts from the People's Republic of China to Cambodia. China invested almost 33 million dollars to honour the 50 years of diplomatic relations between Beijing and Phnom Penh. The building, with a somewhat strange pyramidal structure in the entrance foyer, was built by Chinese workers and almost all materials were imported from China. The building has a floor area of over 30,000 m² and accommodates offices, conference rooms, and a concert hall for 200 people. Around 1,400 employees of the Royal Government work there. The former Council of Ministers building, designed by Vann Molyvann and built in 1963, was demolished in 2009 to give way to the parking lot facing the Russian Federation Boulevard. The slightly curved predecessor building, with its filigree façade, was perhaps not Vann Molyvann's best work, but it had an elegance that the new building unfortunately lacks. It was deservingly immortalised in postcards and illustrated on magazine covers, along with the other new government buildings along Russian Federation Boulevard. Shortly after the inauguration, Prime Minister Hun Sen announced the construction of today's **Office of the Prime Minister** (**058 B**) on the neighbouring site: 'An international conference centre is being constructed next to the Council of Ministers building. I planned the building myself, with a 120-by-45-metre layout.'

Ester van der Laan
Architect
Khmer Architecture Tours,
Space for Architecture Cambodia,
Phnom Penh

Ester van der Laan is an architectural engineer from the Netherlands, specialising in low-cost construction techniques for countries with tropical or desert climates. Ester started her career with UNESCO as an architect in the Cultural Heritage Division in Morocco, Mauritania, and Ethiopia, where she used her expertise in climate-adapted building techniques and knowledge of vernacular architecture. For the last 10 years, Ester has been living in Cambodia with her family, where she joined the team of Khmer Architecture Tours/Space for Architecture Cambodia in 2014, initially as Research and Design Manager and trainer of new guides, then from 2016 as Senior Coordinator as well.

What is Khmer Architecture Tours? Why and how was it started?
Khmer Architecture Tours (KA-tours) is a non-profit organisation that conducts architectural tours in Phnom Penh in order to promote the understanding of urban heritage and modern architecture in Cambodia. Apart from the historical colonial-era buildings, KA-tours focuses on the New Khmer Architecture constructed after Cambodia's independence in 1953, while setting all of these structures in the historical context of Phnom Penh. KA-tours started out in 2003 as a low-key affair, with British architect Geoff Pyle showing friends around town. With

growing demand, he trained Cambodian architecture students to become his guides, professionalised the tours, and added other activities like research, data collection, and technical surveys of valuable architectural sites. In 2009, the need came to create an umbrella organisation for KA-tours with a more inclusive name. So we established Space for Architecture Cambodia (SAC), aiming to broaden the knowledge and awareness of Cambodian architecture for both residents and visitors. By facilitating public events such as festivals, workshops, and conferences, we highlight the built heritage and the need for its preservation. To reach young Cambodians, SAC started giving classes on urban heritage and preservation at universities in Phnom Penh.

What are the architectural highlights that you include in your tours?
The highlights certainly include Vann Molyvann's great works, such as the **Teacher Training College** (121 F) and the **National Sports Complex** (105 E). The way Vann Molyvann set up the masterplan both for the college and the stadium is truly inspiring. He found a way to balance the functions of the buildings, the route of the users, the water bodies, and the vegetation, all while considering shade and ventilation, sun and rain, the bigger concept and the smallest detail, to create a well-functioning complex. The Teacher Training College buildings are each unique in appearance and ambience. They are fit for their purpose and enable the optimal lighting and ventilation by channelling these through perforated brick walls, panels, windows, and specially shaped roof ducts. The indoor stadium is the climax of the National Sports Complex site, where all the ideas and principles of New Khmer Architecture seem to come together. The ingenious construction of the cantilevered roof engenders a magical atmosphere inside: a huge space that feels intimate and comfortable due to the filtered light and cooled ventilation coming through the aluminium wall panels and stadium seating.
Our Colonial and Cultural Architecture Tours present several highlights of

Phnom Penh's older sites. First, the Buddhist Temple **Wat Pipoat Rangsey** (030 A), whose site dates back to the 15th century. This complex embodies the entire history of Phnom Penh. It shows how people of different cultures around the Mekong region came together in the past, settled in Phnom Penh, prayed at the same temple, supported the community, struggled through famines and wars, to finally find a resting place there.

The Chinese temple Xie Tian Gong (029 A) and the **Chinese House** (025 A), both built around 1900 along Sisowath Quay, are beautiful examples of the architecture of that period. The construction, exterior appearance, and detailing of the Xie Tian Gong temple all stem from Chinese traditions. In contrast, in the Chinese merchant's house, only the construction and interior allude to Chinese traditions, and the façade shows influences of French colonial architecture. The **Bank of Indochina** (008 A) on Post Office Square is a well-restored French colonial-style building. It was originally built with a main hall for the customers, bank vaults and offices for the staff, and a large private residence for the bank director and his family. Each of these three parts has its own entrance. Apart from its size, the building is also impressive because of the rich materials used for the detailing and floors, the ornate façade, the vault doors imported from France, and the wrought iron gates and doors.

Over the years, did the focus of your clients change?

We always had a variety of guests, some of whom have often been very specific about what they want to see. Some like everything you show them, some are more interested in history, others in architecture or photography. The guests say they love seeing the old town in a cyclo and walking through the small streets that they would never have found by themselves. It is like stepping back in time to see the old structures and how they have been adapted to modern-day life.

Phnom Penh is normally not the focus or destination of tourists' trips, and they usually don't spend more than two days here, so if they go on one of our architecture tours they are happily surprised that they have seen and learned so much more than they expected. We are also contacted by architects and designers who are very specific about what they want to see. This is why KA-tours stipulates that all its guides be trained as architects or be students of architecture. Our guides are passionate about the subject and love to share their knowledge with the guests. Many of our guests realise that some of the heritage is not well maintained and that it will not last forever, so they advise people to come before it is gone. It is kind of a paradox that seeing the dilapidated old buildings, now housing many families, attracts the artistic or romantic side in us and makes for scenic photos, yet we all understand that both funding and organisational drive are needed to conserve and restore these memories of the past.

Do you think there is more awareness for the built heritage today?

In the past couple of years, we have certainly seen a slight improvement in the preservation of the French colonial buildings around the Post Office area, the old French administrative buildings along the former Canal de Verneville (now Street 106), and some colonial structures on Preah Norodom Boulevard. The restoration works have either been done by the Cambodian authorities or through private investments, which are both positive developments for the city.

However, the iconic buildings of the New Khmer Architecture style of the 1960s have been mostly either demolished or altered beyond recognition. The coming years will be decisive: will the urban heritage be preserved and blended together with the new development, so that it maintains its distinct style and sympathetic character? Or will the buildings testifying to the past be torn down, lakes filled, and parks cemented to such an extent that the city of Phnom Penh becomes void of historical mementos? Hopefully it is not too late to retain some architectural souvenirs of the 1960s and of the colonial days. Only time will tell whether they survive the new construction rage of this rapidly growing capital.

Around the Royal Palace

Portrait: Lu Ban Hap
Interview: Hun Chansan

Facing the confluence of the four rivers, the Royal Palace lies at the heart of the former Cambodian District and is surrounded by key administrative, religious, and cultural institutions of the country. In spite of the ongoing urban transformation, the presence of numerous pagodas and public parks still preserves the airy and green character of the district. While most of the outstanding buildings date from the French-colonial period, some modernist highlights of the time of independence can also be found, such as the Chaktomuk Conference Hall, as well as several interesting contemporary works of architecture.

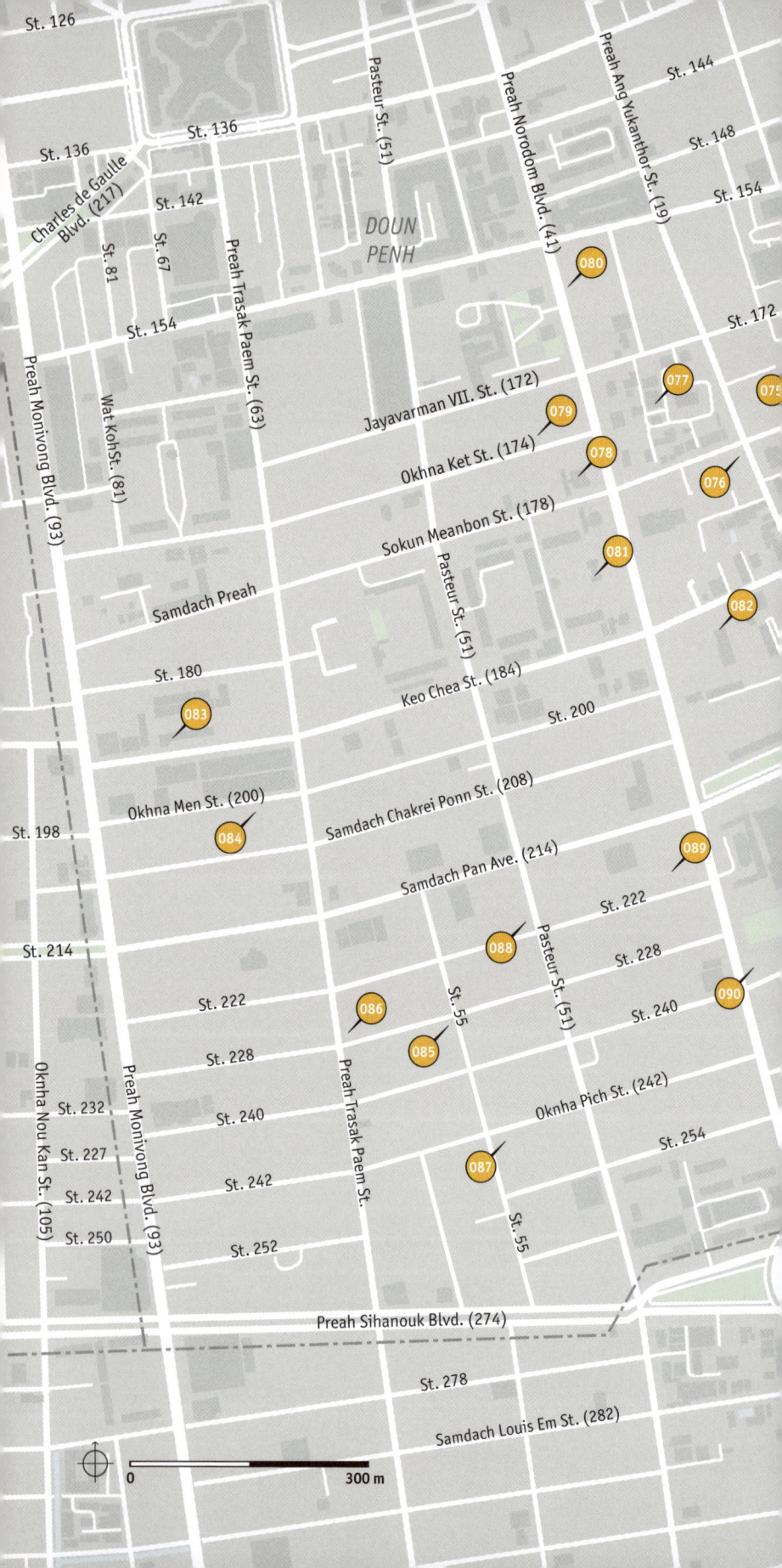

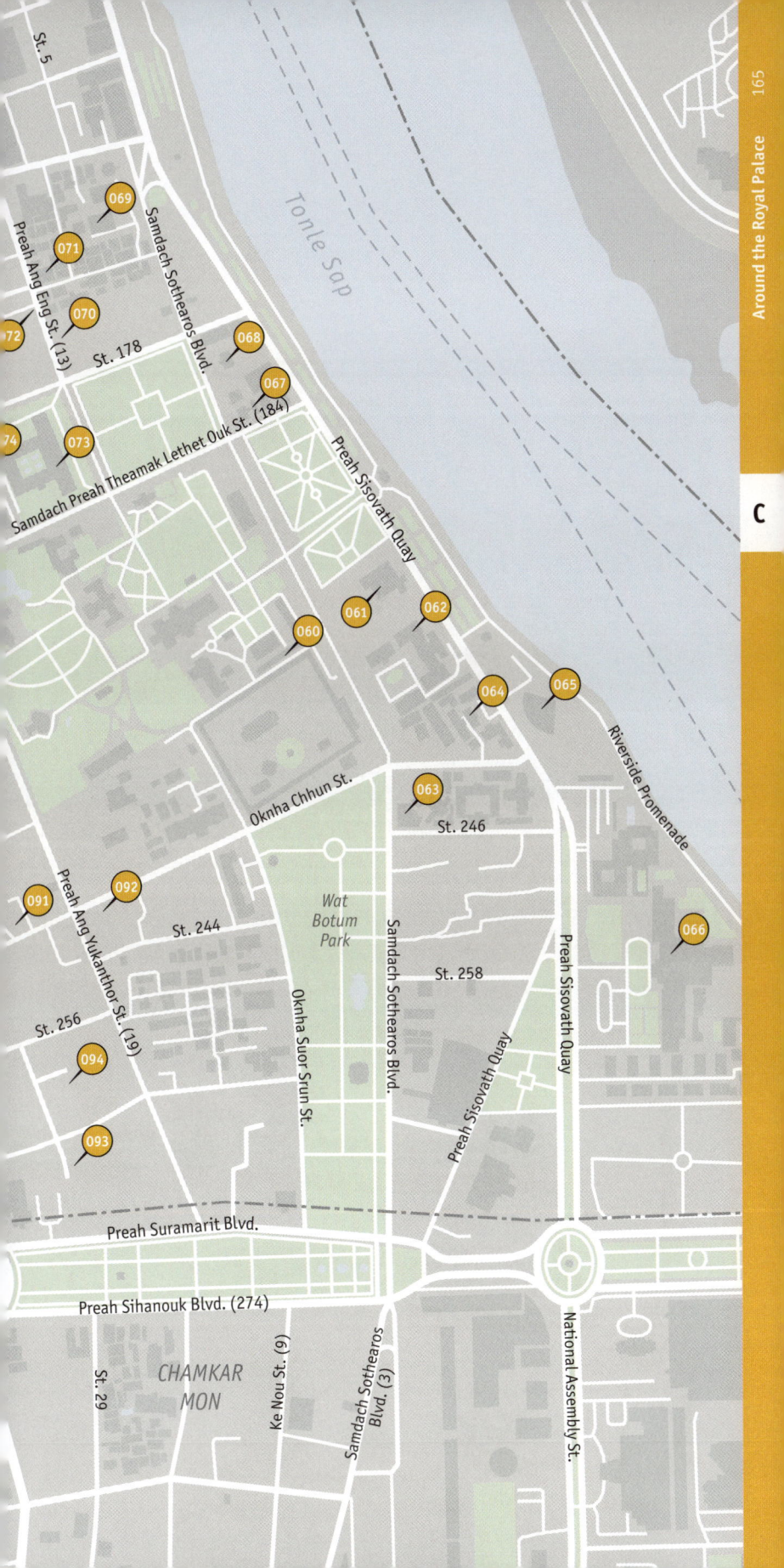

C

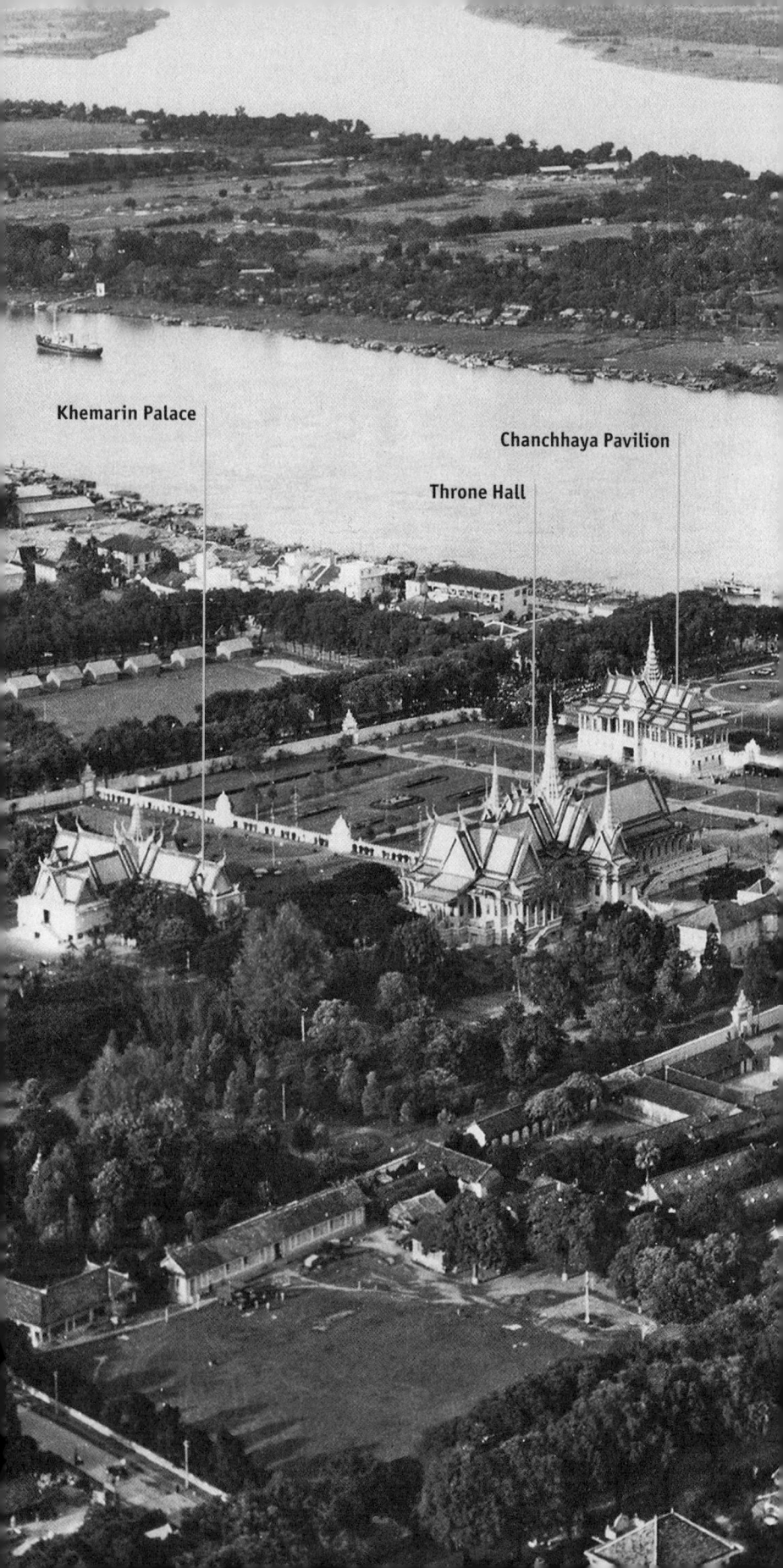

Khemarin Palace

Chanchhaya Pavilion

Throne Hall

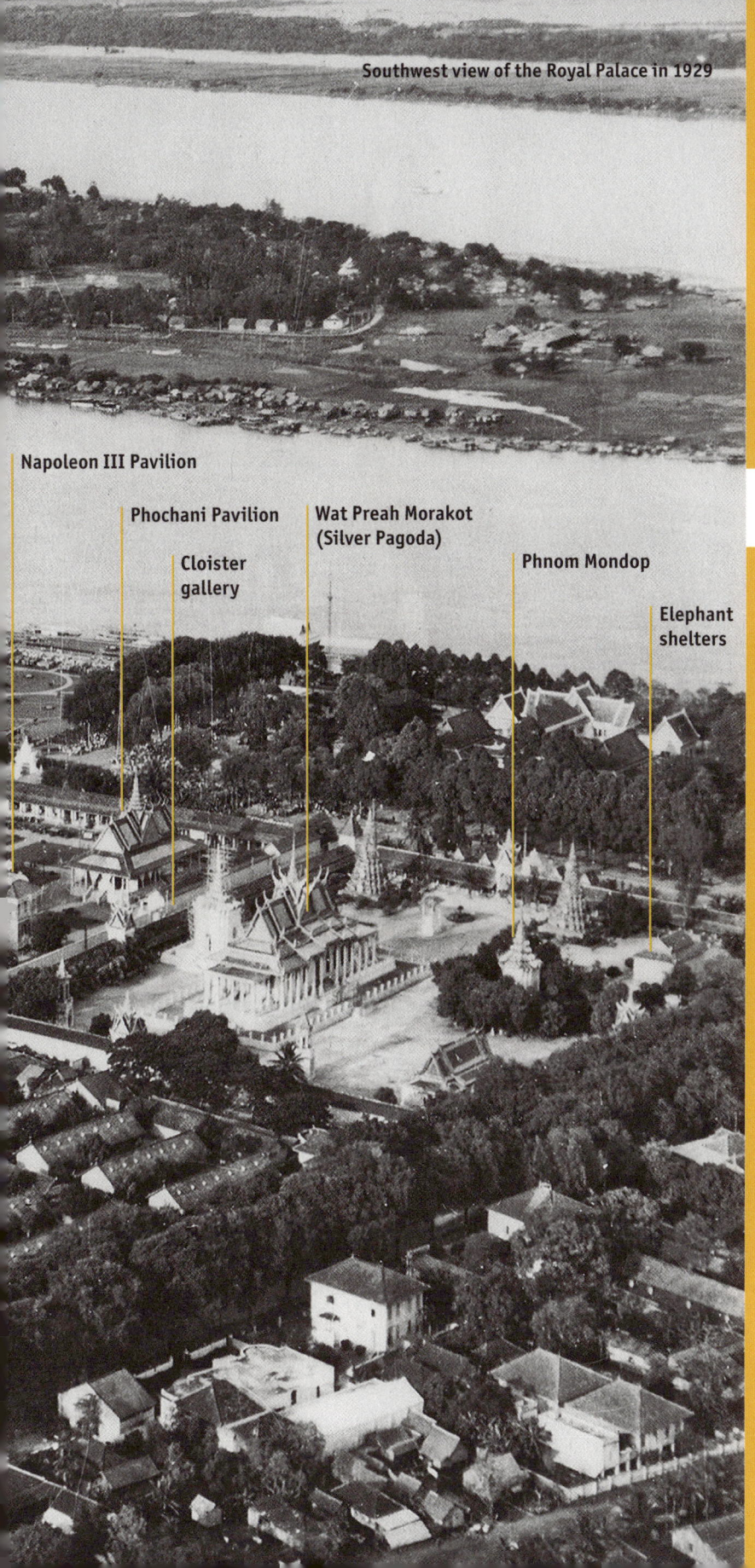

Southwest view of the Royal Palace in 1929

Napoleon III Pavilion

Phochani Pavilion

Wat Preah Morakot
(Silver Pagoda)

Cloister
gallery

Phnom Mondop

Elephant
shelters

C

Royal Palace

Samdech Sothearos Boulevard
Various architects
1860s–1960s

060 C

Set slightly back from the riverfront and facing east, the Royal Palace is both the symbolic and actual centre of the city. With its picturesque buildings and manicured gardens sheltered behind a crenellated wall, the compound is located in a prime geomantic position. Its middle axis was placed in the centre of the Quatre Bras, the intersection of the four rivers (*chaktomuk* in Khmer) at that time. The establishment of the Royal Palace was a comparatively recent event in the history of Phnom Penh. It was not until 1866, after the establishment of the French Protectorate in Cambodia, that King Norodom moved the royal court from Oudong back to Phnom Penh and made the city the country's official capital. The first Royal Palace to be built at the present location was designed by leading Khmer architect Okhna Tep Nimit Mak. It was built by King Norodom with French assistance between 1866 and 1870 and was officially opened on 14 February 1870. The royal court was installed permanently at the new Royal Palace in 1871, and the walls surrounding the grounds (*kampaeng*) were raised in 1873. Several buildings were added over the next decade, most of which were demolished and rebuilt between 1910 and 1927 under King Sisowath to grander designs in concrete, brick, and stucco. These include the early wooden Chanchhaya Pavilion and Throne Hall. The complex became a 'city within the city' with the Throne Hall, the audience and dance halls, the residences, the administrative offices, craft workshops, and barracks. From the late 19th century well into the 20th century, the royal family and the king's concubines, high court officials, and hereditary servants lived inside the Royal Palace. A third phase of transformation took place under King Norodom Suramarit and King Sihanouk, with several structures added and some rebuilt in the 1950s and early 1960s. Many of the buildings of the Royal Palace were built with a distinct combination of traditional (religious) Khmer architectural styles and European features as well as elements inspired by the Grand Palace in Bangkok. This was the outcome of a unique collaboration between the king and the colonial government, with contributions from French and Cambodian architects and artists.

The present complex is divided into four main compounds. On the north side is the **Khemarin Palace** with the private section, or **Inner Court**, adjacent to the west. The central compound contains the **Throne Hall**, while the **Silver Pagoda** is located

Throne Hall

in the south. Visitors can wander around the central compound containing the Throne Hall and Chanchhaya Pavilion as well as the Silver Pagoda compound. The **Khemarin Palace** (*Khemarin Moha Prasat*) is the private residence of King Norodom Sihamoni and members of the royal family. This private compound is separated from the other buildings by a small wall and is located behind the Throne Hall. To the right of the Throne Hall, the main building is topped by a single-spired *prang*. It was constructed between 1927 and 1930 by the famous Khmer architect Oknha Tep Nimit Khieu under the reign of King Sisowath Monivong. From 1960, it was reserved for the use of foreign dignitaries visiting Cambodia, among them Charles de Gaulle, President Sukarno, President Tito, and Chou Enlai. Several interesting buildings from the 1950s and 1960s are hidden in the private gardens of the **Inner Court**, among them the **Damnak Kantha Bopha** located near the west gate, on the east-west axis of the Throne Hall. This elegant bungalow was designed by French architects Leroy & Mondet and inaugurated on 17 September 1956. King Norodom Sihanouk ordered its construction to accommodate foreign guests and to commemorate his favourite daughter Kantha Bopha, who died of fever when she was just four years old.

The **Throne Hall** (*Preah Tineang Tevea Vinichhay*) was built with reinforced concrete in 1917 by the Societé Cochin-chinoise de Béton armé and inaugurated by King Sisowath two years later. It thus replaced a preceding wooden building built between 1869 and 1870 under King Norodom (demolished in 1915). The building has been used for major ceremonies such as the royal coronation and the king's birthday as well as state receptions and audiences granted by the king on national and religious days. The exterior of the cross-shaped edifice is dominated by superimposed roofs, crowned by three spires. The central spire is adorned with the four-faced head of Brahma, inspired by *Prasat Bayon* in Angkor Thom. An imposing front stairway leads up to the surrounding gallery. It is guarded by seven-headed *naga* figures, while the pillars are decorated with *kinnaris* and *garudas* supporting the roof. As with all buildings at the Royal Palace, the Throne Hall faces east. Inside, the Throne Hall contains three royal thrones and golden statues of Cambodian kings and queens from the reign of King Ang Duong onwards. Note the arched ceiling with beautiful frescoes of the *Reamker*, the Khmer version of the *Ramayana* epic. In the middle of the hall, the traditional throne, or *Preah Tineang Bossabok*, is an ancient nine-level classical Khmer-style throne. Each Khmer king sits on it only once in his life, on the coronation day, while wearing the royal regalia. The Throne Hall is

Interior view Throne Hall

flanked by two small buildings erected between 1915 and 1917. On the left, the **Hor Samrit Vimean**, or **Hor Preah Khan**, is used as a repository for royal regalia and costumes. The **Hor Samran Phirun**, on the right, was used as a waiting area for the king before he would mount an elephant for royal processions, and as a storage space for musical instruments and utensils used in the royal coronation procession. This pavilion currently houses a display of gifts from foreign heads of state. The **Chanchhaya Pavilion** (*Preah Tineang Chanchhaya*) dominates the view of the Royal Palace on Sothearos Boulevard, as it was built alongside a section of the palace walls. The current building is the second incarnation of the Moonlight Pavilion. It was built with reinforced concrete between 1913 and 1914 under King Sisowath to replace the smaller wooden pavilion built under King Norodom in 1866. The building has a large open hall on its first floor whose main function before 1970 was as a venue for dance performances of the Royal Ballet. Interestingly, the ceiling

paintings depicting Cambodian dancers and scenes from the *Reamker* were created by French artist Augustin Carrera in March 1913. The paintings were done on large canvases in Paris and then retouched on site so that the colours would fit in with the architectural setting. The building has seen comprehensive restoration works in recent years. It is now used as the place where the king delivers speeches on the National Day or during special events, and occasionally serves as a venue for state and royal banquets. The **Phochani Pavilion** (*Preah Tineang Phochani*) was inaugurated in 1912 as a classical dance theatre for the Royal Ballet. The open hall is adorned with elaborate ceiling frescoes painted by French artist M. Lamorte. It is currently used for royal receptions and meetings. The **Napoleon III Pavilion** was the first permanent structure on the site of the Royal Palace. It was originally erected in Ismailia for Empress Eugénie of France, wife of Napoleon III, for use during the opening ceremony of the Suez Canal in 1869. According to most sources,

Napoleon III Pavilion (under renovation)

Napoleon III presented the building to King Norodom in 1876, and it was reassembled in the Royal Palace in the same year. Entirely made of iron, the prefabricated building was used as an art gallery until its renovation started in 2012 (ongoing at the time of writing).

Located behind the Napoleon III Pavilion, the **Damnak Chan** building (*Preah Reach Damnak Chan*) was constructed between 1953 and 1956 by architect Ung Krapum Phka with a mix of western neo-classical and Khmer traditional styles. Originally meant for the High Council of the Throne, the building has served several purposes since then. Currently, it houses the administrative offices of the Ministry of the Royal Palace.

The **Silver Pagoda** is located in the southern section of the Royal Palace compound, enclosed by high galleries. Upon entering the complex through the north gate, you will find yourself on a vast courtyard, surrounded by a **cloister gallery**. On the walls of the cloisters are murals (frescoes) illustrating the Khmer epic *Reamker*. The 'architect of the palace' Oknha Tep Nimit Mak and about 40 apprentices of the Palace workshops originally painted the frescoes between 1903 and 1904. The legend stretches across 604 m of wall space: reading should start from the east, near the front door, and continue in a clockwise direction. The roof protecting the frescoes was added in the 1960s, based on a design by architect Lu Ban Hap. Nevertheless, weather, microorganisms, and neglect have gradually eroded parts of the paintings. From 1985 to 1992, and then again between 2015 and 2017, a Polish conservation team partially restored the damaged frescoes. The royal temple at the centre of the courtyard is the **Pagoda of the Emerald Buddha** (official name *Preah Vihear Preah Keo Morakot*, commonly *Wat Preah Keo*). Construction of the original pagoda in brick and timber started in 1892, and the building was completed shortly before King Norodom I's death in 1902. It was damaged later, and reconstructed on the same site with reinforced concrete under the supervision of Sihanouk's mother,

Mural at the cloister gallery of the Silver Pagoda

Silver Pagoda and Stupa of HRH Kantha Bopha

Queen Kossamak in 1962. With its elegant multi-tiered roof, the design is based on traditional Cambodian temple architecture. The vihear serves less as a functioning temple than as a repository for cultural and religious treasures. Inside the Silver Pagoda, you can see next to the entrance on the left some of the hand-crafted 5,329 silver tiles weighing a total of 1,125 kg. A dazzling number

Interior view of Silver Pagoda

of Buddhist and historical artefacts are on display, most notably the 90 kg golden standing Buddha Maitreya encrusted in 2,086 diamonds, said to have been cast in the form of King Norodom I. Inside the gilded *bossabok* pavilion is the Emerald Buddha, the image that gave the temple its Cambodian name. Its presence in the pagoda reflects the wish of King Norodom I to match in his own capital the famed Temple of the Emerald Buddha found within Bangkok's Grand Palace. In front of the pagoda itself stands a **statue of King Norodom** on horseback enshrined under a *mondop*, a square structure with a pyramidal pointed roof. It was mounted on its current location in 1892. The **two stupas** (*chedey*) further east were both erected on 13 March 1908, containing the cremated ashes of King Ang Duong (1845–1860) and King Norodom (1834–1904), respectively. The **Temple Library** (*Mondapa of Satra and Tripitaka*) to the north of the vihear houses three collections of sacred Buddhist writings. South of the vihear, the artificial mound known as **Phnom Mondop** symbolises

Kailassa (Kailash) Mountain. On the hill, decorated with 108 small statues representing the 108 past lives of the Buddha, is a shrine, containing a large footprint of the Buddha. Further to the west, the sanctuary (*prang*) for Princess Kantha Bopha was built in 1960 in the form of a traditional Khmer monument with beautifully carved designs in the Banteay Srei style. Next to it, the stupa dedicated to King Norodom Suramarit and Queen Sisowath Monivong Kossomak was built in the same year. Both structures were designed by Vann Molyvann in collaboration with Toeung Veuth, a designer and master sculptor in the Angkorian tradition who also played a fundamental role in designing and building the **Independence Monument** (095 D). The former **Elephant Shelters** (*Raung Damrei*), situated on the way to the exit in the southeast corner of the Silver Pagoda, were built in 1892 and completely remodelled in the early 2000s to become a museum. The current museum includes a small exhibition on the vernacular wooden architecture of Cambodia.

Former Hotel Renakse

40 Samdech Sothearos Boulevard
Architect unknown
1890/1950s

061 C

In a prime location directly opposite the Royal Palace sits a strange compound comprising abandoned buildings in a garden hidden behind yellow ochre walls. Like the nearby National Museum, the Hotel Renakse has a design influenced by traditional Khmer architecture. This can be seen in the proportions and volumes, in the roof composition, in the decoration, and in the way the buildings are organised into pavilions endowed with galleries. The two-floor central entrance building, with one-storey wings, must have been built before 1898, since it is shown in French city plans of that time. In the early twentieth century, this building was flanked by two Cambodian courts ('Tribunaux Cambodgien') of the same style: one on the site of the public garden in the west, and another at the site of the Ministry of Justice (062 C). Under French colonial rule, the building facing the Royal Palace housed the Council of Ministers. It is located precisely on the axis of the ceremonial alley and gate between the Royal Palace and the Silver Pagoda. The two-storey rear building along Sisowath Quay was added in the 1950s and was used to house the Ministry of Foreign Affairs. Its architecture shows an interesting mix of modernist elements at the façade combined with a Khmer-style roof. Lu Ban Hap opted for a similar architectural style 20 years later, when he designed the Hotel Cambodiana (066 C): he tried to make the enormous volume of the hotel blend in with the Royal Palace and nearby pagodas by covering it with a traditional roof. A city map from the 1960s

CAMBODGE

A. T.   22. - PNOM-PENH. - Le Conseil des Ministres

also marks the Council of Ministers as the Ministry of Interior. After the Vietnamese took control of Phnom Penh in 1979, the city became the temporary headquarters of the Kampuchean United Front for National Salvation (KUFNS), an organisation founded in 1978 by opponents of the Khmer Rouge with Vietnamese assistance. In the early 1980s, the Renakse served as a state hotel that hosted international experts and officials. At the same time, it maintained its function as the headquarters of the nascent Party of Democratic Kampuchea. When the Vietnamese administration withdrew from Cambodia in 1989, the building was converted into a private hotel. And in 1992, both buildings became the Hotel Renakse. The hotel, with 35 rooms, left a mark in the history of print media in Cambodia. According to Michael Hayes, founding editor of the *Phnom Penh Post*, the hotel

became the birthplace of the paper in 1992 and later also housed the early offices of the *Cambodia Daily*. The hotel was privately managed under a 49-year lease. After a long dispute that was taken to the High Court, staff and guests were forced to leave the hotel's premises in January 2009 because of its 'age of more than 100 years' and for 'safety reasons'. The edifice is clearly an eminent cultural vestige of the history of Phnom Penh and needs to be appreciated in view of its shared history with the Royal Palace. Rumour has it that the Ministry of the Royal Palace recently appropriated the property. If this is true, one can be cautiously optimistic about the building's future fate. It would be a prime heritage asset for the city, and it could be, for example, repurposed as an exhibition venue for the Royal Palace, with its garden becoming part of the public parks along the river.

MINISTÈRE DES AFFAIRES ÉTRANGÈRES À PHNOM PENH (CAMBODGE)

Ministry of Justice

062 C

44 Samdech Sothearos Boulevard
Architect unknown
1925

The building for the Ministry of Justice is situated on a very prominent location directly opposite the Royal Palace. It used to house the former High Court and Court of Appeals of the French Protectorate. The building was built on the location of the former Tribunal Cambodgien and was inaugurated in 1925. For this public edifice, the French engineers used a neo-classical style with a central portico and symmetrical colonnaded galleries around a three-sided ceremonial courtyard oriented towards the Royal Palace. The courtyard is defined by two protruding secondary wings, which flank the main central block, or *corps de logis*, as in seventeenth century European palaces. Towards the rear of the building, the wings used to enclose two colonnaded interior courtyards on either side of the central building. Interestingly, these courtyards were filled in later with pavilion-like constructions featuring pyramidal hipped roofs. The roofs had ridge turrets, alluding to Cambodian religious architecture, which can still be seen on the left and right of the central portico. The central parapet wall is also decorated with some ornamental plaques and a frieze in an Angkorian style. Even the organisation of the buildings into pavilions with open galleries can be read as a reference to traditional Khmer architecture. The exterior is still in its original condition, apart from the two buildings at the front on both sides of the courtyard, which were added between 2008 and 2012.

The High Court and Court of Appeals in the 1940s

Supreme Court

Samdech Sothearos Boulevard/
Street 240
Architect unknown
1909

 063 C

Diagonally opposite the Royal Palace, there is a group of buildings that once housed the French École d'Administration and the Higher School of Buddhism and Pali. At the corner, you can find what is today the Supreme Court, which was originally constructed as the École de Kromakar, the French School of Administration, in 1909. The striking building makes an important and exotic contribution to the urban landscape of Phnom Penh. With its imposing red-tiled roof, enormous decorated tympanums, and gilded *chedey* spires, the building clearly alludes to traditional Khmer architecture. However, the French architects' use of religious architectural styles for a secular building represents an idea typically applied in 19th century Europe rather than vernacular building traditions. The grand edifice housed the National Assembly for many decades, until the parliament moved to its new building site further south along the Bassac River in 2007.

If you walk further along Oknha Chhun Street towards the river, you will find the next building complex on the right. This used to be the Higher School of Buddhism and Pali (Lycée Bouddhique), built in 1909. Behind a nondescript roadside office building, there are functional two-storey classroom buildings surrounding a courtyard. These buildings replaced the original colonnaded pavilions in the traditional Khmer style that were demolished between 1955 and 1965. In 1962, there were nearly 600 Buddhist primary schools, with an enrolment of over 10,000 novices and 800 monks as instructors, throughout the country. After a long break during the years of war, the compound is used again today by the **Preah Suramarit Buddhist University**.

Finally, on the corner with Sisowath Quay, the **General Inspectorate for National Buddhist Education of the Kingdom of Cambodia** (GINBEC) occupies a building formerly used by the Ministry of Cults

Aereial view with the former École de Kromakar complex to the left, Ministry of Justice to the right, and Royal Palace at the top, 1931

and the Ministry of Foreign Affairs. This is another hybrid example exhibiting a rather peculiar mix of modern and traditional Cambodian architectural motifs. The building was completed in 1965 on the grounds of the former Bibliothèque Royale. This was another French building in the 'National Style', featuring Khmer traditional architectural motifs. It used to mirror the former École d'Administration, as we can see on the left side of the historic aerial photo from 1929 above, and in the French postcard below. The Institut Bouddhique was a research institution formed in 1930 by the Royal Library. The Buddhist Institute contained a library, record and photograph collections, and a museum. Today the institute can be found further south in a new building next to the NagaWorld casino.

Around the corner...
Across Street 240, on the grounds of the Palace Gate Hotel, stands an exquisitely restored French villa that once served as the headquarters of the commander of the French army in Cambodia. It later housed the Central Committee of the Sangkum Reastr Niyum, and then the Office of the President of the National Assembly in the 1990s. In what is today the fine-dining hotel restaurant Mealea, you can find an interesting exhibition of historical photographs.

PNOM-PENH. — Ecole de Kromakar

COLLECTION-HENRY, SERIE A, N° 23

Preah Sihanouk Raja Buddhist University

064 C

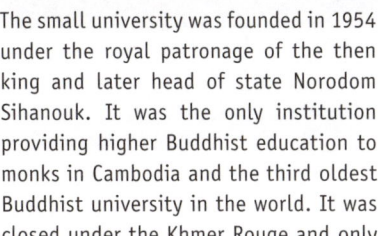

Preah Sisowath Quay
Architect unknown
1958

The small university was founded in 1954 under the royal patronage of the then king and later head of state Norodom Sihanouk. It was the only institution providing higher Buddhist education to monks in Cambodia and the third oldest Buddhist university in the world. It was closed under the Khmer Rouge and only reopened in 1997. In 2006 it became a fully fledged university, capable of enrolling 200 students each year. Constructed on the location of the former Marche Central (see historic aerial photo on the left), the unadorned, two-storey buildings are grouped around a small courtyard. Central staircases, clad with concrete breeze blocks that create a wonderful play of light, open up to symmetrically arranged arcades. Variations of this building type can be found in provincial centres across the country, for example on pagoda grounds in Battambang. The enormous construction programme of the newly independent state in the 1960s led to a similar design approach for school buildings and administrative buildings throughout the provinces, which are often almost identical in construction.

Chaktomuk Conference Hall 065 C

Preah Sisowath Quay
Vann Molyvann
1961

Inaugurated in 1961 as La Salle de Conférence Chaktomuk, this early work by architect Vann Molyvann is certainly one of the finest examples of 1960s New Khmer Architecture. The name of the building refers to the official name of Phnom Penh, *Krong Chaktomuk*, in its short form. It was financed with American money and built on newly reclaimed land along the riverside. The building's floor plan and its folded roof recall the shape of a fan palm. The jagged contour of the rooftop, revolving around a traditional tower, incorporates the triangular gable elements of traditional Khmer rooftops, such as the ones that can be seen at the nearby Royal Palace. Decorative panels in the gables show traditional motifs. From the rear of the building, where there are two large glass fronts, one can enjoy spectacular views of the confluence of the Mekong, Tonle Sap, and Bassac rivers. The building used to be painted white, and the roof, window, and door frames were once made of gold-coloured anodised aluminium. After a renovation project in 2000, which also introduced a couple of spatial alterations and a new orange-yellow coat of paint, the impression is somewhat diminished. The Conference Hall was opened on the occasion of the Sixth Conference of the World Fellowship of Buddhists. In 1979, the tribunal against Pol Pot took place here in his absence. Today the multi-purpose building hosts a wide range of events.

Record cover, 1960s

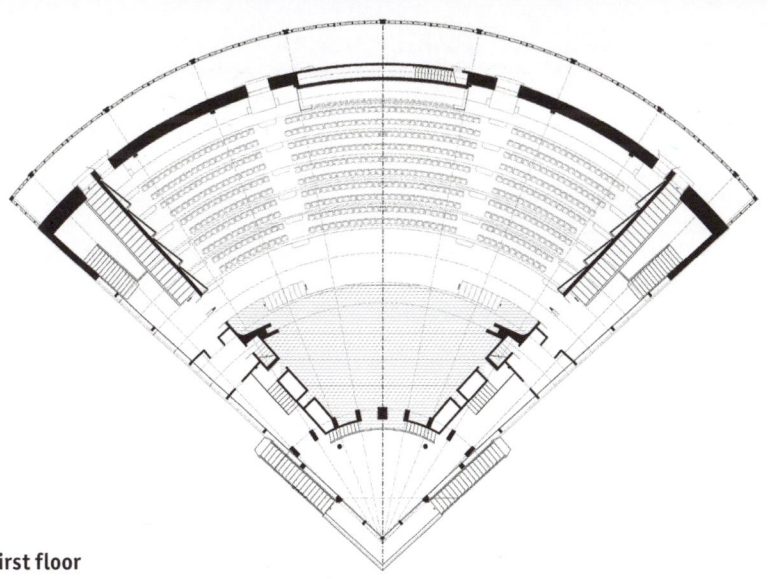

First floor

Hotel Cambodiana

066 C

313 Preah Sisowath Quay
Lu Ban Hap with Chhim Sun Fong
1970/early 1990s

At the time of its construction, Hotel Cambodiana was the largest hotel project in the city. At the time, no one in Cambodia had experience in designing a hotel of this scale. As such, its architect Lu Ban Hap travelled to France for two weeks, at the invitation of Air France, for consultation and assistance. A consortium carried out the construction, with private contributions from Norodom Sihanouk. The hotel was built on the banks of the Tonle Sap, in front of the historic backdrop of the Royal Palace, the National Assembly, and a series of pagodas. Inspired by this environment, Lu gave the large hotel a modernised Khmer-style roof. In an interview with the author in 2015, he recalled that this idea enabled him to win Sihanouk's approval and prevail over a rival proposal from the Ministry of Construction for a tower with ten floors.

The huge structure consists of two staggered wings with hotel rooms and larger apartments at the north and south ends. The central tower performs the service functions. The hotel restaurant lies to the west, where it offers fantastic views of the confluence of the Mekong and Tonle Bassac. Lu placed the building on pilotis, so that the view from the street would extend to the junction of the four rivers. Each room initially had a balcony, which in turn provided shade for the façade and balcony below. Intentionally or not, the building's structure recalls that of **Hotel Le Royal** (**017 A**).

According to Lu, the hotel was to be officially opened in April 1970 after Sihanouk's return from China. But history took a different turn when Sihanouk was deposed by his prime minister Lon Nol in March 1970. Lon Nol turned the hotel into a military camp and walled in the balconies. At times, rural residents who had fled from the Khmer Rouge to Phnom Penh lived in the building. American photographer Al Rockoff, who was in Phnom Penh from 1973 until the Khmer Rouge took over the city, once mentioned that the hotel grounds at that time were home to a 23,000-person

refugee camp. In 1988, a Singapore-based company started to complete the construction. The building was refurbished and expanded before finally being opened in 1990. Today, the ground floor is completely enclosed, which makes the already massive structure appear even bigger and blocks the view of the river. The areas facing the river were recently redesigned as venues for hosting public events. Rumours that this important architectural testimony to the 1960s would be demolished have been circulating for years, but they seem to be unsubstantiated. At the time of research, the author was told that the owner of the hotel had just decided to modernise the building. One can thus hope that financial interests will not triumph over respect for cultural heritage once again.

Hotel Cambodiana under construction, view from the river, late 1960s.

Avec toute mon affection.

N. Sihanouk

Lu Ban Hap receives a medal from Head of State Norodom Sihanouk, 1969

'I could have done so much more for my country'

A portrait of Lu Ban Hap, architect of the Hotel Cambodiana and Head of the Urban Planning and Housing Department of the Municipality of Phnom Penh from 1960 to 1975.

Vann Molyvann (see p. 280) may have been the most radical and perhaps most successful architect of independent Cambodia, with around 80 buildings to his name. But he was not the only one. Alongside him, there were a number of other ambitious architects and planners who, after completing their studies abroad, made important contributions to Cambodia's urban landscapes. Perhaps the most prominent member of this group was Lu Ban Hap. Lu's architectural achievements, which include the **Hotel Cambodiana** (066 C) and the **Chenla Theatre** (116 E), still define Phnom Penh's cityscape. His most famous landmark was the iconic Municipal Apartments, better known as the White Building (demolished in 2018), which he designed in 1963 together with Ukraine-born engineer Vladimir Bodiansky. His lesser known works include: the public gardens that once encircled the White Building; a park around the now filled-in Boeung Kak lake; and the boulevard in front of the Independence Monument. At the same time, as head of Phnom Penh's most important city-planning institution, Lu influenced the shape of the city through more than its buildings and gardens.

Lu Ban Hap was born in 1931 in Kampong Cham province. He moved to Phnom Penh at the age of 14 to attend a secondary school. The young student had difficulty adapting to the monastic daily routines. One day, he ran into the Minister of State, Penn Nouth, by chance. Lu asked him if he could offer him some work. Penn Nouth, impressed by the courage of the young boy, took him into his family, enabled him to finish school, and remained his mentor and friend until his death in 1985.

In 1949, Lu Ban Hap became part of the wave of Cambodian students sent to Paris on academic scholarships. He initially wanted to become an engineer, but on the advice of Vann Molyvann – who had arrived in Paris three years earlier – he enrolled in the architecture programme.

By the time he qualified as an architect, Lu had become intent on travelling to Brazil to work on Brasilia, the futuristic new capital that modernist master Oscar Niemeyer was building at that time. But Sihanouk, whom Lu Ban Hap had met in Paris through his old mentor Penn Nouth, did not want to let the young, well-trained architect go. Lu obeyed Sihanouk's order to return to Phnom Penh in 1960. There, he was immediately commissioned to set up the city's Service Municipal de l'Urbanisme et d'Habitat.

Tep Phan, governor of Phnom Penh at the time, gave Lu carte blanche to modernise the city's urban planning. And Lu relished the vast scope of his tasks: 'When I arrived in Cambodia, the land was languishing. There was no one who cared, no cadres, no administration. French Indochina had been managed from Hanoi, but the French were gone indeed. We had to build everything anew, but for me it was good.' With 12 employees, Lu oversaw everything from urban planning to the design and maintenance of public gardens, through to waste management, street lighting, power supply, and building permits. Under his direction, Phnom Penh edged its way towards becoming a metropolis to be admired. Lu recalled: 'Once, the president of Singapore, Lee Kuan Yew, came to visit Phnom Penh. He was in despair about the state of Singapore and asked me how I managed to keep the city so neat. At the time, Singapore was a dirty city. Phnom Penh, meanwhile, was called the Pearl of Asia.'

Alongside his work for the municipality, Lu established his own architectural practice and later also founded a construction company. His private offices were commissioned to build universities, factories, and the villas for Norodom Sihanouk and Princess Bopha Devi on the Chamkar Mon state compound. Lu's most interesting building was certainly the residential building that he completed in 1963 for his own family,

Wat Botum Park with fountain and bandstand, Lu Ban Hap, 1960s

regrettably demolished in 2006 to give way to the newly constructed Ministry of Land Management, Urban Planning and Construction. The house was dominated by its distinctive roof, which was designed as a ventilated two-shell construction, a novelty in Phnom Penh.

On a study trip to the Soviet Union, Lu learned about the principle of prefabrication. He realised the economic potential of prefabrication and developed a cost-effective modular system with which he managed to build around 40 houses. He also used the principle of prefabrication for a series of school buildings in Phnom Penh. The utilitarian buildings were constructed on a limited budget, but almost all schools are still in use today.

Lu was well into a four-year-long research project, exploring the future direction of development in Phnom Penh, when Lon Nol rose to power in 1970. After this point, all plans for the country fell apart. Some of Lu's colleagues, including Vann Molyvann, foresaw the dark fate looming over the country and emigrated. Lu's wife and children returned to France, but the architect himself remained – a decision he says he made out of a sense of duty to his country. Work became difficult amidst the increasing turmoil caused by the civil war. When the US began to bomb the provinces, there was a large-scale migration from the countryside to the capital. In this context, Lu recalled: 'We could not do anything. More

The public gardens in front of the Independence Monument, Lu Ban Hap, 1960s

Cost-effective prefabricated houses, Kandal province, Lu Ban Hap, 1960s

and more people were coming to Phnom Penh, and I was busy with simply providing them with the basic necessities.' He continued: 'There were no more building materials. One of my clients had to fly in cement from abroad because he wanted to go on with building at all cost.'

In 1975, the Khmer Rouge marched into Phnom Penh, and Lu, like the rest of the population, was sent to work in a rural labour camp. After three months, he executed a daring escape. Accompanied by his niece, he walked – mostly at night – all the way to Saigon. From there, he flew to Hanoi, then to Vientiane, Bangkok, and finally Paris. Once settled in Paris, Lu started to work again, but never at the scale of his Cambodian achievements. In

1978, he designed and built the house where he and his wife live to this day. Next door, he did the same for his old friend Penn Nouth, who had come to Paris in 1979.

Lu returned to Cambodia for the first time in 1989 to support the work of the NGO Médecins du Monde. He made annual visits to the country until 1994 to oversee the construction of orphanages and hospitals. Although he was asked several times, by Prime Minister Hun Sen himself among others, he did not want to return to Phnom Penh.

'I could have done so much more for my country,' he once told the author, 'but my career came to an end when I was 45. I only had 15 years. That was not enough.'

Lu Ban Hap's private residence at Preah Monivong Boulevard, Lu Ban Hap, 1960s

UNESCO Office Building

38 Samdech Sothearos Boulevard
Architect unknown
1910–1920

This building was built as the stately home of a wealthy Sino-Khmer merchant and must have been constructed between 1910 and 1920. Old maps of Phnom Penh and a series of photographs from the 1920s attest to the existence of this house at that time. According to art historian Darryl Collins, a son of Tan Bunpa, the owner of the **Chinese House (025 A)**, once owned the villa, which is presently occupied by UNESCO (United Nations Educational, Scientific and Cultural Organization). Located near the Royal Palace, the outstanding edifice, with an eclectic colonial style, faces the Veal Men (Mount Meru Square) in front of the National Museum. The privileged location suggests the owner enjoyed a high social standing. After the Khmer Rouge regime was defeated, the Vietnamese City Protection Unit was located here between 1979 and 1989. The Department of Conservation, Ancient Temples, Museums and Tourism occupied the building from 1989 to 1991. On November 1991, Federico Major, the then head of UNESCO in Phnom Penh, officially opened the UNESCO office in this building.

The compound consists of two buildings – the main house and an annex – connected by a walkway on the first floor. The villa is made of load-bearing walls in solid brick and concrete slabs. The floor plan is characteristic for the period. One enters the house through an entrance on the spacious porch. The ground floor features an extended foyer with small rooms situated to the rear on the left and right. At the back, a central wooden staircase leads to a gallery on the first floor. The hallway connects the main rooms that overlook the garden and the southern part of the Royal Palace. The building is excessive in ornamentation, characterised by a plethora of stucco decorations and a variety of encaustic tiles used on the floors and ceilings. The columns of the arched verandah on the ground floor show interesting plasterwork: a human face and a phoenix. The moulded head of Rahu eating the moon can be found above the main entrance, probably to fend off evil (Rahu is a demon in Hindu and Buddhist mythology). UNESCO undertook major renovations of the villa in 2008, 2011, and 2016, improving the roof structure and redecorating the walls. The basement was turned into a safe storeroom for documents. The UNESCO library is open to the public, though visitors must register at the reception during office hours.

The Mansion

 068 C

3 Samdech Sothearos Boulevard
Architect unknown
1910–1920

The grand, tired, and enchanting building located on the northeastern corner of the Veal Men (Mount Meru Square) was built as the home of a wealthy Sino-Khmer mandarin with the title of Lok Chhaivary Ly Eng Keng. It was Lok Chhaivary who opened, with his son Tan Pa (see **Tan Pa Residence 035 B**), the branch of the Banque Franco-Chinoise in Phnom Penh. It is said that the first two cars in Cambodia belonged to the king and Lok Chhaivary. The building must have been constructed between 1910 and 1920, just like the similar building located to the south, the **UNESCO Office (067 C)**. Unlike its carefully restored sister building, the majestic edifice is in a fairly decrepit state today. However, despite the years, weeds, and grime, it retains some of the grandeur of its glory days. The edifice is exceptional in its lavishly decorated eclectic colonial style and faded elegance. It is characterised by its rich ornamentation both inside and outside the building: ornate pediment designs and balustrades with decorative vases ennoble the roof. Open hallways on both levels of the front façade are adorned by Ionic columns and elaborate balustrades.

Additional Ionic columns and Corinthian pilasters frame the arched openings of the central entrance portico, which once also featured a balcony with delicate wrought ironwork.

The recent history of the building is chequered. The Vietnamese army used the building following the fall of the Khmer Rouge. In 1989, the villa became the property of the Ministry of Interior, which installed in it the Phnom Penh Municipal Police Office. In 2000, it was acquired by the FCC Group, which runs the Foreign Correspondents Club, but the building mostly remained underused, serving only occasionally as a venue for art installations and expat parties. In 2014, it was revamped as a heritage-themed bar with the name The Mansion. The popular cultural venue hosted regular events such as film screenings and live music and attracted a hip crowd until its gates finally closed in 2017. The building, with its solid brick load-bearing walls, is definitely not beyond repair. Though this key heritage building does suffer from neglect and lack of maintenance, it is in surprisingly good structural shape. Rumour has it that the current owner plans to convert The Mansion into an upscale heritage boutique hotel. One can only hope that the planned renovations, based on thorough studies, will give the mansion a new lease on life.

Wat Ounalom

Samdech Sothearos Boulevard
Architect unknown
14th century (*prasat*) /
1957 and 1966 (*viharas*)

The rather modern looking *vihāra* (main prayer hall, in Khmer *preah vihear*) from 1957, fronting Sisowath Quay, belies the fact that Wat Ounalom is one of Phnom Penh's oldest and most important pagodas. The wat dates back to the reign of King Ponhea Yat in the 15th century, though there is little evidence of its age remaining today. It is probable that the present-day pagoda stands on a foundation created before the Cambodian court abandoned Angkor, some time after 1431. This is despite the fact that the foundation date of this pagoda is often given as 1443, the year of the city's birth. The wat has been extensively rebuilt since then. Few if any of the buildings are more than a century old, with most of them being far more modern. Wat Ounalom is one of Cambodia's two major religious centres and houses the senior abbot of the Mahanikay Order, the principal Buddhist order of Cambodia. (The centre of the Thommayut Order is located at Wat Botum Vaddey). Buddhist pagodas in Cambodia traditionally also served as schools, providing primary and Buddhist education to children and adolescents. In the early 1970s, more than 500 monks lived in the pagoda, which also housed the library of the Institute Bouddhique. It was subsequently destroyed, along with many of the buildings, by the Khmer Rouge. The compound included some fine buildings from the early- to mid-twentieth century, mainly located towards the north of the compound. It resembles a small, peaceful town, a green and car-free oasis in the hectic city. Make sure to wander around to see some of the interesting works of secular architecture on display.

The pagoda gets its name from its role as the repository of an *ounalom*, an eyebrow hair of Buddha's, supposedly still contained in the large *Preah Chedey Thom* (great stupa) behind the *vihāra*. Attached to the rather elaborate stupa are five small sanctuaries, the most revered being

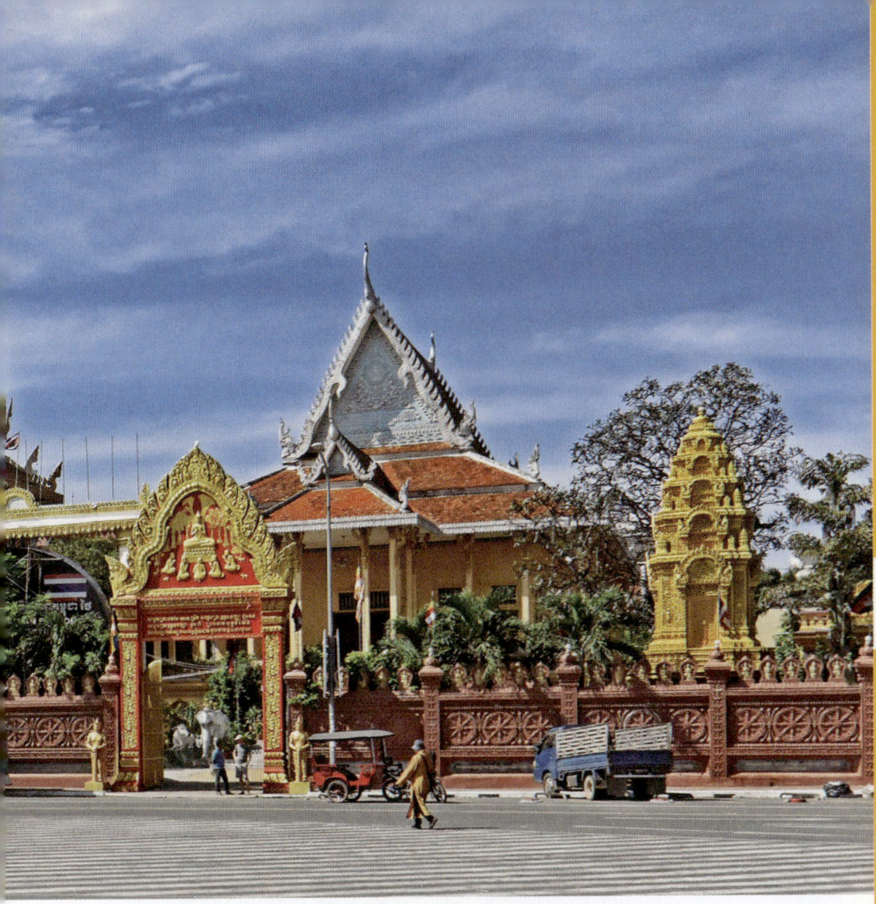

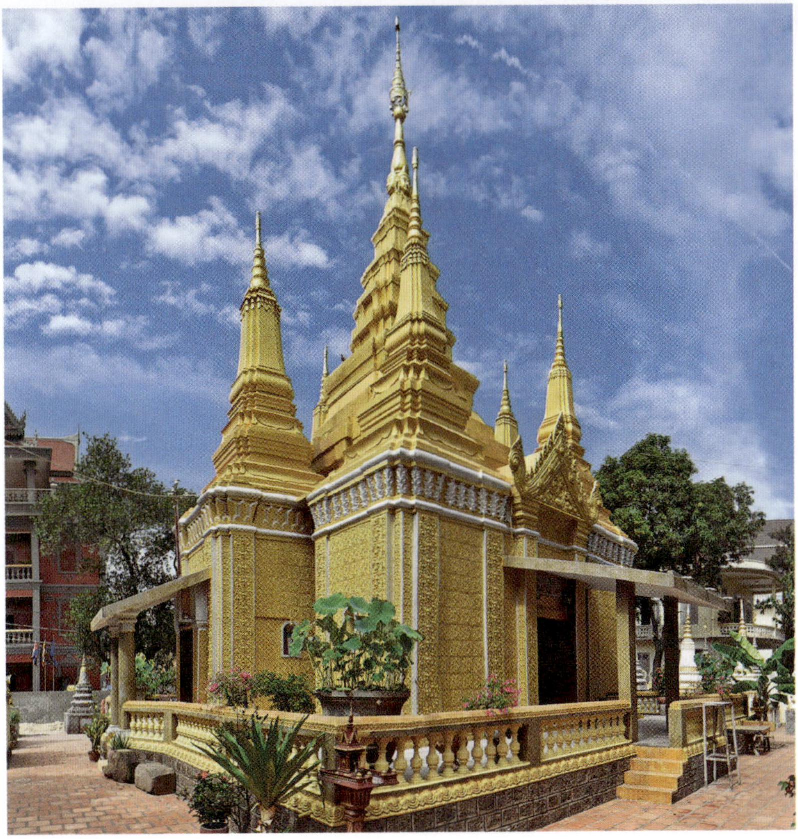

the one facing east, where there is a fine bronze Buddha. The ancient *chedey* in the centre is most probably the oldest existing structure in Phnom Penh, predating the founding of the wat by at least a century. A closer look at the southwest corner of the stupa reveals sandstone blocks (unfortunately recently painted gold) that form the walls of an Angkor-era *prasat*, a Hinduist sanctuary in the form

of a tower. Similar blocks are also inside the stupa's chamber, where a reclining Buddha lintel and an impressive seated Buddha statue postdate the tower.

The unusual building to the south of the main *vihāra* dates back to 1966 and is a somewhat imaginative modern recreation of the original shrine that was constructed in the 15th century. The imposing building is spread over three levels and has an interesting collection of magnificent paintings and cultural relics that throw light on the life of the Lord Buddha. Located in the northeast corner of the pagoda's compound sits the tall, golden Angkor-style stupa of the Venerable Chuon Nath (1883–1969), highly respected patriarch of the Mahanikay sect of Theravada Buddhism. He was also a famous intellectual, who oversaw the translation of the entire Buddhist Pali Canon into the Khmer language and also founded the first modern Khmer dictionary. Nath's other contributions to Cambodia include the current national anthem, *Nokor Reach*, for which he composed both the music and lyrics.

Around the corner:

In the southwest corner of the compound towards Street 13, the **Hiroshima House** (071 C) looms as a somewhat extreme monument for peace above the pagoda grounds, surrounded by traditional Buddhist temple buildings.

Apartment Building, Street 13 070 C

Street 13/Street 178
Architect unknown
1950s

This reinforced-concrete building from the 1950s comprises 17 bays that stretch over a distance of 72 m along Street 13. Its design continuously references the Chinese shophouse typology. Each housing unit, based on a 4.1 x 17.5 m frame, consists of two sections: a 14-metre-deep living area, which is located above the shops and opens onto the street; and a 2.1-metre-deep wet area, comprising a kitchen, toilet, and shower room. The dry and wet areas are separated by a long corridor shared by all apartments on each level. On the last floor, this corridor functions as a communal open courtyard. The upper-floor corridors, accessed via two shared staircases at the rear of the building, communicate with each other, thus ensuring air circulation, ventilation, and temperature regulation throughout the building. Large air vents in the partition walls of the apartments complement the window openings and are incorporated into the design of the main façades. Each of the units features a roadside balcony. The last floor is set back to form a roof terrace that the owners of the apartments have individually adapted according to their own tastes.

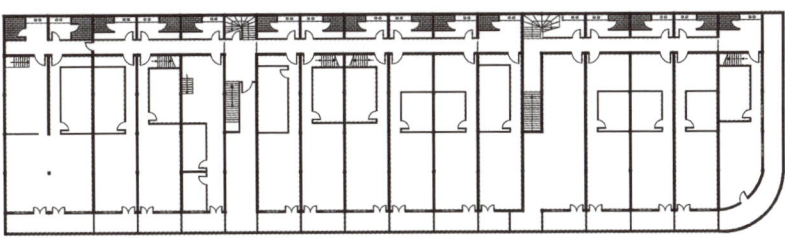

First floor

Hiroshima House

Street 13/Street 172,
on Wat Ounalom compound
Osamu Ishyiama
2006

071 C

The so-called Hiroshima House is one of the most peculiar buildings in Phnom Penh and is in many ways unsuitable for the faint-hearted. The construction of the house was initiated by Keiko Kunichika, a survivor of the atomic bombing of Hiroshima. In 1994, she worked as a volunteer in Hiroshima, helping Cambodian athletes, who were participating in the Asian Games for the first time in 20 years. She was moved by the words of a Cambodian athlete at the end of the sporting event, who expressed his hope that Cambodia could rebuild itself after the atrocities of the Khmer Rouge and make its children as happy as those in Hiroshima. With a group of volunteers, Kunichika founded the Association for Exchange between Hiroshima Citizens and Cambodians, which spent over a decade building this strange edifice until it

finally opened in 2006. Japanese architect Osamu Ishyiama explains:
'After the atomic bombardment of Hiroshima, an American peace activist Dr. Schmoe rebuilt several houses in the destroyed city. They were called "Hiroshima Houses". In them were portrayed the most radical liberty and dignity of architecture. The Hiroshima House, which the citizens of Hiroshima are now building in Phnom Penh, might be seen as an international extension to Dr. Schmoe's Hiroshima Houses. It will function as an archive gallery, documenting both Hiroshima's destruction and the holocaust by Pol Pot. It will contain an orphanage, school of peace, accommodational facilities, and a woodwork studio. Architecture is not everlasting, but for some moments in history it could function as a resting place for the memories of the people.'
Architecture professor Thomas Daniell has described Osamu Ishyiama as an outsider architect who works for outsiders – as an exemplary member of the so-called 'Red School' of Japanese architecture.

This term, coined by Terunobu Fujimori, denotes a visceral, warm, heavy, thick, rough, and handmade architectural style that contrasts with that of the 'White School', described as cerebral, cool, light, sharp, transparent, and machined. The 'Red School', characterised by the incorporation of traditional materials and craft techniques, client involvement in the construction process, intuitive on-site improvisation, perpetual incompletion, and an endearing awkwardness of form, tends to emphasise processes above results.

Hiroshima House today offers lodging as well as educational programmes. Children who cannot afford to go to school receive lessons in English, Khmer, social studies, and arithmetic. Unfortunately, the larger part of the facilities is not in use today. Visitors can enter the giant cube, located in the northwest corner of the Wat Ounalom compound, covered with a structure reminiscent of traditional Khmer roofs. Once they climb up the stairs, they find themselves in an inner courtyard that is used as a sports area.

Despite the raw appearance of the building, you can see surprising details in many places, such as the remains of lamps carefully planned within wall niches. Especially on the upper floors, the labyrinth of narrowing staircases, inclined supports, and absurd details stimulates the senses to an extent that can make this space almost unbearable. This is not the only reason to be careful while visiting: the 'do-it-yourself' construction method and inadequately detailed planning mean that some components are rather fragile.

Friends Futures Factory

072 C

72 Street 13
*Architect unknown / Atelier Cole
(renovation)*
1920s / 2019 (renovation)

Mith Samlanh ('Close Friends' in Khmer) was established in August 1994 as a non-religious organisation working with street children in Phnom Penh. It became a local NGO in 1999, and its mission is to alleviate the harsh living conditions of street children in Phnom Penh. The organisation quickly expanded to become Friends-International, which today provides holistic social support to over 18,000 children, youths, and families each year, helping them claim their rights to health, safety, family care, and education. The main compound of Friends-International, on Street 13, may well be one of the oldest remnants of Phnom Penh's early industrial history. Most of the buildings, including the factory hall and the villa facing the street, date back to the 1920s. When Friends-International moved its education and training programmes into the complex in the 1990s, the premises were simply the empty facilities of a former bicycle factory. The space included old metal punching plates that have since been incorporated into the design of the compound. As such, the space retains its connection to its historical context. Unfortunately, little further information exists about the history of these buildings. The former factory building has a filigree metal frame structure held together by rivets. Rumours say that this structure may have been the work of the famous engineer Gustave Eiffel – a claim that is not entirely far fetched but needs verification. The building might have been constructed by Société de Constructions de Levallois-Perret (S.C.L.P.), formerly Eiffel et Cie, founded by Gustave Eiffel (1832–1923) in 1868. The company carried out public infrastructure projects in French Indochina. In Cambodia, it built the bridges of the Battambang-Mongkolborey railway line, the Banam Bridge (1935–1936), and, in Phnom Penh, the Tonle Sap Bridge (1956).

Between 2018 and 2019, the historical complex was converted into Futures Factory, an exciting multi-functional space with co-working and market spaces, food outlets, and a cooking school. The remodelled courtyard functions as a central public square. Around it, three major renovation projects have taken place. On the left, behind the Friends restaurant, a former medical building was transformed into a café and hospitality school. In the building on the right, the architects sensitively restored the exposed historical steel structure. They also gave a modern addition, inserting a new concrete slab to create a first floor that new social enterprises can use as a workshop. The ground floor was designed as a 'market place' in which to test products in a commercial setting. One can find all kinds of items here, from hair products and nails to designer clothes and upcycled goods. There are also movable 'co-working pods' that can be bolted together to allow residents to expand their businesses if needed. The project aims to support small businesses sponsored by Friends-International.

Outside, the entire upper floor of the roadside factory has been clad in perforated metal screens. These reflect heat during the hot morning hours before opening up at midday to allow greater airflow into the building.

The Futures Factory is an outstanding example of adaptive reuse. The architects retained the historic and aesthetic characteristics of the industrial heritage buildings, while developing economically, socially, and culturally viable new uses. As such, the resulting space makes a large contribution to the identity and physical condition of its urban surroundings.

C

National Museum of Cambodia 073 C

Street 13 / Street 178
George Groslier
1920

This building is perhaps the most elegant work of colonial architecture in Cambodia. It stands on the Veal Preah Meru (or Veal Preah Man) square, where the royal cremations and religious festivals take place. George Groslier (1887–1945), historian, architect, curator, and author, spearheaded a renaissance of traditional Cambodian arts and crafts during his time in Phnom Penh, and it was he who designed this building, which is today perceived as a work of 'traditional Khmer' architecture.

The imposing edifice is a prime example of how the French interpreted Khmer temple architecture. Many aspects of the building exemplify a fusion of French and Khmer architectural traditions: its proportions, volumes, and decorations; its arrangement into pavilions lined by galleries; and the interplay of its magnificent roofs.

The museum was inaugurated on 13 April 1920. George Groslier, who was at the time the director of the School of Cambodian Arts, also became the museum's curator and held this position until 1942. The museum was named Musée Albert Sarraut, after the then Governor General of Indochina. The French managed the museum for over 30 years, until control

over the museum was handed over to the Cambodians in 1951. However, the directorate remained in French hands for a long time, and it was not until 1966 that the museum was entrusted to its first Cambodian director, Chea Thay Seng. The building was renamed the National Museum in 1966. It lay abandoned during the Khmer Rouge regime, before being renamed the Archaeological Museum in 1979. It reverted to its former name, the National Museum of Cambodia, in the late 1980s.

The building has the quadrilateral layout of a cloister. Open galleries surround the garth, a symmetrical courtyard garden, which has four water basins as well as a small pavilion in the centre. The original rectangular design of the building was slightly altered in 1924, when wings were added to both ends of the eastern façade. This alteration extended the length of the building to 97.09 metres. In 1968, the central section of the eastern façade was renovated under the supervision of Cambodian architect Vann Molyvann. Students of the then École des Arts Cambodgiens created the carved woodwork on the doors and windows as well as the shutter paintings in the main entrance galleries. Helen Grant Ross and Darryl Collins aptly describe the building's architectural qualities in their book *Building Cambodia: 'New Khmer Architecture' 1953–1970*:

'The National Museum in particular is a successful design in the way it transcends certain elements of Cambodian religious architecture into a fresh innovative composition. The majestic portico with its colonnade, high ceiling and monumental doors opening onto an inside courtyard has no parallel in traditional architecture. Yet it serves the purpose of a museum extremely well. The large expanse of roofs layered on top of each other is directly inspired by the traditional prayer hall but attains a grander scale and proportion. The way it is set into the urban plan reflects the grand perspective element of French town planning that evolved from the 17th century onwards.'

The building is also a great example of how colonial-era architecture was adapted to local weather conditions. Note the offset vertical openings, directly above the windows and doors, that are mainly there for ventilation. The awnings attached to the windows outside the galleries shield the interior from direct sunlight and torrential rainfalls. Meanwhile, the large verandah on the eastern façade and the interior open walkways offer protection against the harsh sunlight while ensuring good ventilation. The peaceful atmosphere of the garden courtyard offers a respite from the traffic-choked Phnom Penh, and the masterly architecture provides an appropriate home for the nation's art treasures.

Today the museum houses the world's finest collection of Khmer art – particularly works in bronze, stone, and wood – dating from prehistory through to the pre-Angkorian, classic Angkorian, and post-Angkorian periods. Its collection includes over 14,000 items. Some 1,900 of them are on display in the 2,800-square-metre exhibition space, while the rest are kept in secure storerooms.

Around the corner...

We highly recommend visitors to explore the traditional performing arts of Cambodia. To this end, visitors can take a look at the daily performances organised by the local NGO Cambodian Living Arts on the open air stage on the north side of the museum compound.

Royal University of Fine Arts 074 C

Street 178/Street 19
*George Groslier/Vann Molyvann,
Chan Lay Heng (1960s extensions)*
1918–1935/1960s

The **Royal University of Fine Arts (RUFA)** celebrated its centennial in March 2018. The institution was founded in 1917–18 as the École des Arts Cambodgiens (*Sala Rajana* in Khmer) under its first director George Groslier, who was also the architect and curator of the adjacent **National Museum** (073 C). Though Groslier was the official director of the institution, he transferred control over the school to the former royal architect Tep Nimit Mak, whom he instated as the 'indigenous' administrator of the school.

In January 1965, the School of Cambodian Arts merged with the National Theatre College and the National College of Music to become the University of Fine Arts. Before 1965, *Sala Rajana* was not a university, but rather a school offering courses in fine art and handicrafts such as sculpture, painting, silversmithing, and weaving. The university was closed during the Khmer Rouge period and reopened in 1980 as the School of Fine Arts. In 1988, the school once again became the Royal University of Fine Arts.

The university occupies an entire block directly behind the National Museum. Like its prominent neighbour, the buildings on the campus are finished in rust-red limewash and topped with traditional clay tile roofs. They feature large windows with wooden louvred shutters topped by air vents. The buildings are clustered around green courtyards dotted with sculptures, though these spaces are regrettably interrupted by the seemingly unavoidable car parks. The single-storey buildings in the northern half of the compound are probably the oldest. They are slightly elevated from the ground on tiled-brick platforms and surrounded by clay-tiled awnings supported by slender timber columns. The small building surrounded by open galleries today houses several faculty offices, but it used to be the private residence of George Groslier. In 1928, Paul Boudet, then director of the Libraries of Indochina, described Groslier's Phnom Penh home as 'very un-colonial, more like a Pompeian villa ... [with] books all along the walls.' The building later became the home of Madeleine Giteau (1918–2005), who was a member of the École Française d'Extrême-Orient, the last French curator of the National Museum (serving between 1956 and 1966), and author of the *Guide du Musée National de Phnom-Penh*.

Further south towards the Royal Palace, there is a one-storey U-shaped building complex that was added later, probably in the second half of the 1920s. In 1965, the newly founded university required more classrooms for the department of architectural decoration. This led to the Glass Hall project, which resulted in the extension required for an interior design studio. The project also resulted in a new southern gate to the school. The architect and painter Chan Lay Heng (1934–2011), who was himself teaching at the School of Cambodian Arts at the time, designed a rational building with continuous rows of windows. The building stands on columns above open walkways on the ground floor and thus complements the western side of the courtyard

formed by the 1920s building complex. Lay Heng had studied traditional architecture, architectural decoration, and poster design at the former *Sala Rachana* between 1954 and 1961. After receiving his degree, he worked at the Service Municipal de l'Urbanisme et de l'Habitat under its director Lu Ban Hap and mayor Tep Phan, before teaching at the School of Cambodian Arts (later Royal University) between 1964 and 1970. He later returned to the school to teach communication design between 1979 and 2011.

When the Royal University of Fine Arts was launched, under the patronage of Norodom Sihanouk, in 1965, the university offered programmes not only in fine art but also in traditional dance, music, archaeology, architecture, and urbanism, which are still on offer today. If you stroll through the campus, you will see groups of students working on creative projects in and between the buildings. They are likely hunkering over their laptops or architectural models, drawing and painting, or practising on traditional musical instruments. The architect Vann

Molyvann, who himself served as the first rector of RUFA between 1965 and 1967, once recalled his interdisciplinary approach to designing the building:

'When I helped to establish the Royal University of Fine Arts, I didn't want to break up the *Sala Rajana* [the existing art school] into separate parts. I wanted to keep the different sections together to produce a symbiotic effect ... In such an environment, students learn not only about their own area of specialisation, but also about the fields of study of their friends. They invite each other to help out with theatre and music performances, take one another to exhibitions of painters and sculptors, and share ideas about art movements ...'

The two-storey building on the right side of the main entrance on Street 178 was added in the 1960s based on a design by Vann Molyvann himself. With its hipped roof, shuttered windows, and protruding canopies, the building blends in with the earlier buildings on the campus.

In 2017, the Cambodian government announced its decision to relocate the

C

Royal University of Fine Arts from its historic location. It announced that it would build a new campus on four hectares of land in the Chrouy Changvar district, and that the old university buildings would be used for the necessary expansion of the National Museum. The pending relocation has irked some members of the public, who value the university's historical significance in the area and argue that the relocation might change the school's identity. However, at the time of this book's writing, the original campus was still very much alive.

PNOM-PENH — *École des Arts cambodgiens. Vue d'ensemble des ateliers de dessin et d'orfèvrerie*

Hyatt Regency Hotel (former Royal Villa)

55 Street 178
Architect unknown /
SCDA Architects
1900–1910 / 2020 (scheduled)

075 C

A highly unorthodox heritage conservation project was taking place at the heart of Phnom Penh while this book was being written. The site, a plot at Street 178 across the National Museum, has a chequered past. The grand French colonial mansion was originally built as a royal residence. According to Prince Ravivaddhana Monipong Sisowath, it was the former home of Princess Sisowath Pindara, favourite daughter of King Sisowath. Little is known about the building's fate during the years of war. A year after the government of Cambodia and rebel groups signed a UN-sponsored peace treaty on 23 October 1991, intended to end Cambodia's long civil war, the beleaguered, impoverished city experienced, of all things, a restaurant boom. Almost every week, a foreign-owned, foreign-run restaurant opened somewhere in Phnom Penh to serve the 22,000-member UNTAC peacekeeping force and the rest of Cambodia's newly returned and free-spending expat community. In 1992, Thierry Dauptain, a French manager of many first-class restaurants across Southeast Asia, repurposed the renovated villa to open the famous No Problem Café. The restaurant and bar soon became perhaps the most popular venue for UN workers during the peacekeeping operations in Cambodia between

1992 and 1993. Later on, the building was used for art shows and as the Cambodian branch of a French property fund that owned the building at the time. The property was later sold, and in 2016, the new owner, the Chip Mong Group, a local conglomerate, signed a management agreement with Hyatt Hotel & Resort. In March 2017, construction of a five-star hotel, designed by Singapore-based SCDA Architects and Meinhardt engineers, got underway. The renderings show a 14-storey, 50-metre-high and 80-metre long building towering behind the historical building shell, on top of three underground floors. The hotel will offer 247 rooms as well as a rooftop swimming pool and bar, likely with splendid views of the National Museum and the Royal Palace. Incomprehensibly, the royal villa meanwhile has been completely gutted. Only its outer façade has been retained. This approach reduces heritage preservation to mere façadism and destroys any hope that the mansion's elegant historical legacy and integrity will be maintained during the property's transformation. In principle, it would have been a fine solution to keep the building as a historical feature while adding more commercial space behind it. This could in theory make it possible to take advantage of the land value while simultaneously supporting conservation. But here, the disproportionate dimensions of the newly constructed building masses will have a ruinous impact on the historic urban landscape of Phnom Penh, right at the heart of the royal district. The hotel is scheduled to open by 2020.

C

Royal Villa (former Residence Penn Nouth) `076` C

Street 178/Street 19
Architect unknown
1920s

This part of the city, near the Royal Palace, was known as Village Cambodgien during the era of the French Protectorate. This was the area where high-ranking Cambodian officials and their families, particularly those with direct links to the royal court, lived in stately villas. The mansions were built on demand, in various neo-classical styles that were popular in Paris at the time.

The compound at the corner is a typical example of the residences built for wealthy people during this period. Its two-storey main house has a north-facing front façade and is connected to an outhouse containing the kitchen, bathrooms, and further bedrooms towards the southern perimeter of the plot. Neighbouring the plot is a row of Chinese shophouses. In recent years, new structures were built in the front garden to provide additional space for commercial uses. These structures unfortunately obstruct the view of the ground floor of the historic building. Despite these alterations, the building certainly has its charm. The curious traveller might enjoy taking a closer look at the antique shop on the ground floor. You enter the old building through an impressive porch flanked by a pair of columns. Inside, there is a stunning example of colonial-era interior architecture, with elaborate and well-preserved encaustic floor tiling. Do have a look at the front gate. Its wrought-iron bars bear the initials 'PN', which stand for Penn Nouth, the veteran Cambodian statesman who once resided in this villa.

Penn Nouth, born in 1906, completed his studies at the **French Administrative School** (**063** C) and served in the colonial administration before taking active part in Cambodian politics. In 1940, he worked as the deputy minister of the Royal Palace, before serving as the governor of Phnom Penh from 1946 to 1948.

He was a senior figure in Prince Norodom Sihanouk's Sangkum Reastr Niyum (People's Socialist Community) government, and served as prime minister several times between 1948 and 1969, when he was replaced by General Lon Nol. It was under Penn's direction that some of Cambodia's leading architects of the period, including Vann Molyvann and Lu Ban Hap, were sent to receive their formal training in France. Penn Nouth's later residence (demolished), located on Russian Boulevard, was designed by Vann Molyvann. He broke with Sihanouk in the late 1970s after the prince allied himself with the communist Khmer Rouge in an effort to oust the Vietnamese from Cambodia. Penn then emigrated to France where he died in 1985 at his Parisian home, which was designed by his neighbour and long-time friend Lu Ban Hap, who had emigrated to Paris in 1975.

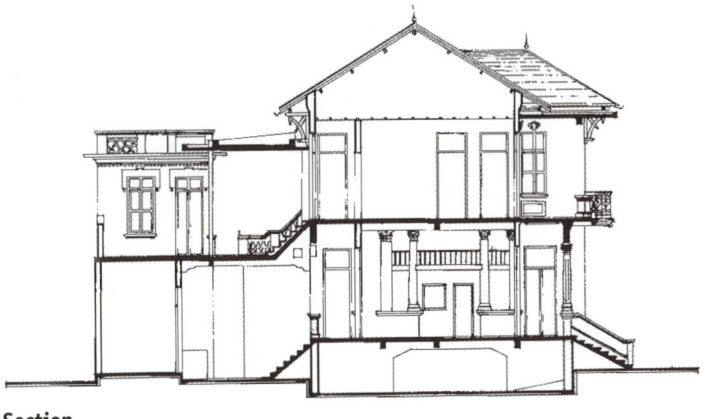

Section

Wat Saravoan Techo (Wat Saravan)

077 C

Street 19/Street 178
Architect unknown
1890s/1926

Wat Saravan, located behind the Royal Palace, is said to be one of the five oldest pagodas in Phnom Penh, with its foundation dating back to 1818. The compound still retains a number of original buildings, though several new structures have been added throughout the years. Wat Saravan contains the largest library of ancient Buddhist scrolls in the country. It is said to have over 3,400 manuscripts written on parchment, even though a great many were destroyed or lost during the civil war in the 1970s. The main sanctuary was built in 1926 and is a fine example of a brickwork *vihāra* built during King Sisowath's reign. Outside, the Angkorian-style gallery with wide columns sits on a moulded basement and can be accessed via double stairs on each side. The large wooden doors, brightly painted with traditional Khmer motifs, open onto four sides of the sanctuary. Their moulded casings are topped by elaborate triangular plasterwork inspired by Angkorian pediments. Inside, the wooden ceiling follows the shape of the roof. The chief nave has six bays, whose horizontal panels are decorated with Khmer *kbach* medallions. Note the golden stencil ornaments on the 14 black lacquered columns. They were created using a traditional technique that was very popular until the mid 20th century and was capable of achieving the most stunning effects with very simple means. The floor and the walls underneath the windows are covered with beautiful encaustic (inlaid) tiles. The tiling technique, invented in southern France in 1828, entails adding mineral pigments to cement and pouring the resulting mixture into metal moulds. The figures are thereafter cold-pressed and dried in the sun.

The pagoda also has interesting mural paintings from the late 1920s, arranged on two levels. Depicted at the top are scenes from the life of Buddha. Meanwhile, the murals between the window and door openings illustrate scenes from the past reincarnations of the Buddha, the *jakatas*. Clumsy and sloppy restoration works were carried out in the 1990s. With no respect for the artworks, wall sockets and wires were nailed in many places directly onto the murals.

One striking structure on the site is a red-brick tower (*prang*), probably dating back to the 1890s. The pyramidal building, comprising three levels, was clearly refurbished just recently with copious amounts of cement. The original plastered balustrades were unfortunately removed, but the edifice still shows an eclectic mix of Angkorian decorative roof elements and colonial-style windows. The building could be about 100 years old, and its original function was probably as monks' quarters. Look out for the small greyish rectangular stupa (*chedey*) behind the tower: it is decorated with panels that feature inscriptions in Thai and Khmer writing, as well as the year '1936' in Arabic numerals. A stone stele with Chinese engravings completes this remarkably multi-ethnic ensemble.

Former Huynh Tho Residence 078 C

75 Preah Norodom Boulevard/
Street 178
Architect unknown
1915–1925

This stately private mansion, built for a wealthy business agent of a foreign company, was known as the Huynh Tho Residence. The name Huynh Tho suggests that the original owner was of Vietnamese, not Chinese descent. The building housed the Japanese embassy in the 1990s and is now a privately owned building that has been meticulously preserved by its owner. Penny Edwards describes this type of villa in her book *Cambodge: The Cultivation of a Nation, 1860–1945* as a typical building for a specific clientele: 'In the 1930s, many wealthy Cambodians and retired Chinese business tycoons preferred to build ornate European villas in what the art administrator George Groslier termed the "comprador style".'

These colonial villas were built on demand, following Parisian models. They demonstrate great eclecticism, with their neo-baroque, neo-classical, or regionalist architectural styles. The designs include elements such as turrets, bow windows, and large cantilevered roofs. Their façades might be decorated with loggias or porticos, or display decorated gables, which all add to the stately character of these edifices. Here, the symmetrical front façade of the main building is oriented towards Norodom Boulevard. A three-floor turret added later marks the corner with Street 178. The villa, which has an almost Palladian layout if one ignores the tower, shows striking similarities with the **UNESCO Building** (067 C) as well as **The Mansion** (068 C). The building footprint on the French map of 1925 indicates that the two-storey outhouse, located along the western border of the property, is original. The building must have housed the kitchen and staff rooms. It is connected to the main building via a covered passageway.

French-Colonial Buildings
North of Sisowath High School

Street 174 and Street 178,
between preah Norodom Blvd
and Street 63
Architects unknown
1920s–1930s/1960s

Just around the corner of the marvellous **Huynh Tho Residence** (078 C), two parallel streets are dotted with French-colonial villas and shophouses built between the 1920s and 1940s. All of these villas are conveniently located on a small loop between Street 63 (Preah Trasak Paem Street) in the west, and Norodom Boulevard in the east. The area once belonged to Village Cambodgien, the former Cambodian District surrounding the Royal Palace. At the intersection of Street 174 and Norodom Boulevard, there is a small cluster of yellow-ochre Chinese shophouses, probably dating back to the late 1920s, which were renovated in 2013. The first floor, featuring balconies and a parapet roof, still retains its original appearance. Meanwhile, the commercial space on the ground floor has been heavily altered: the units have been merged, and large shop windows have been added. Across the street, there is another similar group of shophouses, most likely dating back to the early 1920s.

Further along the north side of Street 174, at No. 33, stands a very peculiar modern building that was built as a Chinese Catholic church in the 1960s. It later became the cinema Reaksmey Bophea ('Rainbow of Light'), before becoming a

military storage facility in 1993. Shortly thereafter, it was converted one last time into a residential building. The former church space on the first floor was subdivided into apartment units, while the front façade remains by and large unchanged. The cantilevered balcony frame and large screen wall on the upper floor shelter the main entrance on the ground floor and enable air ventilation and provide shading towards the south.

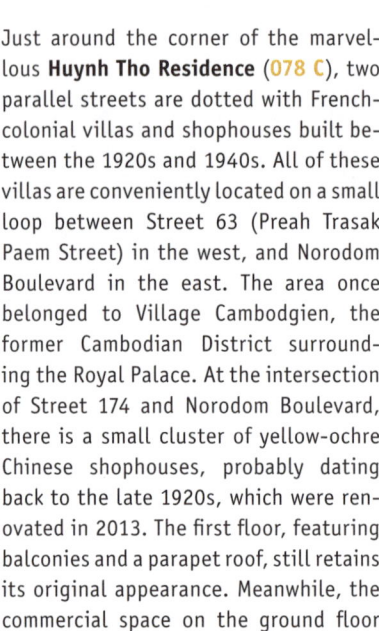

If you cross Street 51 (Pasteur Street) towards the west, you will find another cluster of traditional Chinese shophouses from the early 1920s at No. 41–45. These still remain intact with their small-scale commercial spaces on the ground floor. For more information on Chinese shophouses see 038 B and 091 C.

50 metres further down, at No. 74 on the opposite side of the street, there is a beautifully restored French-colonial villa from the 1920s or 1930s with Art Deco influences hidden behind large trees. This is Romdeng, a social enterprise and

training restaurant run by **Friends** (072 C), an international NGO working since 1994 to help former street children and marginalised young people in Phnom Penh.

including the roof balustrade with its ornate arched pediment, are still in place, and give an idea about the wealth of its former inhabitants.

C

At No. 82, the wine bar and restaurant Le Bouchon occupies another small but pleasant colonial residence. Colonial Phnom Penh saw much construction activity in the 1920s. The villa is a typical example of the upscale residences built during this period. Much like vernacular Khmer wooden houses on stilts, the villa is raised from the ground by concrete pillars. It thus allows air to circulate, and the spacious front verandah is elevated from the street. The main façade retains most of its original elements; only the large glass door was added later during a renovation project.

Around the corner, at No. 53E, Street 178, stands another residential villa from the 1930s, with some features of the Art Deco style. It features a curved balcony above the entrance, a rounded cornice, and a roof, as well as a parapet wall and four urns, all of which overlook the original limewash enclosure. The window designs are a great example of how colonial-era architecture was adapted to local weather conditions. Awnings attached to most windows shield the interior from direct sunlight and torrential rainfalls. The offset horizontal openings directly above are mainly there for ventilation.

Our last building on Street 174 is located next to the intersection with Street 63. It houses the offices of the Poste del la Police Phsar Thmei III in an almost identical, but rundown villa. However, here, all the original embellishments,

Ambre, an upscale fashion boutique by designer Romyda Keth, occupies a sumptuous 1924 colonial villa with an outhouse further east, at No. 37. The owners have meticulously remodelled the building to make it fit for its new purpose.

C

Former Villa of Sirik Matak

50 Preah Norodom Boulevard
Henri Chatel
1950s

080 C

Sisowath Sirik Matak (1914–1975) was a member of the Cambodian royal family. He was cousin of Prince Norodom Sihanouk, who later became Cambodia's head of state. In 1970, Sirik Matak staged a coup, together with the then prime minister Lon Nol, against Sihanouk. He thereafter acted as deputy prime minister in the newly proclaimed Khmer Republic. Later, he withdrew from politics and, in 1973, was placed under house arrest as a result of wide-spread protests against his involvement in government. However, he was later reintegrated into government business. Between 1954 and 1956, Sirik Matak was the Foreign and Defense Minister of the Cambodian government and headed the Ministry of Defence and Education. Henri Chatel, who came to Cambodia in 1949, was appointed architect of the Ministry of Defence in 1954, which explains why he was commissioned to design Sirik Matak's residence. The villa is one of the few buildings that still refer to the once low-density character of the district. The street-side façade of the upper floor features strictly geometric brise-soleils and thus forms an interesting contrast to the playfully designed roof. Interestingly, an almost identical villa can be found at No. 6, Street 242, though little is known about it at this time. On 12 April 1975, the last remaining Americans in Phnom Penh left the city by helicopter. They thus left the fate of the city's two million inhabitants, and of the entire country, to the Khmer Rouge. The Americans offered to take Sirik Matak out of the country, so that he may seek political asylum in the US. However, Sirik Matak rejected the offer, even though he was on the list of the 'seven traitors' published by the Khmer Rouge. In a letter to the US ambassador John Gunter Dean, he wrote:

'As for you and in particular for your great country, I never believed for a moment that you would have this sentiment of abandoning a people which has chosen liberty. You have refused us your protection, and we can do nothing about it. You leave us. It is my wish that you and your country will find happiness under the sky. But mark it well that, if I shall die here … in my country that I love, it is too bad because we are all born and must die one day. I have only committed the mistake of believing in you, the Americans.'

A few days after capturing Phnom Penh, the Khmer Rouge forced the French embassy to hand over Sirik Matak, who had found temporary refuge there. On 21 April 1975, he and others were executed in the swimming pool of the Cercle Sportif, the current location of the US embassy.

Preah Sisowath High School  `081` `C`
Preah Norodom Boulevard,
between Streets 178 and 184
Architect unknown
1900–1910

The Preah Sisowath campus occupies a large, sprawling four-hectare plot on Norodom Boulevard. It dates back to the period in which France consolidated its colonial rule over Indochina. The French-language École du Protectorate was founded in 1873 as the first modern Franco-Cambodian school in the country. The school was renamed Collège du Protectorate (middle school) in 1893. It then became Collège Sisowath in 1905, named after King Sisowath I, before becoming Lycée Preah Sisowath (middle and high school) in 1933.

The French colonial administration created a system of elite schools across Indochina in the early 20th century to foster a class of civil servants. The exclusive Lycée Preah Sisowath was one of them. It prepared students for service in the French colonial and indigenous administrations as well as the judiciary. During the years of the French Protectorate, the school was heavily dominated by Vietnamese immigrant children. The first Cambodian students graduated from the Lycée with baccalauréats in 1939. However, only 144 Cambodians had completed the full baccalauréat by 1954. The school was closed and used as an army warehouse under the Khmer Rouge regime. It was then officially reopened again on 21 January 1980 with the name Phnom Daun Penh High School. In 1993, the faculty requested the Ministry of Education to change the high school's name back to its original name, Lycée Preah Sisowath, to preserve its historical legacy.

The school is significant not only for displaying a well-preserved ensemble of colonial architecture but also for the role it played in modern Cambodian history. Saloth Sar, better known as Pol Pot, failed the school's entrance exam in 1943, but gained admission in 1947, only to study there for a short year. He was not a very successful student and switched to a technical school in Kampong Cham to study carpentry. However, it was at Lycée Sisowath that Sar befriended Ieng Sary and Khieu Samphan, who would later become the Khmer Rouge's Foreign Minister and Head of State, respectively. Sar was also joined at the Lycée by Lon Non. Lon would later become Head of Security in the government of his brother Lon Nol, who overthrew Prince Sihanouk and was President of Cambodia from 1970 to 1975. **Lon Non's private residence** (032 A), probably built around 1970, can still be found close to the roundabout in front of the old stadium. The Lycée Sisowath alumni list isn't all bad though. Famous Khmer architects Vann Molyvann and Lu Ban Hap, and Cambodia's queen mother, Norodom Monineath Sihanouk, were also

C

schooled here, as was Cambodian opposition leader, Sam Rainsy.

The compound comprises eight classroom buildings, two of which are later additions. It forms a symmetrical ensemble arranged on an east-west axis around two large courtyards that are today used as sport fields. The main entrance towards the east was originally designed as a formal park (see historical photo). This park led to a grand central building with administrative offices. This building was flanked by two elegant French-style villas for the headmaster and the treasurer in the north-east and south-east corners of the block. Most of the existing buildings of today's Sisowath High School

probably date back to 1925–1928. Like many French administrative buildings, they feature a utilitarian design that borrows elements from local architecture. These elements include the large cantilevered roofs and covered galleries and walkways. The architecture is also adapted to the tropical climate of Cambodia: every classroom has three large windows and an entrance door with louvred wooden shutters to enable air circulation. Each building has two old wooden staircases that have remained intact until today. The buildings were recently renovated, and fortunately, most of the original architectural features and the French colonial style have been maintained.

The gardens of Preah Sisowath Highschool in 1931

Plantation Urban Resort & Spa

082 C

28 Street 184
Architect unknown /
Asma Architects (renovation)
1940s–1990s / 2011 (renovation)

French hotelier Alexis de Suremain saved four historic buildings from demolition. One was a colonial villa, dating back almost 80 years, and all four represented Cambodia's modernist style of the 1960s. The hotelier hired Asma, a local architectural practice, to transform the buildings into a stylish hotel while preserving their distinctive design. Plantation Urban Resort & Spa opened in November 2011. A lotus pond welcomes you on arrival.

It is surrounded by an open gallery, and the Pergola restaurant and a bar are situated to the left. The oldest building of the complex stands behind the pond. The elegant villa dates back to the 1940s. It was badly damaged during the late 1970s and was used by the Ministry of Labour as office space for some time. The building's exterior features, such as the generous front porch, the clay tiled roof, and louvred wooden shutters, were carefully restored to their original condition. Meanwhile, the building's naturally ventilated interior was thoughtfully remodelled to house the hotel reception. A delightful maze of leafy footpaths leads you further into the sprawling property, to

C

the other buildings dating from the 1960s to 1990s. These were converted, with as minimal demolition as possible, to accommodate 72 hotel rooms. Balconies and sunscreens were added to the façade to create shade and provide cooling. Perforated walls and bamboo pergolas perform a similar function. The plantation feels modern and historic, spacious and intimate, with lush gardens and plants throughout. It has a restaurant, a lotus pond bar, and a smaller pool, which are open to non-residents and are often used to host art exhibitions around the lotus pond. Its simplicity, functionality, and emphasis on clean lines make this an intelligent example of contemporary tropical modernism, adapted to the local climatic conditions. Moreover, the hotel illustrates that historic buildings are not only an important cultural and architectural heritage; they can also become a financial asset, for example in the hospitality sector, if they are given a unique sense of place with historic depth. Old, historic buildings may become unsuitable for their programmatic requirements over time. But it is possible to rehabilitate them in a sustainable manner. Clever adaptive reuse of existing (historic) buildings lowers energy consumption and reduces waste, which would otherwise result from demolition and reconstruction with new building materials.

Institut Francais

218 Street 184
Architect unknown/
Asma Architects (renovation)
1990/2013

083 C

The French Institute of Cambodia opened in October 1990 in what used to be the former private hospital of Dr. Keo Chea. The institute was initially named Alliance Française, then Centre Culturel Français, before finally becoming the Institut Français du Cambodge (IFC) in January 2011. Funded by the French Ministry of Foreign Affairs, it plays a key role in what would be called 'cultural diplomacy'. It supports the cultural, artistic, and educational cooperation between France and Cambodia and promotes the French language as well as French literature, cinema, and culture. Each year, around 5,000 students enrol at the institute's language centre across the street to learn French. The institute offers a diverse cultural programme. Moreover, it has been giving enormous support to Cambodian artists who are seeking to define their country's cultural identity. In 2012, the Institut Francais launched an extensive renovation programme that has transformed its buildings on Street 184. The buildings now enclose the ground-floor hall on one side of the street. On the other side, a glass-cube reception area, an outdoor bistro, and an indoor restaurant have been newly constructed. When the renovation project began, the architects found the garden behind the buildings abandoned and inaccessible. As such, they added a drainage system to provide access to the open space in the rainy season and covered the soil with gravel so that it would absorb rainwater. They also set up a mound of grass for children to walk and play on. Moreover, they moved the bookstore to the front of the building and added a modest black steel pavilion, for the new indoor restaurant, at an angle around the existing bamboo grove in the rear garden. The new garden and the restaurant, Le Bistrot, were finally inaugurated in March 2014. The architects' design has brought a sense of calm and modernity to the compound. Today, students can sit in the leafy garden along the library and take advantage of the air-conditioned exhibition hall in the midday heat. We highly recommend visitors to enjoy a cold beverage in the peaceful ambience of the garden café.

Bophana Audiovisual Resource Center

064 Street 200
Architect unknown /
Heritage Mission (renovation)
1960s / 2006 (renovation)

084 C

Just one block south of the **Institut Français** (083 C) lies another cultural hotspot of Phnom Penh. The Bophana Audiovisual Resource Center (BARC) is the brainchild of two Cambodian filmmakers: Ritty Panh and Ieu Pannakar (1931–2018). Pannakar was a senator and minister of the Royal Palace, who devoted his life to cinema and broadcasting in Cambodia. Pannakar was also in charge of the state's film, photography, and broadcasting services between 1955 and 1970. Rithy Panh, a documentary film director and screenwriter, became the first ever Cambodian filmmaker to be nominated for an Academy Award with his movie *The Missing Picture* in 2013. In the same year, he received the Un Certain Regard prize at the Cannes Festival. The French-schooled director's films focus on the aftermath of the genocidal Khmer Rouge regime in Cambodia. Rithy's works stem from his personal experiences, as his own family were expelled from Phnom Penh by the Khmer Rouge in 1975 and subsequently died of starvation or exhaustion in a remote labour camp in rural Cambodia.

The BARC was inaugurated on 4 December 2006 with funding from the French government. It was named after the courageous young woman, portrayed in Rithy's early docudrama *Bophana: A Cambodian Tragedy*, who was executed by the Khmer Rouge. The central mission of the BARC's collection is to preserve the country's history as captured on film, in photographs, or in audio materials. It thus aims to help Cambodians and foreigners who wish to explore the country's audiovisual memory and learn more about its past glories and terrors. The centre organises regular events such as screenings, exhibitions, debates, and workshops to bring the archives to life. From the very beginning, the centre has also been training young Cambodians for careers in filmmaking, broadcasting, and new media. The trainees obtain the skills required to work with local and foreign directors.

The BARC is housed in a 1960s building that was thoughtfully renovated by the Heritage Mission (see 041 B) in 2006. Owned by the Ministry of Culture and Fine Arts, the building used to be a film-training centre before the war. The three-storey building is slightly set back from the street as well as from the lateral plot boundaries. With a large footprint of 18 × 22m, the building has a small interior courtyard providing natural light and ventilation. The renovation project preserved all the details on the front façade: the horizontal brise-soleils, the filigree concrete frame, the air vents, the elaborate door and window grilles, and the balcony railings. The roof terrace is topped by a sizable but elegant trellis made of reinforced concrete. The ground-floor interior has an open layout and is used as a multi-functional space. Note the original features such as the stylish open staircase behind the front desk, the walls made of glass bricks or concrete blocks, and the chequered cement floor tiles throughout. The first floor houses the archive and a small exhibition of cinematic items. The BARC is worth a visit even when there is no special exhibit taking place. Visitors can learn more about the centre's work and breathe in the cultural atmosphere of a 1960s space that has been adapted to contemporary times.

C

Lumiere Hotel

26 Street 55 / Street 228
Re-Edge Architecture and Design
2017

085 C

The Lumiere heralds the entry of skyscrapers in a district otherwise still characterised by low-rise buildings. The 15-storey hotel, commissioned by Singaporean investors, comprises 88 rooms, event spaces, a public skybar (with a commendable panoramic view), a gym, and Phnom Penh's first-ever rooftop jacuzzi. The architects, directed by princiapl Hun Chansan, divided the structure into three towers on an irregular site measuring almost 500 m² in order to provide the corridors with natural light and give the building a slimmer appearance. The off-set levels were intended to dissolve the traditional block typology and break it down into a human scale (see interview with Hun Chansan on p. 244). At the same time, the rotation of the floors directs the eye to a series of attractions in the city's skyline, such as the **Vattanac Tower** (**011 A**) or the **Independence Monument** (**095 D**). Hun Chansan has been pursuing the idea of off-set parts within a structure ever since he worked on his master's thesis, entitled 'Re-Edging Retails'. He is one of the relatively few local young architects who have managed to establish themselves in Phnom Penh after finishing their studies abroad. All of his projects demonstrate a playful approach to massing. His buildings foreground their three-dimensionality and attempt to create a lively façade through the coordination of light and shadow.

Ministry of Economy and Finance, State Property Department

Street 63 / Street 228
Architect unknown
1960s

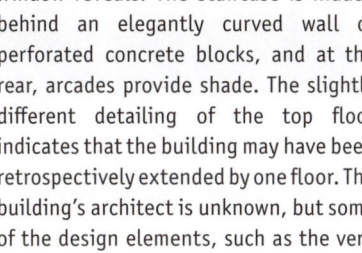

086 C

C

This small office building was probably built in the late 1950s or early 1960s and is well adapted to the tropical climate. To the south, the offices are shielded from the sun by loggias and protruding window reveals. The staircase is hidden behind an elegantly curved wall of perforated concrete blocks, and at the rear, arcades provide shade. The slightly different detailing of the top floor indicates that the building may have been retrospectively extended by one floor. The building's architect is unknown, but some of the design elements, such as the very particular window reveals, can be found in a similar form in buildings by Henri Chatel or René Nguyen Khac Scheou.

House for Norodom Sirivuth's Mother

087 C

22 Street 242/Street 55
Vann Molyvann
Late 1950s

This building was being remodelled at the time of writing. Yet the authors nonetheless decided to include this early work by Vann Molyvann as a form of documentation. The villa was planned for Khun Kim An Yeap, mother of Prince Norodom Sirivuth. The house originally had a cubic form and comprised two stories. A cantilevered balcony used to wrap around the upper floor. Vertical slats originally covered this gallery on three sides, and the residents could adjust them in accordance with the position of the sun to facilitate the desired amount of light and air-flow. Though the northern façade has been altered, the movable slats are still visible on the façade towards Street 55. Originally, one entered the house from the west through a large entrance hall, where a dramatic spiral staircase led to the upper floor. Renovation of the house started in 2013, which led to a new floor being added on top of the formerly flat roof. Since then, the building has been significantly altered. The garden, which originally surrounded the house, is now almost completely filled with newer constructions. The elegantly vaulted canopy, originally marking the entrance, is regrettably also no longer existent. The glazing that almost entirely surrounded the ground floor has also been lost.

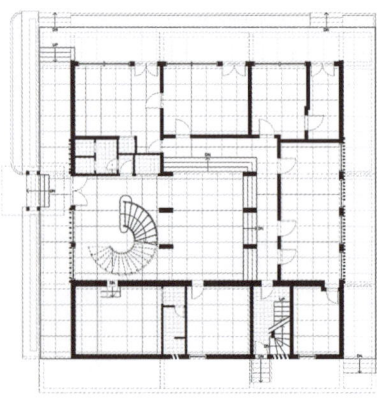

Ground floor

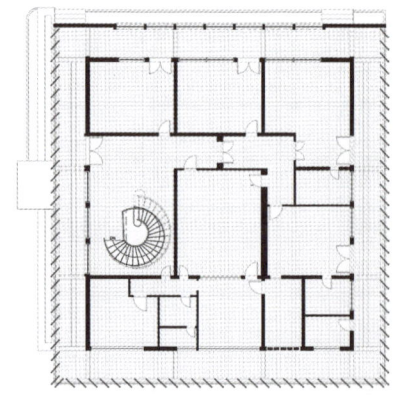

First floor

Villa for Samdech Son Sann

088 C

Street 51/Street 222
Mam Sophana
1970

Mam Sophana frequently stresses that he prefers curves to right angles (see **Round House 102 D**). Yet his houses are often composed of straight lines. This is also true of the villa he built in the late 1960s for Son Sann (1911–2000), an important figure in Cambodian history. Son Sann obtained a degree in economics in Paris before returning to Cambodia in 1933. He later held various government positions during the pre-independence period as well after 1953. He founded the National Bank of Cambodia in 1955, served as prime minister from 1967 to 1968, and later became Sihanouk's personal economic advisor. After Lon Nol took power, he went back to Paris and only returned to Southeast Asia after the Vietnamese invasion. He served as prime minister of an opposing coalition government that was not acknowledged by the UN. He also helped negotiate the 1991 peace treaty. In 1997, he emigrated again to Paris, where he died in 2000.

Mam Sophana received the commission for this house when he was still a young architect, just after he had returned from his studies in the US. He recalls having to carry out all tasks himself, from the drawings to the calculations, since he could not afford any employees at that time. Like many of Mam Sophana's buildings from this period, the house was clearly influenced by the architect's studies in the US and in particular by the works of Frank Lloyd Wright. The house combines these influences with elements designed to cope with the country's tropical climate.

At the time of research, the house stood empty after having served as a boutique hotel for a while. One can only hope that this wonderful villa, by one of the most distinguished architects of his time, will not fall victim to the demolition ball. Yet Mam Sophana himself shows little sentimentality: 'The change is a must ... It is only possible to preserve old structures if the country determines that they illustrate traditional or French colonial architecture. They include Angkor Wat, old temples, and other works of a similar nature.'

Russian Center of Science and Culture

103 Preah Norodom Boulevard
Architect unknown
1945–1955

089 C

The Russian Center of Science and Culture occupies an elegant villa in a *Streamline Moderne* Art Deco style, on the intersection of Norodom Boulevard and Street 222 (Samdech Preah Sangkreach Tieng Street). The building is set back from the boulevard behind a lush garden. The main building is attached to another building on the northern perimeter of the plot. The expressive white-washed plaster façade of the main building undulates with several setbacks and rounded corners. Its stylish façade is further accentuated by grey horizontal roughcast bands. The frieze on the second floor encloses the air vents, and the cantilevered cornice provides shade to the façade. A single window located just below it indicates that there is a mezzanine floor inside.

Relations between Russia and Cambodia began in the 1850s, when Russia's last tzar, Nicholas II, travelled to Southeast Asia and sent an official envoy to Phnom Penh. Diplomatic relations in the late 1950s led to the erection of the **Khmer-Soviet Friendship Hospital** (117 E). By 1964, the **Institute of Technology of Cambodia (ITC)** (119 F) had been designed by Russian architects and built with Soviet funds as a gift to Cambodia.

In 1979, after the fall of the Khmer Rouge, the occupying Vietnamese army conducted rescue efforts with the aid of communist allies in Eastern Europe and the Soviet Union. East Germany and the Soviet Union sent not only material aid but also teachers to work at the city's university. They also sent specialists to build infrastructure connecting the port of Kampong Som to the south coast's railroad. This was necessary for the supply of much-needed materials to the country. One year later, the Russian Centre of Science and Culture opened in two locations on Norodom Boulevard. The centre originally built scientific equipment and conducted laboratory work, but the nature of its tasks changed over the years. In 1982, the USSR established a scholarship programme to send Cambodian students to study at Soviet universities free of charge. According to the Russian embassy in Cambodia, over 8,000 Cambodians have since received their degrees in Russia and in the former republics of the Soviet Union.

The purpose-built wood-panelled theatre on the northern side of the ground floor was the city's only venue for classical music in the 1990s. Inside, there is an imposing lobby, filled with photographs of past events as well as enamelled folk items and babushka dolls. The hall, like the centre, has lost much of its former glory and was regrettably no longer in operation at the time of writing.

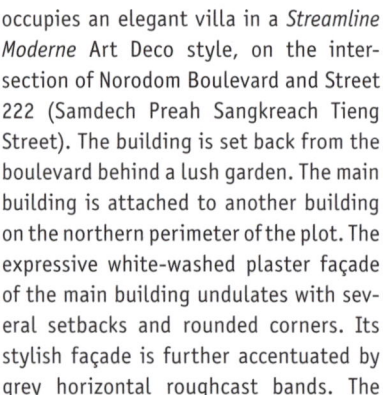

Former Residence Ing Kieth   090 C

90 Preah Norodom Boulevard
Georges Kondracki
1971

Georges Kondracki (1928–2001) worked as a United Nations expert in Cambodia from 1965 to 1970. Before studying architecture at Cornell University in the US, he worked with Le Corbusier and as an assistant for the ATBAT group. In Cambodia, he was involved in the construction of the railway stations at Sihanoukville (in collaboration with German architect Georg Lippsmeier) as well as at Kep and Takeo. Later, he worked in Jakarta, the Philippines, and Ethiopia. His villa for Ing Kieth is well hidden behind walls and trees. The well-proportioned building with its elegant brick façades shows the talent of the architect and his aim to adapt the house to the tropical climate. Cantilevered roofs, hovering above an open attic, and deeply recessed windows protect the house from sunlight.

It is worth taking a look at Ing Kieth's career too, as it reflects the upheavals Cambodia went through in its recent history. Born in 1926, Ing Kieth studied at the Ecole Spéciale des Travaux Publics et des Bâtiments in Paris. In 1954, he returned to Cambodia and became head of the School of Public Works and Mining, but soon went back to Paris to enrol at the Ecole Nationale des Ponts et Chaussées. There he obtained the highest grade in France as an engineering student. Back in Cambodia, he held a number of positions, including that of Minister of Public Works and Telecommunications, and was involved in several urban planning and transport projects. In the mid-1950s, he played a major role as an engineer in the construction of the **Independence Monument (095 D)**. After being sentenced to death by Lon Nol, he fled to Canada in 1974. In the 1990s, his career continued to flourish. He was appointed Deputy Prime Minister and Minister of Public Works and Transport in the new royal government set up under Norodom Sihanouk in 1993. Sihanouk once described Ing Kieth as one of his long-time companions, alongside architect Vann Molyvann and Kheat Chhon, originally a nuclear engineer who also held important positions in his government in the 1960s and continued his political career into the 2000s as Minister of Economy and Finance.

C

C

Row of Shophouses, Street 240 `091` `C`

29–39 Street 240
Architects unknown
1920s

The iconic Street 240 is at the heart of Phnom Penh's expat life, with its specialty boutiques, bars, and eateries. Here you can find a well-preserved ensemble of traditional Chinese shophouses, some of them restored with very good taste. The street was formerly known as Okhna Chhun Street, named after one of the first Cambodians to act as interpreter for the French administration in Phnom Penh. It is located within a stone's throw of the **Royal Palace** (`060 C`). The royal elephants, whose stables were also located nearby, used to make their procession down this street in historical times.

Let's start with the building at No. 39, housing The Shop, a bakery and coffeeshop founded by Belgian Griet Lorré in 2001. What makes it quite unusual for a semi-commercial shophouse is that the building and its neighbours are set back from the street to make room for a small leafy front yard. Its characteristic features include: the ground-floor arcade with rectangular columns; the façade with symmetrical louvered shutter windows and a loggia on the first floor; and the pitched roof with clay tiles. Inside, the coffeeshop is pleasantly cool without any air conditioning, thanks to the natural cross-ventilation and high ceiling. The rear courtyard separates what was once a small outhouse for the kitchen and bathroom from the main building. The Waterlily boutique used to be next door. It had been open since 2003, still with the beautiful original encaustic floor tiles, though it recently closed. Hopefully the next owner will preserve the integrity of the building. Over the years, the owner of The Shop opened The Chocolate Shop, another tastefully renovated Chinese shophouse, at No. 37, two doors down the street. Go down the small alley on the left into the block to see a completely different world. Over the decades, the block's interior has been completely filled with small-scale housing, somewhat resembling a hyperdensified urban village. Another special building is located at No. 29, a little further down the street. It mediates between the setback row of shophouses and their neighbouring buildings directly lining the street. The century-old building used to belong to a Chinese-Khmer merchant. In 1996, Australian designer Cassandra Harper meticulously restored the building and opened the Bliss boutique. A spa took over the back of the house in 2004, keeping the small courtyard and gracefully worn wooden staircase. Note the various patterns of the original encaustic floor tiles and the Chinese sliding wood pole door that was used to secure the property at night.

Penh House Hotel

34A Street 240
Asma Architects
2018

Penh House occupies a narrow plot of land, south of the Royal Palace, stretching between Street 240 and Street 244. The hotel has a modest height: the architect Ivan Tizianel distributed the 52 rooms over five (six to the back) floors in two buildings. Set back from the street, the main façade is composed of a large glass-fronted foyer and undulating balconies on top. Inspired by the wonderful trees lining the street, the hotel's façades are covered with lush fauna. The two parts of the hotel are connected by open corridors on each floor crossing the courtyard. Clad only with raw wooden slats, this breezeway ensures ventilation and light as well as privacy for the adjacent rooms.

The architects chose modest materials throughout the building: a simple, white paint for the façade, beige tiles and reddish-brown-coated floors in the public areas, and a lot of dark wood. A highlight is hidden on the rooftop – the infinity pool is set back from the street and offers magnificent views over the tree canopies. It thereby brilliantly uses the Japanese design principle of 'borrowed scenery' (*shakkei*).

C

The Jungloo
22 Street 264
Alexis de Suremain
2018

093 C

The Jungloo (for 'jungle igloo') is the brainchild of Alexis de Suremain, a Frenchman who came to Cambodia in 2001 with the non-governmental organisation Pharmacists Without Borders. Today he works in the hospitality industry and manages a number of quite attractive hotels in Phnom Penh and Siem Reap. He says that creating the Jungloo, a 'bio-climatic tented bungalow', had been a childhood dream.

The bungalow can be realised on land or be made to float on water. It represents an ambitious attempt to minimise the ecological footprint of tourist developments while maximising the comfort of guests. The prototype stands on the leafy property of the Hotel Kabiki. It is the result of years of experimenting with tents and light bungalow structures. The Jungloo, measuring approximately 35 m², stands on a wooden platform supported by a foundation. It comprises a rather robust support structure made of simple PVC water pipes. Above it is a double-shell roof, made of textile sheets, which efficiently cools the interior and provides humidity with its rear ventilation. As such, the design limits its energy-intensive air conditioning in the sleeping area. All furniture is made of bamboo and recycled wood. A dual bio-digestion septic system treats the wastewater in an ecologically friendly manner. You can find a floating version of the Jungloo on Phnom Penh's riverfront. Additional ones were under construction at the time of writing.

Around the corner ...
One of the few remaining wooden houses in the city centre stands on the opposite side of Street 264. Such works of vernacular architecture used to be a common sight along the streets of the inner city until the 1990s. Outside the city and in the countryside, traditional wooden houses on stilts still make up the predominant form of housing.

The Pavilion Hotel
227 Street 19
Architect unknown/Marie and Alexis de Suremain (renovation)
1920s/2006 (renovation)

094 C

The Pavilion Hotel stands out in this city, where architectural heritage is often disregarded in favour of modernisation and quick profits. This 1920s French-Khmer property was once a private retreat of Queen Consort Sisowath Kossamak, the late King Sihanouk's mother. Hoteliers Marie and Alexis de Suremain fell in love with this villa and transformed it into an exquisite hotel in 2006. The rear part of the building probably stems from an extension project in the 1930s. The main building within the complex serves as the Reception Villa. The renovation and remodelling were carried out with great respect for the building's original character. As such, the encaustic tile floors with their intricate designs, the high ceilings, and the stylised Corinthian columns in the reception hall were all preserved. The yellow-ochre façade still features the original window and door formats with their subtle metal grilles. It is lavishly decorated with whitewashed Khmer ornamentation that was possibly added later, in the 1950s. The ornamentation includes: pediments above the windows and doors; medallions on the pedestals of the balcony balustrade; and decorations along the main ridge and eaves of the roof. These *kbach rachana* elements were traditionally moulded in plaster or carved in wood by craftsmen for religious or royal buildings. They typically featured foliage motifs and often drew inspiration from Buddhist or Hindu cosmology. The patterns here are reminiscent of those used by carvers during Angkorian times for sections of temple galleries that didn't have bas-reliefs. Starting in the late 19th century, these decorations were also used on important public buildings of the French Protectorate and sometimes on private mansions of wealthy Cambodians.

The hotel has slowly expanded over the years. It now offers 36 additional rooms in three more buildings that have been added to the property: The New House, previously the residence of the chief veterinarian of the Royal Palace; The New Villa, the former private residence of a Cambodian senator; and The Sun-Pool Villa, the latest addition which used to be the lodgings of diplomats based in Phnom Penh. Each one has its own style and atmosphere, with distinctive architectural features such as an elaborate wooden stairway and intricate wrought-iron railings. With its leafy gardens surrounding the buildings and pools, the hotel has retained its intimacy and tranquillity. It is a fine example of successful adaptive reuse of a group of existing (historical) private mansions.

C

Hun Chansan
Architect
Re-Edge Architecture + Design
Phnom Penh

Cambodian architect Hun Chansan received his master's degree from Northeastern University in Boston after finishing secondary school in Singapore. In 2009, he returned to Phnom Penh and began to work as a lecturer at various architecture schools. Though he had no concrete plans to stay in Cambodia, he was surprised to find a potential market and many opportunities in the country. In 2011, he established Re-Edge Architecture + Design, characterised by a passion for shaping the built environment in a growing Cambodia. In 2018, he was named 'Cambodia Real Estate Personality of the Year' at the Cambodia Property Awards and listed as one of '50 Asians to watch' by the Straits Times.

What is it that makes Phnom Penh special among other cities in Southeast Asia?
For me, Phnom Penh is special for many reasons. The city's name and history can be traced back to a historical legend. Moreover, Wat Phnom is situated on one of the most special rivers in the world, the Chaktomuk River, where the Mekong meets the Tonle Sap. The water flows in and out of the Tonle Sap and cuts islands and peninsulas out of the land. The way the Royal Palace sits within this unique geographical situation offers a great example of how architecture, religion, culture, and physical environment can come together and form the starting point for urban planning. Unlike many modern cities, Phnom Penh went through many ups and downs. However, that makes the city more interesting. Phnom Penh shows many layers of civilisation, history, architecture, art, and cultural exchange. Another great aspect of Phnom Penh is its modern architecture from the 1950s and 1960s, which still exists in large numbers and shows the progress of Cambodia – the continuation of its innovative power. It is also fascinating to see how Cambodia was influenced by the West at the time but nevertheless held onto its traditions.

What challenges do you see for Phnom Penh's future development? And where do you see opportunities for positive development?
The city must accommodate a group of very different people and meet their specific needs. Its infrastructure must keep pace with a rapid construction boom. As the urban population increases, modern, safe, and smart public transport is needed. However, existing urban spaces, sidewalks, and building regulations are not yet adapted to this growth. Positive developments include the opening of shopping malls, better hospital facilities, and modern skyscrapers. These developments offer new options, enabling better lifestyles and broader dissemination of knowledge. Thanks to rising incomes and economies of scale, they improve the standard of living of both the older and younger generations of Cambodians.

How do you see your place as a young Cambodian architect in this environment and what is your personal approach?
I think this free, open, and yet complicated environment gives me the courage to meander my way through all things architectural, business, and regulatory. It makes me more spontaneous, more open minded, but also more persistent. I think it's about making the right decisions, learning from mistakes, and moving on to better days.
I also think I am fortunate for having started early, for having found my own place as a young Cambodian architect in today's environment. I think every project and every client wants more than just a good concept. Clients need to build up their brands, and they have to show their

uniqueness, their place in the growing economy. That's why they want their architect to be trustworthy and responsible, have a good track record, and add value to their investment. I think they want to team up with architects/designers who have a similar brand value, so establishing Re-Edge as a brand early in my career turned out to be an advantage for me and my team. Our brand communicates more than just good concepts and fresh ideas. We are young and responsible, and we pave the way for others. I also think that teaching, sharing my knowledge, and learning from all things around me helps to build bridges, spread my name, and extend my network.

What should architects visiting Phnom Penh pay particular attention to?
Phnom Penh is unique in that its built environment is not uniform. We see the pagodas, the Royal Palace, the museums, French colonial architecture, Chinese shophouses, the Art Déco style of the Central Market, Chinese temples, and even Muslim mosques. But architects should pay particular attention to the Modern Khmer architecture from the 1950s and 1960s by Vann Molyvann and his peers. These buildings are significant to architects around the world. They show how connected Cambodia was before the war as well as how western influences can be translated into the Cambodian context and climate.

What are your favourite buildings or places in the city, and why?
I have a deep connection with the **Olympic Stadium** (105 E) because my primary school and secondary school were nearby. I remember a carefree childhood when I went to the stadium to swim and play tennis. Of course, the stadium's architecture itself is also fascinating. It is an iconic public structure that is timeless and can serve as a case study for passive design for many generations of architects. The stadium seating, both indoors and outdoors, proves that form follows function, but at the same time, it is designed to allow reflected light to penetrate deep into the spaces, let the wind flow through, and divert the warm air in the roof. The

integrated drainage concept directs rain water into the basin surrounding the indoor stadium, just below the seating areas. Evaporation creates a convection effect that cools the indoor spaces and surroundings. The **Royal University of Phnom Penh** (118 F) is one of the few university campuses in Cambodia that feels like a real campus. You'll find a mix of simple academic buildings and interesting modern architecture that shows influences from the west as well as from Cambodian architecture. I like the spaces between and under the buildings and the huge trees. There are also outdoor cafés, pavilions, and ponds for students to relax in. I hope for some new additions that will modernise the campus, reflect time and context, and update it to keep pace with other campuses around the world.
I grew up in front of the **Central Market** (033 B), and I still remember the coconut trees and gardens that once surrounded the dome structure. The bright yellow dome is influenced by Art Déco architecture, but the louvre systems were designed to mimic the traditional Khmer temple towers. Inside, it is equally amazing. The natural light, reflected by the louvres, illuminates the retail booths. The openings from below and above also promote airflow, making the building breezy and comfortable. The symmetrical dome structure stands out from the surrounding shophouses and new highrise buildings. There are a few other buildings and areas such as the **Chinese House** (025 A), a mixture of French colonial architecture and Chinese immigrant culture. I like the architecture of the **National Museum** (073 C), its boutique scale, which is less intimidating than most museums and galleries. I like the atmosphere, the nature, and the flow of the gallery with the open courtyard. **Boeung Keng Kang 1** is known as the café district and lifestyle neighbourhood. The area has opened up to new developments that are increasingly becoming the new iconic buildings of Phnom Penh. The riverside shows a unique geography unlike other cities. The natural phenomena occur directly in front of the Royal Palace where the rivers meet to form *Chaktomuk*, the 'four faces'.

C

Boeung Keng Kang 1 and Tonle Bassac Area

Interview: Hun Sokagna

The district directly south of the Independence Monument is divided by Preah Norodom Boulevard into the Boeung Keng Kang 1 (BKK1) area to the west and the Tonle Bassac area and Diamond Island to the east. The western part, particularly BKK1, has been considered an expat hotspot since the 1980s. It is characterised by a mix of coffee shops, restaurants, and NGO offices often located in converted 1960s villas, as well as numerous newly built apartment towers. The eastern part features some small but interesting contemporary architecture and design projects around Bassac Lane and the massive new urban development of Diamond Island (Koh Pich).

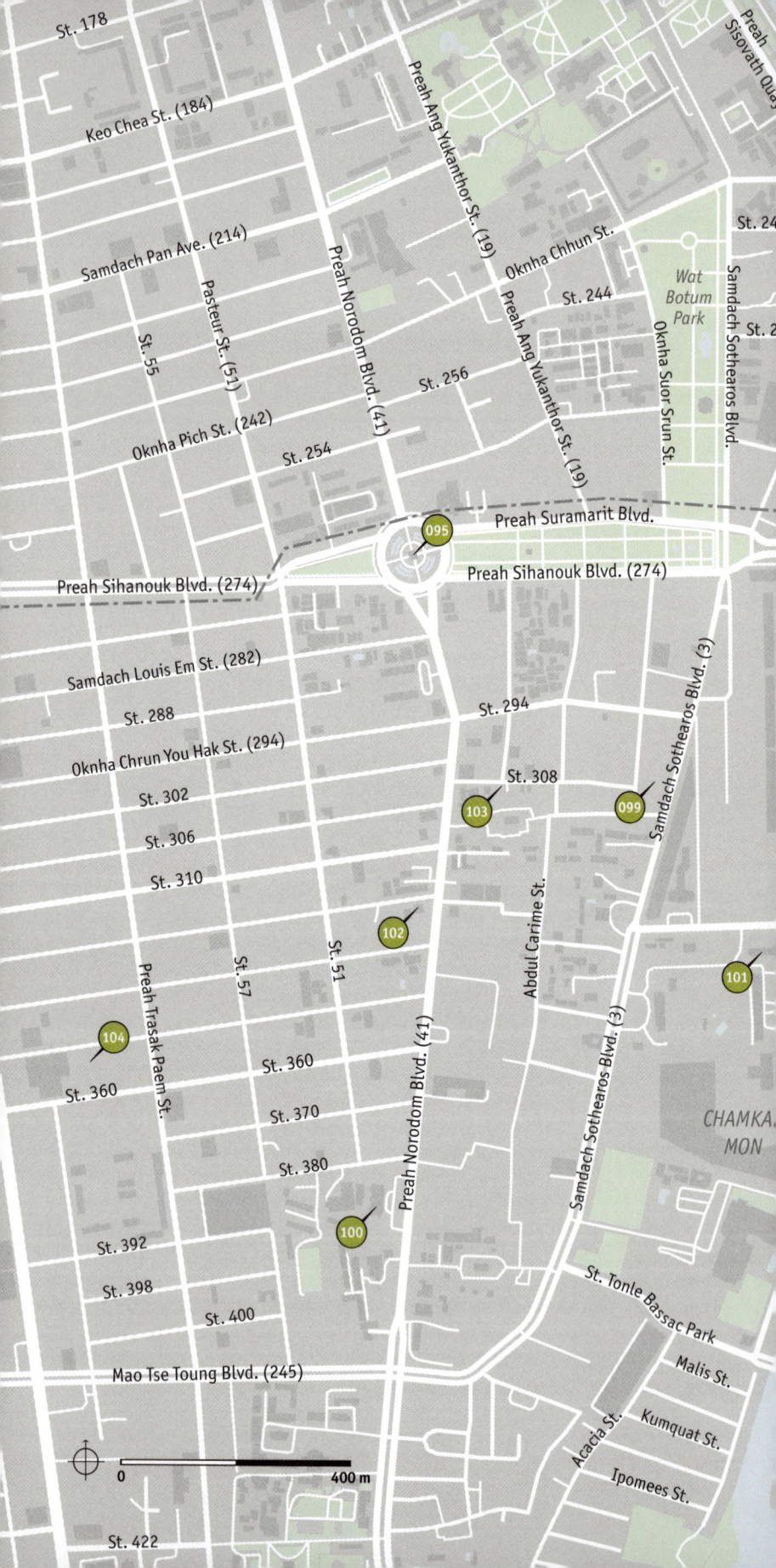

Mekong

Riverside Promenade

Twin Dragon
Bridge

098

National Assembly St.

Samdech Hun Sen St.

Sopheak Mongkol Rd.

Koh Pich St.

096

Exhibition Rd.

Koh Pich St.

097 St. 78

Swan Bridge

Xiao Long St.

Park Ave.

Diamond
Island Park

Bassac

La Sene Rd.

Newton Rd.

Darwin St.

Harvard St.

Elite Rd.

Berkeley

Princeton Rd.

St.

Koh Pich St.

Yale Rd.

Bassac

CHBAR
AMPOV

Independence Monument

095 D

Intersection of Preah Norodom Blvd and Preah Sihanouk Blvd
Vann Molyvann
1962

The Independence Monument, maybe the most significant symbol of the young Cambodian nation and still probably one of the most important symbols of the country, was planned as early as the second half of the 1950s, though it was not inaugurated until 9 November 1962, nine years after independence. Vann Molyvann was responsible for the design as a young architect. He was entrusted with the task by the head of state Norodom Sihanouk in 1957, shortly after he had returned from his studies in Paris. The two figures first met each other during a meeting in which Vann Molyvann showed Norodom Sihanouk samples of Chinese marble to be used for the monument. This meeting became the starting point for Vann Molyvann's wildly successful career as Cambodia's most important architect.

Preah Sihanouk Boulevard was inaugurated at the same time as the Independence Monument. It was designed by Lu Ban Hap and the Service Municipale de l'Urbanisme et de l'Habitat. The monument is the centrepiece of the boulevard, which, with its fountains, sculptures, and colourful flowers and trees, has to be seen as a whole. It aptly symbolises the country's independence which was won in 1953 after over 90 years of French rule.

The Independence Monument stands in the middle of a roundabout in the axis of Preah Norodom Boulevard. The boulevard runs from **Wat Phnom (001 A)** towards the south and ends at the intersection with Sihanouk Boulevard. It thus symbolically bridges the gap between the foundation of the city and the attainment of independence.

The construction of the traditional Khmer *prasat* tower was obviously a tricky matter, since Sihanouk Boulevard lay on a banked branch of the Bassac River. During the excavation of the monument's foundation, an old bridge with the name Spean Kon Kat ('mixed child bridge') was discovered. The first building contractor failed to completely demolish the bridge, and failed even after two years to build a solid foundation for the monument. The successor company was more successful. It built the support structure using reinforced concrete and subsequently clad it with decorative elements (*kbach*). The surface originally consisted of a granite-like material made of crushed red marble, but it has since been sadly painted over with a dark red tone. Grey Chinese marble was used for the steps and the pedestal, and a French goldsmith crafted the 'flame' inside. The monument's red colour and overall design were inspired by the ancient temple of Banteay Srei, which was built around 20 km northeast of Angkor in the second half of the 10th century and rediscovered only in 1914. Vann Molyvann and his collaborators visited Banteay Srei to select suitable motifs. Around 20 sculptors produced the ornaments with the use of moulds. They were led by Toeung Veuth, a master sculptor and mason from Battambang who also created the heads of the *nagas* (mythical serpents). This first collaborative effort between the sculptor and architect was very successful. And subsequently, the two figures created the *chedey* (stupas) dedicated to King Suramarit, Queen Kossamak, and Princess Kantha Bopha on the grounds of the Silver Pagoda next to the Royal Palace. Vann Molyvann once revealed that he drew inspiration not only from the famous Khmer temple Bantaey Srei but also another, in this context quite astonishing, model: 'The monument, conceived in the Angkorian tradition, drew on Le Corbusier's Modulor for its proportions.'

In the following years, the Independence Monument became the central stage for Sihanouk's annual political processions. In 1964 for example, delegations from all the kingdom's provinces drove past it in a parade to honour the king, and the monument was often illustrated on the cover of Sihanouk's various self-glorifying journals, including *Le Sangkum* in September 1967. In October 2013, the 27-metre-high Norodom Sihanouk Memorial was inaugurated in the park to the east of the Independence Monument to commemorate Sihanouk's role in liberating the country from the French Protectorate.

Ministry of Environment

48 Preah Sihanouk Boulevard
Architect unknown
2016

096 D

The palatial new building for Cambodia's Ministry of Environment, decorated with domes and towers, was inaugurated with a Buddhist ceremony in January 2016. It is located opposite **Diamond Island** (**098 D**), in the immediate vicinity of the NagaWorld casino complex.

The 6,750 m² plot was reportedly a gift from Prime Minister Hun Sen. According to official figures, 8 million dollars were invested to construct a floor area of 18,000 m² for 600 employees and to increase the productivity of the ministry. Before, only 3,000 m² were available, which is why, according to the ministry, many employees often didn't come

to work – they simply wouldn't have had enough workplaces. According to a ministry spokesperson, the new building has been designed with both traditional Khmer elements and modern concepts that reduce power consumption and are more environmentally sustainable.

The architectural concept, which was born out of an invited competition, shows a clear break not only from traditional Khmer architecture but also from early colonial modernism and from the New Khmer Architecture of the 1950s and 1960s. In the past, the norm was to build climate-adapted architecture using passive design concepts, which included enabling cross ventilation, providing shading, and orienting buildings based on the position of the sun. In contrast, the focus of this new building is clearly on compensating for climatic conditions by technical means. In terms of design, the central dome and the turret forms venture into a new stylistic territory. Thus, the Ministry of Environment and similar buildings such as the **Norton University** (**128 G**) and the **Office of the Prime Minister** (**058 B**) represent a contemporary attempt to combine modern technologies with building forms and decorative elements that are intended to reflect a distinct national identity.

The Bridge

National Assembly Street
*CK&A Consultancy International
Pte Ltd*
2018

The Bridge is the exact opposite of the massive, historicist work of architecture that is the adjacent Ministry of Environment. According to its developers, the building features contemporary elements that are new to Cambodia's architectural landscape, such as full glazing across the entire SOHO tower façade. SOHO, for 'Small Office Home Office', is described as 'a lifestyle apartment where young couples can stay in comfort and have a small work section, which they can convert into a room when they have a child.' There are 963 of these units in Tower 1 and 746 residential units in Tower 2. The massive podium houses over 1,000 parking lots, over 500 retail units, and 32 shophouses. The Bridge, featuring 45 storeys and measuring over 150 metres in height, is one of the many structures in Phnom Penh that break from the scale of the city's urban fabric, recalling the towering structures in Singapore. It stands next to The Peak, a development that will contain 55 storeys upon completion. The two buildings, together, almost completely obstruct the view of the urban space to the south and to the east towards the water. The same joint venture developed both buildings. It comprises a Cambodian logistics group, which is eyeing new business areas, and a Singaporean holding, which, according to its CEO, relocated its business due to the harsh measures implemented against property developers in Singapore in 2012. The Singapore-based architecture firm CK&A is responsible for the planning of both The Bridge and The Peak.

Diamond Island (Koh Pich)
Various architects
2006/ongoing

098 D

Legend has it that a ship sank some time in the mid-twentieth century where the northern end of the island is located today. It is said that sand accumulated around the sunken ship over the following years, gradually forming a piece of alluvial land measuring around 68 hectares.

Families first began to settle on the island in 1979. They were mainly families of fishermen who also cultivated vegetables on the fertile soil. Other inhabitants gradually followed suit, and this idyllic settlement lasted for many years. But in 2004, the Overseas Cambodian Investment Corporation (OCIC) approached the city council with a proposal to develop the land under the name Koh Pich, which means 'Diamond Island' in Khmer. In 2005, after controversial negotiations, relocation contracts were concluded with most of the 300 families living on the island. The residents had to leave their land, in exchange for a few dollars of compensation per square metre, to make way for one of Phnom Penh's most expensive and spectacular urban development projects to date.

A tour of the island is particularly worthwhile for those interested in contemporary interpretations of French, Greek-Roman, or Baroque architecture. One might even call it a form of 'Asian post-modernism' that blends all these architectural styles together. You can complete the tour on foot in around 90 minutes, though going by bike or in a tuk-tuk is recommended. If you enter the island via the bridge behind the enormous NagaWorld complex, you arrive in the northern tip, which has only been built up loosely so far. Here you will find amusement parks and all kinds of facilities dedicated to distraction. These

D

include the Convention Centre, an enormous shed used to host concerts, international trade fairs, and lavish wedding ceremonies. The building has been embellished with turrets, arches, and all kinds of decorations. Things become more exciting towards the south. We recommend circling the island clockwise on Koh Pich Street. Once you have passed the leisure and children's parks, where a substantial proportion of the city's residents seem to gather on weekends, you arrive at the **Riviera**. This is the name of a 700-million-dollar complex, which actually bears little resemblance to the Italian Riviera. It has much more in common with the Marina Bay Sands complex in Singapore, which clearly inspired the design of the Thailand-based architectural practice A-Seven. The completed complex will comprise three 33-storey condominium towers – with an infinity pool, a shopping mall, a hospital, an international school, and two pedestrian shopping streets – along with two additional 29-storey condominium towers. The buildings will not have a 4th, 14th,

24th, or 34th floor: Chinese superstition considers the number four unlucky. The **Diamond Island Parc**, a few metres to the right, attracts the visitor's eye with its baroque green area filled with pavilions, putti, and horse carts. Behind the park lies the **City Hall**, a 10,000-m² creative dream, also by Thai architecture firm A-Seven. The stylistically versatile firm is responsible for a whole series of other buildings on the island. Past the golf course to the left stands the **Diamond One** apartment complex, offering a floor area of almost 57,000 m². The triangular building is the prelude to the gated community behind it, aptly named **Elite Town**. This area's streets are named Columbia, Harvard, and Princeton Streets, and it offers security and cleanliness, which are both highly prized characteristics in Cambodia. The area, shielded behind high walls, is intended for the country's emerging upper class and employees of foreign companies. The undisputed highlight of the island tour is the OCIC's **Èlysée** project, located opposite **Elite Town**. The complex stands on a plot measuring

around 76,000 m² and contains 270 residential units along with a number of facilities. It will cost between 890,000 and 1.3 million dollars to complete, and is arranged around an office building in the shape of the Arc de Triomphe in Paris. This still-ongoing project is aimed at younger, more affluent Cambodians as well as foreigners seeking to invest in the country's real-estate sector. The small eco-park at the southern tip of Diamond Island is unique. It features two ponds and a little green, which are intended to improve the ecological balance of the development, though this is obviously an unsolvable task. We recommend following Elite Road back north. Once you pass the attractive building housing the Canadian International School, you will notice the portal-like structure of **Casa**, a mixed-use development built with funding from Hong Kong. The 122-metre-high twin towers contain 33 floors with 512 luxury units as well as retail and office spaces. According to the company's website, the towers incorporate the ancient principles of *feng shui*. The building resembles an ancient spade coin, a symbol of wealth. The opening between the towers symbolises a dragon's gate, which is intended to induce good health and prosperity for the residents. The Korean embassy at the foot of the tower is unspectacular, but its architecture is modern and fortunately avoids folkloric echoes. The last stage of our little tour takes us back to France. **La Seine** bewitches with its attempt to bring Parisian charm to the tropics. From here, one can leave the island by crossing the poetically named Swan Bridge. At first sight, it might seem surprising how Koh Pich seems to be filled with neo-classical buildings, vaguely mimicking French colonial architecture, even 60 years after the country's independence. However, Cambodians are not the primary target group of this development. A good share of the money comes from China, which is also the origin of many of the developers and construction companies as well as the buyers, courted by sales executives fluent in Mandarin. Even the street signs bear Chinese characters to help the new clients orient themselves.

Tronum Serviced Apartments

099 D

59B Street 3 (Samdech Sothearos Boulevard)
Vannak Architects
2017

In Cambodia's booming construction industry, 'size does matter', as an article in the *Nikkei Asian Review* stated in 2018. This makes the ten-storey Tronum tower a downright modest example of its building typology. It contains 14 uniquely designed serviced apartments, office spaces, a public rooftop restaurant and bar, a pool and jacuzzi, laundry and food-shopping services, and a spa. Architect Seng Vannak, who studied at the École des Beaux Arts in Paris and also holds the position of Deputy Head of the Urban Management Division at Phnom Penh City Hall, developed the building with his business partner Xavier Beaur. The Tronum tower was designed to meet the increasing demand for apartments in the luxury segment. According to Seng Vannak, *tronum* is a term Cambodian poets use in songs to evoke a sense of home. The L-shaped plot, measuring 580 m², is almost completely built up. The tower is set back from the street, which leaves space for vegetation at the front – a small gesture that seems almost generous in today's Phnom Penh. According to Seng Vannak, he drew inspiration from Phnom Penh's architecture of the 1960s, especially the famous White Building (demolished in 2018), for the building's design. The architect also wanted to give the building a green façade to reflect the city inhabitants' habit of placing flowerpots everywhere on their balconies. It remains to be seen whether green façades will catch on as a trend. This project obviously makes up only a small proportion of the construction taking place in Phnom Penh. Yet it represents an important first step towards improving the city's microclimate and reducing the urban heat island effect.

Tiger Beer Villa

100 D

Preah Norodom Boulevard
Architect unknown
2008

This private residence, located on the southern section of Norodom Boulevard, displays an architectural style that recalls the image of European castles. It offers an estimated 2,500 m² of gross floor area along with a further 1,000 m² in an adjacent building. One imagines that an entire mountain must have been mined in order to procure the granite required for the façade and the massive walls enclosing the property. Rumours have it that the building belongs to Cambodia's distributor of Tiger Beer, one of the richest businessmen in the country, and his wife. One might say that it exemplifies the desires of the country's nouveau riche to show off their wealth with a merry mixture of eclectic neo-classical styles, liberally sampled from the rich history of architectural pattern books with unbounded glee.

Russian Embassy Apartments 101 D

Samdech Sothearos Boulevard/
National Assembly Street
Henri Chatel, Jamshed Petigura
1963

These two apartment buildings, designed by architects Henri Chatel and Jamshed Petigura, are the last remaining apartment buildings from Front de Bassac, the most visionary urban development project of the 1960s in Phnom Penh. Henri Chatel was one of the busiest architects of his time. He arrived in Phnom Penh in 1949 as a representative of Maurice Masson's firm in Saigon. He thereafter became involved in the construction of the National Bank of Cambodia and Phnom Penh Cathedral (both destroyed by the Khmer Rouge) as well as the Khemara Cinema. In 1954, he was appointed as principal architect of the Ministry of Defence. He thereafter built, among others, the building for the Ministry of Defence on Russian Federation Boulevard and several apartment buildings. He also oversaw the conversion of the **Hotel Le Royal** (017 A). The work of this extraordinarily talented architect, who later worked in Europe and the Middle East, still awaits full documentation. Chatel won the competition for the apartment buildings in 1959, but he handed over the project to his colleague Jamshed Petigura in 1961, as he had to leave the country for personal

National Bank apartments, 1960s

reasons. The buildings were originally intended to accommodate employees of the National Bank of Cambodia. In 1979, they were handed over to the Russian Embassy in exchange for the Cambodian Embassy in Moscow. Today, they accommodate the staff of the Russian Embassy. The buildings are still in excellent condition, thanks to its sheltered location and an extensive renovation project in the 1980s. It is said that Chatel always sought architectural solutions suited to Cambodia's tropical climate. He regretted having to use concrete, a climatically unfavourable material, since brick was not sufficiently available at that time. Nevertheless, the ensemble is a wonderful example of climate-adapted building. The folded roof element, so typical of Cambodian modernism of the 1960s, was supposedly used here for the first time, and it protects the top floor against direct sunlight and heavy rain. The elevated ground floor enables air circulation and creates shaded recreational areas.

The Round House

171 Preah Norodom Boulevard
Mam Sophana
1971

'My style is curved. Why curved? I hate angles. Angles are easy to draw.' This is what the architect Mam Sophana told the author in an interview in 2016. His Round House on Norodom Boulevard is probably the best example of his idiosyncratic style, which he in fact was rarely able to realise (see also **National Technical Training Institute 139 G**). Mam Sophana was one of the few Cambodian architects who lived in the country in the 1960s and early 1970s. During this time, he carried out many large-scale projects with his own firm. He studied in the US, where, in his own words, he 'learned freedom and independence'. He returned to Phnom Penh in 1965, and planned a variety of public and private buildings in Phnom Penh and other cities. The influence of American architects such as Frank Lloyd Wright shows in much of his work (see **Villa for Son Sann 088 C**). In contrast, his colleagues such as Vann Molyvann and Lu Ban Hap, who had studied in France, brought with them ideas of European modernism, principally of Le Corbusier.

In 1974, Mam Sophana moved to Singapore, where he played a key role in planning the city's Changi International Airport. Today, he lives in Phnom Penh once more, where he runs a small practice and works as an urban-planning consultant for the government. The columns on the porch of the Round House have a curved design that looks rather strange. But this seems to be the result of an inadequate brief from the client. According to Ross and Collins, the architect once stated: 'If you don't tell me what you want, I will give you bent columns.' The small house has lost much of its former charm, due to a number of unreasonable and awkward alterations that have been made. Yet it is an intriguing example of the almost touching attempt by a young architect to establish his own style in the booming city of Phnom Penh in the 1960s. In 2002, a replica of the Round House was erected on Street 214 without the participation of Mam Sophana.

Micro-bar Alleys

Bassac Lane, off Street 308/
Langka Laneway, off Street 51
Various architects
2013–2019

103 D

For decades, Phnom Penh's night-life has been dominated by consumers of cheap beer near the Mekong riverside. But in recent years, an 'alley culture' has emerged, breathing new life into the after-dark scene of the capital. Many of the places have been crafted by young architects and designers. During the day, Bassac Lane, an alley off Street 308, sees local residents going about their daily lives at a leisurely and relatively quiet pace. When night falls, however, the same sleepy area becomes one of Phnom Penh's most eminent night-life haunts. Bassac Lane began to undergo considerable transformation, or gentrification, in 2013. This is when the brothers George and William Norbert-Munns, from New Zealand, opened a series of micro-bars. The first was Seibur, opened in 2013, which was followed by several others. Today, around half a dozen trendy bars and eateries occupy the alley. Further establishments can be found on the adjacent Street 308, each drawing its own stream of regular clients and tourists in the know. The themed bars, each with a distinct character, somehow have the air of a movie set. Seibur, located on the entrance corner to the left, is a breezy, open-fronted venue. As the first to arrive on the scene, it sparked the alley's evolution into the bustling night-time hotspot that it is. Next to it is Cicada, an insect-themed bar serving infused gins, and some steps

further on the corner is The Library, fitted with shelves full of books, where one can enjoy a range of daiquiris. On the opposite side there is Harry's, a vintage-themed, elegant little bar that features framed historic maps of Phnom Penh. Closeby is Hangar 44, resembling an industrial-chic motorbike workshop. The latest addition is Phnom Penh Yacht Club, which opened with a Mediterranean theme on the corner with Street 308.

Outside Bassac Lane, at No. 32, Street 308, one finds Le Boutier, an elegant cocktail bar in a purpose-built three-floor glass box with large show windows overlooking the street. This retro-style bar's theme is Cambodia's 'Golden Age'. It serves aptly named drinks such as 'Don't think it's forgotten', named after the 2015 documentary film of the same name, which tells the story of Khmer rock in the 1960s and 1970s before the Khmer Rouge destroyed the country's emerging pop music by killing nearly all of its musicians. In 2016, Le Boutier was opened by US-born Annemarie Sagoi together with David Chhay, a Parisian of Cambodian descent. When he was a child, Chhay's mother lived a few blocks from the bar, which cemented his desire to set up a place in the area. Elbow Room stands at No. 35. This bar, which opened in 2016, features an elegant interior and street-art-style décor. A ten-minute stroll down the maze of tiny residential alleys further south of Bassac Lane takes you to No. 9B, Street 830. Here, the Samai Rum Distillery occupies an interesting industrial-style, barn-like building, where its award-winning Cambodian-produced premium liqueur is distilled, bottled, and served to the public.

Another cluster of tiny bars and eateries can be found in an alley off Street 51, just opposite the intersection with Street 288. The alley surrounds the stylish Patio Hotel, newly built by Korean architect-cum-entrepreneur Oh Byung Hee in 2013. The alley somewhat recalls the narrow Isakaya alleys of Tokyo, with their miniature gastro-pubs. Here you can find Katanashi, a Japanese vintage-themed tapas bar, the miniscule No Style yakitori counter, and the posh SushiLab, each located just a few steps from one another. Meanwhile, Bistrot Langka, an intimate restaurant squeezed into a narrow building, has been serving upmarket French cuisine since 2016. A vintage Coca Cola machine tucked away in an alley corner nearby hides the entrance to Battbong, a speakeasy-themed bar and restaurant started by French-Khmer co-owner Klanetra Ching in 2016. The name of the bar translates into 'my lost friend', which is a reference to its clandestine motif. The quirky venue has managed to attract a diverse clientele in a city where Khmers and expats often frequent separate bars.

Embassy Central

34 Street 352
Hok Kang Architects
2019

104 D

The Embassy Central tower is the second condominium tower, after the Embassy Residences at Street 41, that the young architect and entrepreneur Hok Kang realised, both as a developer with his company Urbanland and as a designer with Hok Kang Architects. The architect, who was also behind the Brown Coffee and Bakery chain (see 114 E and 123 F) founded Urbanland in 2013 with a vision 'to create aspirational spaces for the community', as he explains. Since then, Urbanland's developments have included, in addition to the two apartment buildings, the Treeline Hotel in Siem Reap and the **Raintree** (012 A), an innovative office building in Phnom Penh, which has received numerous awards from the real estate industry.

Located in the heart of Phnom Penh's hip BKK1 district, the 25-storey Embassy Central tower occupies a plot measuring 1,328 m². The residential tower sets new standards both with the design of its façade and with the layout of its floor plans. Deep balconies provide the apartments with a certain amount of natural shading and individual outdoor space, despite the fact that all units are air conditioned. The elegant lines of the vertically meandering pilaster strips and the three-dimensionality of the façade make the tower stand out positively from the mass of mushrooming high-rise buildings filling up the city's skyline, most of which are designed purely to maximise floor space. What particularly defines the tower is the 'sky gardens', each several storeys high, cutting into the building's volume. Embassy Central residents have access to a private clubhouse comprising a fitness centre, infinity pool, sauna, and changing facilities. They also have access to the signature elevated garden and private function area designed for entertaining guests. Three aboveground and three underground parking levels, praised as some of 'the most generous in BKK1', ensure that none of the residents will have to search for a parking space in Phnom Penh's chronically congested streets. Prices for the 119 condominiums are between 222,000 dollars for a 61 m² one-bedroom apartment and 713,000 dollars for a 196 m² three-bedroom apartment.

D

Hun Sokagna
Architect and researcher
Roung Kon Project,
Space for Architecture Cambodia, Khmer
Architecture Tours,
Phnom Penh

Hun Sokagna holds a BA in architecture and urbanism from the Royal University of Fine Arts. She is an independent researcher and tour guide for Space for Architecture Cambodia and Khmer Architecture Tours. She co-founded the Roung Kon Project, where her tasks include public relations, research, and web development and where she was responsible for the Ciné Lux drawings. Sokagna is also a part-time lecturer at Limkokwing University of Creative Technology Cambodia.

What exactly is the Roung Kon Project?
The Roung Kon Project was founded in 2016 by a group of architects and architecture students. It is a multi-disciplinary project that aims to research, document, promote, and educate about all the heritage cinemas in Cambodia, that is, cinemas that were built before 1975. The documentation takes several different forms, such as architectural drawings, interviews (with filmmakers, scholars, and ordinary film-loving people), new and archival photographs, film, written archival documents, and historical maps. The project explores the urban form of Cambodia's cities through cinemas. It studies how this urban form reflects the ideology of Norodom Sihanouk's Sangkum Reastr Niyum regime, and how the regime's city planning was intertwined with cultural engagement. All the materials collected and produced by the Roung Kon Project will be free to access online for researchers, students, artists, architects, and urban planners for educational purposes and as a tool to help promote knowledge about Cambodia's built heritage of movie theatres. Our hope is to help preserve this built heritage.

Why and how did you start this project?
Most of us have volunteered for the Vann Molyvann Project since 2015. One day, we realised that the Capitol Cinema, which was remodelled by Vann Molyvann, was being prepared for demolition. We were sad, so we launched this project to archive documents about cinemas in Phnom Penh before everything disappears.

Where can one see some of the old cinemas in Phnom Penh?

Phnom Penh had 33 cinemas from the French colonial period to the 1970s. Most of them are gone now. A few cinema buildings are still standing but they are not used as cinemas anymore. They have been renovated to serve other uses – as clubs, karaoke bars, or parking lots for example – and some have been demolished. **Hemakcheat Cinema** (046 B) has been changed to house a slum community. **Ciné Lux** (048 B) and Kirirom Cinema are under demolition (as of January 2019). The former **Chenla Cinema** (116 E) is a state cinema, but it is not really in use.

Which is your favourite Cinema?

Ciné Lux is my favorite cinema. It was probably built in 1938 and has a splendid modern Art Déco style. It was once one of the most famous cinemas in Phnom Penh. Ciné Lux was in use until the early 1990s for a variety of activities including film screenings and theatre performances. It has a total of 800 seats. It re-opened in 2001, after renovations, but stopped screening in 2016. Unfortunately, its demolition began in early 2019. Every time I went to this cinema to make architectural drawings for the Roung Kon Project, I loved it more. I discovered that it was not only a cinema, but also a residence for artists. As the Lux was used for performances too, it also had changing rooms for actors.

What are your favourite buildings or places in the city, and why?

I really appreciate the **Olympic Stadium** (105 E), by Vann Molyvann, because it is the building that aroused my interest in studying architecture. I live closeby, so I always go there for my training. The design concept and the history of the stadium are amazing. The **Independence Monument** (095 D) is a memorial monument and an important landmark of Phnom Penh. And finally there is the **Institute for Foreign Languages** (121 F), the former Teacher Training College, another unique design by Vann Molyvann.

The Southwest

Portrait: Vann Molyvann
Interview: Pen Sereypagna

The districts of Boeung Keng Kang 2 and 3, and Toul Tom Poung (south of Mao Tse Toung Boulevard) are situated to the south of the National Sports Complex, perhaps the most emblematic building of the New Khmer Architecture of the 1960s. These areas were developed during the western extension of the city in the 1950s and 1960s. While BKK2 is the location of the Tuol Sleng Genocide Museum, Toul Tom Poung centres around the Russian Market, popular with visitors of the city. The surrounding area is the latest place-to-be for expats, dotted with an increasing number of hip coffee shops and bars, souvenir shops, and apartments. Besides several small but interesting contemporary architectural projects, the iconic House of Vann Molyvann and the vast modernist complex of the Khmer-Soviet Friendship Hospital are located nearby.

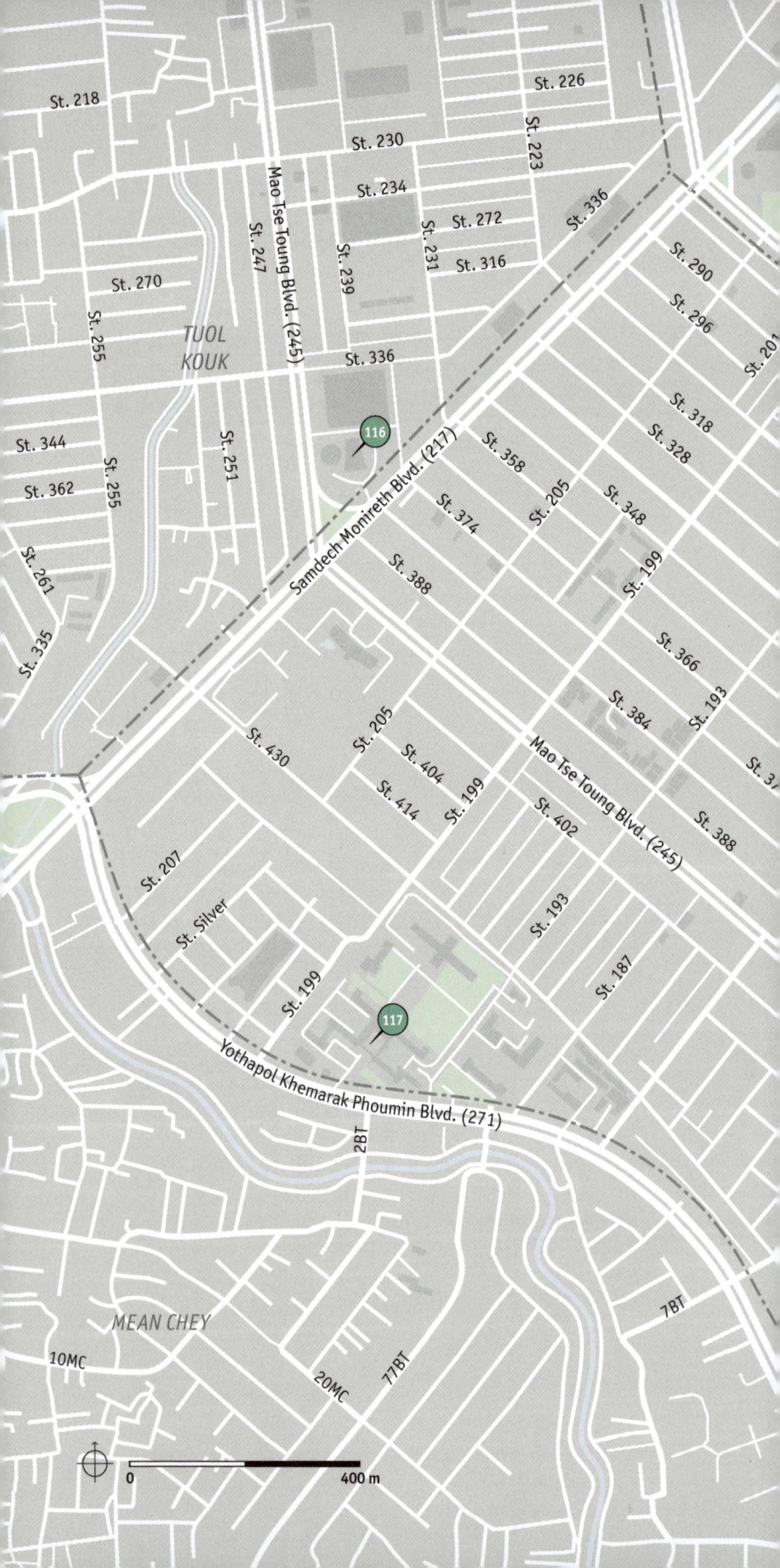

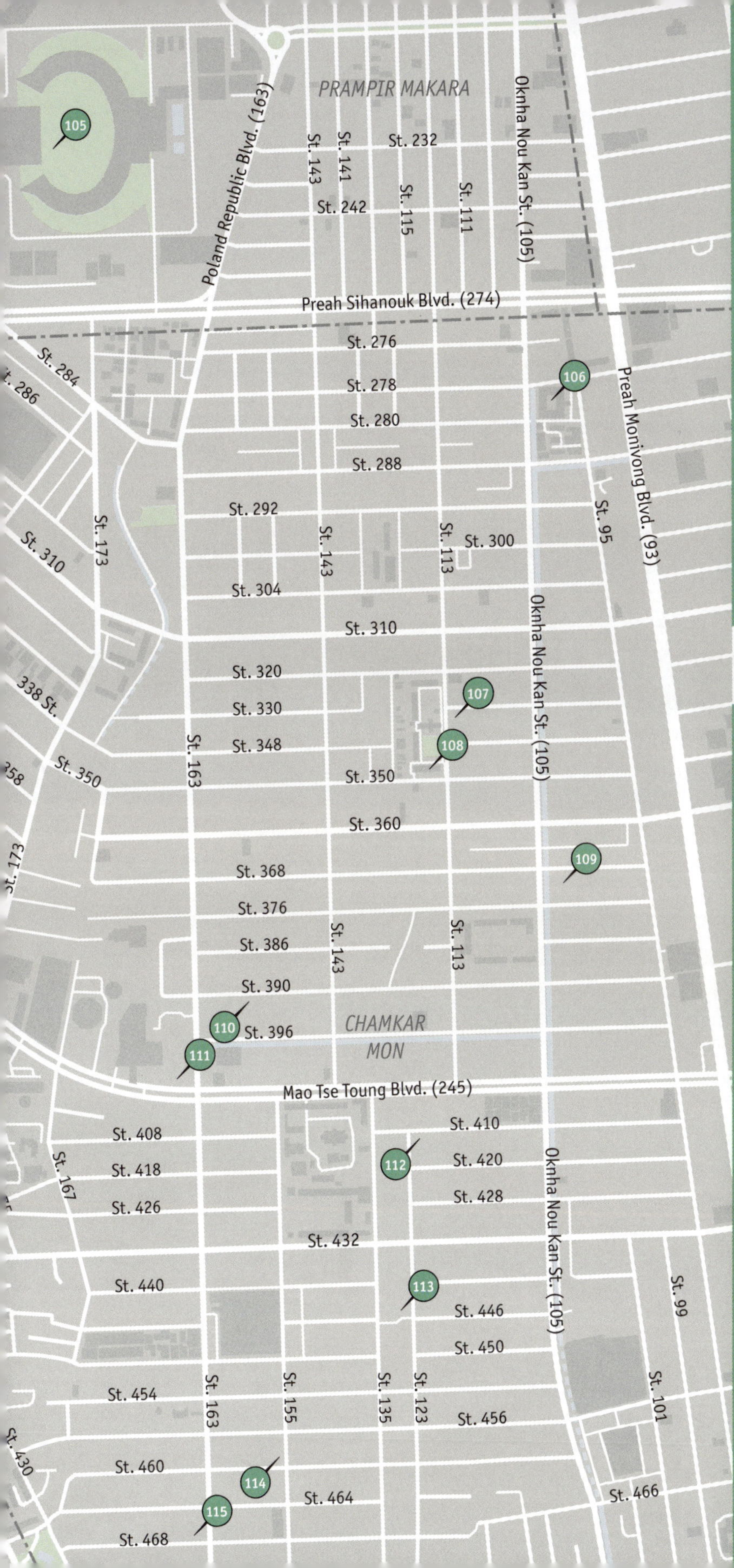

PRAMPIR MAKARA

105

Poland Republic Blvd. (163)

St. 143
St. 141
St. 232
St. 242
St. 115
St. 111

Oknha Nou Kan St. (105)

Preah Sihanouk Blvd. (274)

St. 284

St. 286

St. 276

St. 278

St. 280

St. 288

106

Preah Monivong Blvd. (93)

St. 95

St. 173

St. 310

St. 292

St. 143

St. 113

St. 300

St. 304

St. 310

338 St.

St. 320

St. 330

St. 348

St. 163

St. 350

358

Oknha Nou Kan St. (105)

107

108

St. 350

St. 360

173

St. 368

St. 376

St. 386

St. 143

St. 113

109

St. 390

St. 396

110

111

CHAMKAR
MON

Mao Tse Toung Blvd. (245)

St. 408

St. 418

St. 426

St. 167

St. 410

St. 420

112

St. 428

St. 432

St. 440

Oknha Nou Kan St. (105)

113

St. 446

St. 450

St. 99

St. 454

St. 163

St. 155

St. 135

St. 123

St. 456

St. 101

St. 430

St. 460

114

115

St. 464

St. 466

St. 468

E

National Sports Complex (Olympic Stadium)

Street 217 (Charles de Gaulle Boulevard)

Vann Molyvann

1964

105 E

The building complex is commonly referred to as the Olympic Stadium, even though Cambodia has never actually hosted the Olympic Games. It has served as an important symbol for the emerging country since the 1960s. During the stadium's inauguration ceremony, the then head of state Norodom Sihanouk gave a speech, bursting with national pride, to 100,000 spectators. He proclaimed:

'Our achievements and progress in all fields, as well as our national unity, have shown the world that we are not a bastard nation deprived of intelligence, courage, and energy, as our enemies have often pretended. Despite the criticism and slander of some of our neighbours and their imperialist masters, we have proven our capacity to transform our ancient kingdom into a modern nation.'

The project included a water sports complex (now demolished) on the banks of the Bassac River. Accommodation buildings were also built to house the athletes. These included: the Olympic Village Apartments (now transformed), also called the Grey Building due to its grey granite cladding, and the Municipal Apartments (demolished in 2018), also called the White Building, which was later marketed as low-cost housing. The stadium was originally intended for the 1963 Southeast Asian Games, though the event was cancelled for political reasons. Had the event taken place, the project would have surely ended in embarrassment, for the stadium wasn't

E

even half completed by that time. After Sihanouk commissioned the project, Vann Molyvann quickly assembled an international team. He appointed the Russian-born Vladimir Bodiansky, who had worked with Le Corbusier on the Unité d'habitation in Marseille, as head engineer. Since Cambodia did not have the required planning infrastructure at the time, the architects Claude Duchemin and Jean-Claude Morin drew up the plans in Paris. The construction posed an enormous challenge, since 40 hectares of land had to be almost completely transformed. The building site was a swamp, which meant most of the work had to be performed manually and with ox carts. Many building elements were prefabricated in order to speed up the construction process. The aluminium cladding of the hall, for example, was manufactured in France. The project cost a total

of 30 million dollars, a huge sum for the small country. Yet it was financed entirely with the national budget, partially with the help of an additional tax levied on ice cream and alcohol.

The complex comprises the stadium with 60,000 seats and a grandstand, a sport hall, a swimming pool with a grandstand, and a podium for medal winners and the Olympic flame. These coherently integrated areas are surrounded by open spaces containing tennis, volleyball,

The National Sports Complex, 1960s

and basketball courts as well as areas for water management. The architectural configuration of the building, which appears as archaic as it is monumental, shows clear allusions to the temples of Angkor. The structures, axially lined from east to west, have an almost inverted layout of the national sanctuary. The indoor sport hall recalls the courtyard complexes that form the entrance level to Angkor Wat. And it is covered by four enormous roofs that refer to the four-part division of the temple's entrance area. The stadium forms a giant, empty shell for receiving the masses, recalling the terraces in the centre of Angkor Wat which grow upwards to evoke the image of the holy mountain of Meru. Like the rear of Angkor Wat, where there are three exits, the rear of the stadium has a roof comprising three concrete square umbrellas that cover the tribune of the swimming pool.

After its opening, the stadium was used for all kinds of activities. In 1966, it hosted the second Games of The New Emerging Forces, and in the same year, Charles de Gaulle gave a highly acclaimed speech to tens of thousands of spectators. Things changed dramatically after Lon Nol's assumption of power, and the stadium was repurposed as a field hospital. In April 1975, when the Americans performed Operation Eagle Pull to evacuate the city, their helicopters took off from the stadium, leaving the city to its fate in the face of the imminent invasion of the Khmer Rouge. The Khmer Rouge regime used the former playing field as an execution site and the indoor stadium as a gathering point. After the fall of the Khmer Rouge, the stadium lay abandoned for a long time, until Cambodia began to recover in the 1990s. Since then, the stadium has been closed, reopened again, and partially renovated. The population makes intensive use of the structures, and the stadium has been a source of inspiration for many architects. There have been rumours of a planned demolition for years. This would be a great loss, and not only for Cambodia, since the National Sports Complex is a crucial witness to the history of the country.

'They didn't know what an architect was'

A portrait of Vann Molyvann, Cambodia's first and most famous architect, and the man behind the Olympic Stadium.

The new, post-colonial chapter of Cambodia's history was accompanied by a new architectural culture. Nowhere else in Southeast Asia has a country's architecture so successfully mirrored and influenced its history as a whole. Particularly emblematic is the work of Cambodia's only 'starchitect' to date, Vann Molyvann (1926–2017). Vann Molyvann was born in Ream, Cambodia, in 1926. He went to Paris in 1946 on a French scholarship, initially to study law. But after a meeting with Henri Marchal, the curator of Angkor for the École Francaise d'Extreme-Orient, he decided to become an architect. In March 1948, he was admitted into the Ecole Nationale Supérieure des Beaux-Arts. After completing his studies, he returned to Cambodia in 1956, where he became the first trained Cambodian architect in the country. Molyvann's once described the difficulties he faced in the early years of his professional career:

'... when I came back, at first, no one knew what my profession was. I had obtained my diploma in France, but no one in Cambodia wanted to hire me. They didn't know what an architect was.'

But this lull was not permanent. A short time later, Norodom Sihanouk appointed him as Head of Public Works and as State Architect. From this point onwards, Vann Molyvann was responsible for all of the state's building tasks. This enabled him to forge the architectural identity of the emerging country.

Vann Molyvann

Preah Suramarit National Theatre, Phnom Penh, late 1960s

Vann Molyvann once described the atmosphere of the Cambodia after his return from Paris as follows:
'There was an unprecedented creative dynamism in my country after a long period of decline. Everyone was aware that it was necessary to rediscover our origins ... and that Cambodia, as a country with an ancient tradition, should reassert its own personality. The cultural movement we presently see ... bears the mark of this spirit. Obviously, this did not mean reproducing artistic creations of the Angkorian past; rather, it meant being inspired by them. It meant transcribing and adapting them to a new reality.'

In Vann Molyvann's view, Cambodia's architectural culture at the time was driven by a wish to recollect the country's history and to reconstruct and renew the lost identity of the Khmer people. This view, in fact, fits seamlessly into the (French) narrative of Angkor's lost civilisation, which seems to have been a powerful point of reference for Cambodian identity from the colonial era to the present day.

The architectural programme at the École des Beaux Arts was still strongly influenced by western classicism. As such, the young student from Buddhist Cambodia found himself having to draw Doric and Ionic columns as part of his education. However, Paris, with its outstanding collection of architectural works and pool of experts, was also the place where Vann

Molyvann was able to pursue his interest in the culture of his own country. And of course, it was inevitable that he would confront the ideas of modernism, which at the time was shaping the architectural debates throughout Europe. Molyvann studied the buildings of Frank Lloyd Wright and Paul Rudolph and came to know the works of Le Corbusier, whom he once called his 'most talented and skilled teacher'. He recognised, in Corbusier's buildings raised from the ground, similarities with the architecture of his homeland. And the Modulor, a system of proportions devised by Le Corbusier, later guided Molyvann's choice of dimensions for his buildings. However, Vann Molyvann always maintained a critical outlook. He once commented: 'We could not simply repeat things as they were once done in Europe. We had to think of new ideas, with a Cambodian perspective.'

Almost all of Molyvann's works reveal his attempt to combine Cambodian traditions with his French education. His buildings incorporate the principles of order found in Angkor's famous temples as well as elements of traditional Cambodian décor. They also stem from vernacular building methods, which have been shaped by the local climatic requirements for centuries. Molyvann frequently used water as a design element, oriented his buildings based on the position of the sun, and raised them above the ground to enable natural ventilation.

All of these recurring design elements show a consideration of the specific geographical and climatic conditions of Cambodia. At the same time, Molyvann also made radical and innovative use of reinforced concrete as a building material. His thoughtful use of materials and careful detailing have protected his buildings against rapid decay in the tropical climate. In this way, he not only succeeded in combining the design principles of western modernism with local conditions; he also found his own architectural language. The International Style became Khmer Modernism.

Vann Molyvann built over 80 buildings throughout the country. He was also an urban planner and oversaw the expansion of Phnom Penh and the establishment of the seaport at Sihanoukville (Kampong Som). He designed exhibitions in Cambodia and many other countries of the world and choreographed public performances. In addition, he held a number of important public positions: he served both as secretary of state and as minister, and was the founding director of the Royal University of Fine Arts. Last but not least, he ran his own architectural practice. Some of his buildings can still be seen in Phnom Penh, such as the **Independence Monument** (**095 D**), the **National Sports Complex** (**105 E**), the **Chaktomuk Conference Hall** (**065 C**), the former **Ministry of Finance** (**127 F**), and the **100 Houses** (**138 G**) in the Tuk Thla district. The wonderful buildings on the government premises (Chamkar Mon Compound), the State Palace, and the State Reception Hall unfortunately cannot be visited. Many of his buildings have sadly fallen victim to the ongoing construction boom, which has been accompanied by the relentless demolition of existing buildings.

Perhaps the most painful loss was the demolition of the Preah Suramarit National Theatre. This building was erected in the 1960s, as part of a major urban development project on the banks of the Bassac River, on land wrested from the river. The building had tapered interiors, spread across several floors, which were naturally ventilated and dimly lit by a sophisticated slat construction. Inside, one could enjoy spectacular views of the surrounding landscape through narrow windows. The back of the theatre behind the stage could be opened to provide a view of the landscape. The floor plan had a triangular form, which itself reappeared as a motif throughout the building: the floor of the foyer was covered with triangular tiles, the ceiling was divided into a triangular grid, and the roof of the stage resembled a pyramid. Like the Chaktomuk Conference Hall and the National Sports Complex, the design of the theatre was based on Le Corbusier's Modulor. A fire partially destroyed the theatre in 1994. It was then completely demolished in 2008,

Council of Ministers (demolished), Phnom Penh, 1960s

State Palace at Chamkar Mon Compound, Phnom Penh, detail, 1960s

in spite of its architectural value. Vann Molyvann's Olympic Village Apartments (the Grey Building), a residential project on the same site, was completely remodelled and destroyed in the 1990s. The Council of Ministers, an early work of the architect, had to give way to the parking lot of the new **Council of Ministers** (**059 B**) in 2008, and in 2018, the Capitol Cinema disappeared in a cloud of dust.

Vann Molyvann's productive phase in the country ultimately lasted only 14 years. In March 1970, Norodom Sihanouk was deposed during a trip abroad. This heralded the end of the country's short period of prosperity. The Khmer Rouge's rise to power a few years later catapulted Cambodia back into pre-industrial times. As early as 1971, Molyvann fled from the imminent unrest to Switzerland, home of his wife Trudy. There he soon found himself working for an architectural practice in Lausanne on the competition for the École Polytechnique Fédérale de Lausanne. Later, Molyvann worked for the UN in Africa and Indonesia. After his return to Cambodia in 1991, he was appointed as Minister of State for Culture, Fine Arts, Land Management and Urban Development. And in 1995, he became Director of APSARA (Authority for the Protection and Management of Angkor and the Region of Siem Reap) – a position he held until 2001. In 2003, he published *Modern Khmer Cities*, and in 2008, at the age of 82, he published his doctoral thesis on the history and future of Southeast Asian cities. In 2011, the renovation of the Central Market in Phnom Penh was completed, a project that Molyvann carried out together with the French practice Arte Charpentier. In 2013, Molyvann won the Nikkei Asia Prize 2013 in the culture category. He died on 28 September 2017, at his home in Siem Reap.

State Reception Hall, detail, 1960s

National Center for Tuberculosis and Leprosy Control

106 E

Street 95/Street 278
Pacific Consultants International and K. Ito Architects and Engineers Inc.
2001

In the late 1990s, Cambodia asked the Japanese government for support in expanding its medical facilities for the treatment of tuberculosis. One of the outcomes was the National Center for Tuberculosis and Leprosy Control, which was built with technical support from the Japan International Cooperation Agency (JICA). The building was designed by Japanese architects and engineers and erected by a Japanese construction company. The design brief stipulated that the building should not be too ostentatious. This requirement was by and large met, if one overlooks the tall tower section. The building impresses with its pared-down architectural language and its modest range of materials, which consist of concrete, bricks, and simple plaster for the surfaces.

The building measures just over 3,000 m² and comprises two blocks that accommodate consultation rooms, laboratories, offices, and storage rooms. It has an interesting structure: a ring-shaped gallery around a small courtyard connects the two building sections. These open walkways are placed in front of the functional rooms as a structure made of reinforced concrete. A reinforced-concrete skeleton, filled in with perforated clay bricks, is placed in front of the street-facing sides. It thus forms a simple but effective climate buffer in front of the façade.

JICA and Pacific Consultants International, in collaboration with the Technical School for Medical Care, have developed another building for Phnom Penh's healthcare sector. Located right next to the **Khmer-Soviet Friendship Hospital** (117 E) at Street 271, the modest building is another example of functional, climate-adapted architecture.

Office Building
32 Street 330
Truong Khinnin
2017

107 **E**

Writing an architectural guide on a city such as Phnom Penh requires a great deal of historical research and extensive networking. Yet it also, to a large degree, depends on chance. We were fortunate enough to discover this building during one of our many forays into the city. It is pleasing to see that there are still clients in Phnom Penh, today increasingly characterised by enormous leaps in scale, who attach importance to buildings that consider the height of their surroundings. The building is situated on a street corner directly opposite the Tuol Sleng Genocide Museum, formerly the S-21 torture prison run by the Khmer Rouge. The building's unusual façade immediately catches the eye. Cantilevered plant troughs, staggered balconies, and concrete sun-protection screens cover the slightly recessed glass façade, thus forming an effective climate buffer. This small office building features a modest range of materials and a climate-adapted design, which together make it a successful example of contemporary architecture in Phnom Penh.

Tuol Sleng Genocide Museum (former Chao Ponhea Yat High School)

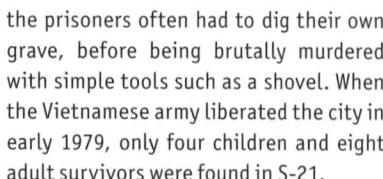

108 E

Street 113
Lu Ban Hap (original school buildings)
1960s

We hesitated for a long time before deciding to include the Tuol Sleng Genocide Museum in this architectural guide. There are many good reasons not to report about such a horrific place in this specific context. However, buildings are ultimately a reflection of the social and political conditions in which they were built, and of the historical changes that took place around them. Since this relationship between architecture and its socio-political context is one of this book's concerns, we decided, in the end, that it would be important to mention the building.

This building was called S-21 – the 's' stood for 'secret office' – in Pol Pot's Democratic Kampuchea. It was one of the 196 prisons run by the Khmer Rouge. It was the central site of the regime's interrogation and detention system and was used to imprison, torture, interrogate, and execute those who were deemed a political enemy. Around 18,000 people were interned here from April 1976 onwards. Most of them had been accused of betraying the Khmer Rouge Party or the communist revolution. The inmates were usually subjected to cruel torture methods intended to force confessions. They were then taken away to be executed at Choeung Ek, one of the infamous killing fields outside the city. There,

the prisoners often had to dig their own grave, before being brutally murdered with simple tools such as a shovel. When the Vietnamese army liberated the city in early 1979, only four children and eight adult survivors were found in S-21.

This simple ensemble of five utilitarian buildings was initially built for an entirely different purpose. After Cambodia gained independence from France, Norodom Sihanouk launched an unprecedented initiative to support education. Schools and universities were built across the country, and Chao Ponhea Yat High School was one of them. But Phnom Penh was a poor city, and building so many schools put a strain on the municipal budget. Lu Ban Hap, who had been director of the Service Municipal de l'Urbanisme et d'Habitat since 1960, went on a trip to the Soviet Union to study the principles of prefabrication. Upon returning to Phnom Penh, he developed a modular system with which he then built almost all of the city's school buildings until 1960s. His prefabrication system nearly halved the construction costs for the schools.

The Khmer Rouge, however, didn't believe in education. The regime closed down schools and universities, murdered teachers and intellectuals, and transformed what were once places of hope into places of horror. Today the complex is open to the public as the Tuol Sleng Genocide Museum, and it is still a difficult place to bear.

Further reading:
Chandler, David P., *Voices from S-21: Terror and History in Pol Pot's Secret Prison.*

Black Shophouse

16E Street 368
Architect unknown
2014

109 E

The Loft

54 Street 390
Din Somethearith
2017

110 E

When you walk through the streets of Phnom Penh, it sooner or later becomes clear that many of the shophouses in the city have undergone a radical spatial transformation over the years. What we call the Black Shophouse, on Street 368, is an exceptional example. It is the last unit on a row of nondescript two-storey shophouses that probably date from the late 1990s. It has clearly undergone a complete transformation. New balconies have been cut into the middle section. In addition, the right half of the building has been torn down. A black steel construction has taken its place, now featuring an open staircase that leads to an additional floor. This unusual spatial arrangement is accentuated by the reduced geometry of the new components and their dark paintwork. Meanwhile, the remaining balcony slabs, which now protrude, somewhat unsupported, away from the façade, have retained their stucco coating.

This small apartment building is located in one of the rapidly developing areas in Phnom Penh's Boeng Keng Kang 3 district. The architect Din Somethearith was one of the founders of the Frangipani Hotel Group. In the 2000s, he recognised the potential of the many 1960s villas remaining in the city, and introduced a reappreciation of those villas by converting them into small boutique hotels.

The present building was originally one of the city's typical narrow shophouses, measuring just over four metres in width. The architect added a third floor, and inserted several loft-like apartments inside to be leased. Each unit has a spacious balcony, a high ceiling, and a gallery level in the form of a suspended steel construction. Din Somethearith also opted for perforated metal panels and wooden screens instead of the more commonly used concrete brise-soleils. The apartments and the small roof garden are accessed via arcades and an external staircase.

E

Vann Molyvann's House
107 Mao Tse Toung Boulevard
Vann Molyvann
1968

It took over ten years after Vann Molyvann returned from his studies in Paris before he could afford to build this house. As a civil servant, he received only a modest salary from the state, which he had to use to support his wife and six children. It wasn't until he received a private commission to build a brewery in Sihanoukville that he had enough money to buy the 1,000 m² plot and start planning. But the family could not enjoy living together in this house for long. Shortly after the fall of Norodom Sihanouk in 1970, the family decided to leave the country. In 1991, they returned to their home, where they lived until they moved to Siem Reap in 2014.

The building's main structure was built in reinforced concrete. The ground floor used to house the architect's private studio. The two upper floors, standing on a square platform rotated by 45 degrees, were reserved for his family. Like with many of Vann Molyvann's buildings, the composition of this house is based on Le Corbusier's Modulor system. The basic square measures 18.3 x 18.3 m, and the inner square measures 12.94 x 12.94 m. The complex interior, with its staggered levels, is barely visible through the building's brick-clad façade. But on closer inspection, you can make out an offset in the looming ceilings, a discreetly protruding balcony, and a slight recess in the façade. The most striking feature of this house is the roof. The double-shell construction takes the form of a parabolic hyperboloid. It was inspired both by the vernacular Brazilian architecture that Vann Molyvann explored for his diploma thesis as well as by the formally experimental buildings of the 1950s and 1960s such as the Philips Pavilion by Iannis Xenakis. The whole house, and in particular the roof, was the product of a great experiment. Vann Molyvann enlisted the help of his 26-year-old brother-in-law, Walter Amberg, who had recently qualified as an engineer, to carry out the calculations required for the construction. The exuberant composition of the façade and the complexity of the interior make it clear that Vann Molyvann was far from being a minimalist. It is often claimed that Vann Molyvann's works, and New Khmer Architecture in general, are directly connected to European modernism or to Germany's Bauhaus movement. Yet this house makes such views highly questionable. Indeed, such views represent a post-colonial perpetuation of Eurocentric modes of interpretation, which hardly do justice to the uniqueness of this architectural work and its manifold references.

Coupled Villas

Street 123, between
Streets 410 and 420
Asma Architects
2017 / 2018

 112 E

Today, most clients who commission such a large private residence as this one in Phnom Penh are seeking a home with an ostentatious exterior that reflects the financial means of the owners. But this generous house, which is actually two houses linked by an open corridor on the first floor, is different. Although the volume itself is quite impressive, the exterior completely renounces the usual eclectic mixture of architectural decorations that characterise most new upper-class residences. The building, with its unobtrusive and almost enigmatic façades, does not reveal its interior easily. It is composed of white cubes that are playfully interlaced with large screens made of dark-grey concrete. From the street, you can only catch a glimpse of the glass elements and plants hidden behind the perforated walls. It is the playful arrangement of volumes, the skilful use of light and shading, and the elements of tropical building that make this ensemble worth seeing. The two houses face one another and are separated by a garden behind high walls. The living rooms are arranged on the ground floor and first floor, while the upper floors are more private, with bedrooms, ensuites, and dressing rooms. A small roof garden is situated at the top.

E

Kinin Collective
24 Street 123
Thim Sophal
2018

113 E

Kinin is a charming gastronomy project run by a young collective of Cambodians and expats. It is located in the Tuol Tom Poung district, near the Russian Market. The building, renovated in 2018, is a pre-war vernacular wooden house, located in the back of a leafy courtyard that, in the words of architect Thim Sophal, 'tries to marry nature and a living space – something we tend to forget when we live in a city such as Phnom Penh'. Just 15 to 20 years ago, many of the buildings lining the streets of Tuol Tom Poung and the BKK2 and BKK3 districts would have been traditional wooden houses just like the one here. But today, you need to look around quite persistently to find the few that remain, which are sometimes hidden behind roadside constructions and newly added concrete façades.

Thim Sophal graduated from the Royal University of Fine Arts. He worked at local architecture firm HKA (see **Brown Café TTP 114 E**) for several years before becoming self-employed. The ground floor of the traditional wooden house and the tropical garden oasis in front accommodate three different businesses: fusion restaurant Khumbhaka, cocktail bar Yemayâ, and wine store Prasada Sora. During the construction process, the architect tried his best to only reuse and repurpose the found materials on site and resources from other demolished buildings. Situated in a rather quiet side street, Kinin is a wonderful pocket-sized oasis that is pleasing both to the eye and to the palate.

Brown Café TTP
175 Street 155
Hok Kang Architects
2017

114 E

Brown TTP is one of the 19 branches of Brown, a Cambodian café chain, which are spread across Phnom Penh and Siem Reap. It is located in Tuol Tom Poung, one of Phnom Penh's trendy neighbourhoods. All branches are housed in a building with an affectionate design. Some branches are in a new building, such as Brown TTP and the **Brown Roastery Toul Kork** (123 F), while others are in a repurposed building such as the former **Bureaux des Messageries Fluviales** (006 A).

The Brown TTP branch, like all branches of the chain, was designed by Hok Kang, one of Brown's founders. The double façade, with exterior wall screens made of simple concrete blocks, displays architectural elements drawn from the New Khmer Architecture of the 1960s which can still be found everywhere in Phnom Penh. The folded concrete roof can also be interpreted as a reference to the many buildings from that time, of which this particular roof shape came to be seen as a kind of signature feature. The interior is dominated by wood and exposed concrete. One can also see effective use of polished steel, for example in the carefully crafted workbench-like table on the upper floor. The Cambodian artist and architect Sothea Thang created a remarkable wall installation on the first floor. It depicts a giant tree branch created from natural hemp rope and iron. The artist explains his work as follows:

'The branch consists of several parts, each one crafted uniquely so that no single leaf or fruit is like any other. I paid particular attention to the ties that bind fruit and leaves to their branch. I modelled the fruit, leaves, and main branch after their real forms found in nature, but at a giant scale. I used materials that have become a kind of signature for me: natural hemp rope and iron. The work's accuracy and realism contrast with the fantastical feelings that its scale and materials evoke.'

Sothea Thang has now collaborated with Hok Kang for many years and also has a series of successful exhibitions to his name. He is also a co-owner of the tiny but beautiful **TINI Café**, located not far away at No. 57, Street 450, which he also designed himself.

E

Java Creative Café TTP

53 Street 468
T3 Architects
2018

115 E

Dana Langlois came to Phnom Penh in 1998, where she soon became engaged in the local art scene. In 2000, she opened the Java Creative Café, a café and community art space, on the first floor of an old colonial building on Sihanouk Boulevard. The café's verandah, overlooking the public gardens, is still one of the most relaxed places in the city. Since 2000, Dana Langlois has been actively curating, researching, and producing hundreds of exhibitions, and supporting new artists by showing their work at the Java Café gallery. In 2008, she founded Our City Festival. The event, which took place every year until 2014, brought together creatives from Cambodian cities to discuss the influence of urbanism on contemporary culture. Today, the Java Creative Café has three locations, the latest of which opened in Tuol Tom Poung in 2018. The new café-cum-event space sets new architectural standards as well. Designed by the architecture firm T3, the café is housed below the metal roof of a former warehouse. Underneath the roof, the rooms of the café are stacked on top of one another like toy blocks. The architecture of the space incorporates bio-climatic design principles. It limits the use of air conditioning and instead relies more on ceiling fans and natural ventilation. As such, the design makes the building both comfortable and energy efficient. Above the building, the architects placed an additional layer of cement boards over the existing metal panels to create a double ventilated roof. The building's airy layout and its open courtyard in the back enhance the natural ventilation. The use of natural materials, such as wood, balances out the industrial character of the building. The architects used second-hand hardwood to avoid contributing to the deforestation of Southeast Asia. A tiny theatre with 54 seats is housed in a black box spanning the courtyard. It is used to host concerts, readings, and regular performances of the two resident theatre groups: the Sophiline Arts Ensemble and Prumsodun Ok & Natyarasa, Cambodia's first gay dance company. Another Java Café, which also hosts exhibitions, can be found in the Toul Kork district.

Phnom Penh Cultural Centre (former Chenla Cinéma d'État)
Street 245 (Mao Tse Tung Blvd)
*Lu Ban Hap with Chhim Sun Fong
and the Service Municipal de
l'Urbanisme et de l'Habitat*
1969

116 E

Chenla Cinéma before renovation

Cambodia's former head of state Norodom Sihanouk was obsessed with film. He was involved in around 50 films as an actor, producer, or director. He also had a small movie theatre at his seat of government, in the Chamkar Mon compound, but he nevertheless approached Lu Ban Hap with the idea of building a small cinema for 20 people. The scope of the project grew larger with every meeting between the two figures, which eventually led to the inauguration of a stately movie theatre with 800 seats. The construction cost around four million Riehls, around ten times the originally planned amount. The cinema has an almost brutalist form and comprises a relatively small stage and orchestra, as it was mainly intended for film screenings. The exterior is even more monumental: two huge pylons made of concrete support a crossbeam. Suspended on this crossbeam is a large cantilevered steel roof.

The State Cinema was opened on 14 November 1969, when it was used to host the second Festival International du Film Phnom Penh. As he had done the previous year, Sihanouk used the festival, chaired by Vann Molyvann, to present his own films. He had already been awarded the main prize of the festival in 1968, for which he received a large golden Apsara figure. In 1969, he was also given the award for his latest film, *Crepuscule*, in a special category created for him as the sole participant. The film's presentation came at a time when Sihanouk's excessive filmmaking was causing ever-more concern both among Phnom Penh's elite and broader public. In 1966, he had presented his first feature film, *Apsara*. He shot a total of nine films until 1969, for which he wrote the screenplays and regular performed as an actor. This was an astonishing body of work for the head of state of a country embroiled in internal conflicts and stricken by global political events. In January 1970, Norodom Sihanouk left Cambodia, and he was shortly thereafter deposed as head of state. The cinema lay abandoned until it was renovated in 2002 with funds from the Canadia Bank.

Khmer-Soviet Friendship Hospital

Street 271
Guiprazdrav Institute /
Ms. Gordienko and Ms. Erchov
(full names unknown)
1960

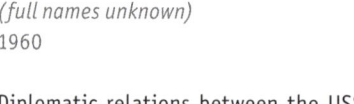

117 E

Diplomatic relations between the USSR and Cambodia were established in 1956. In the following years, Cambodia received substantial support from the Soviet Union. Cambodia was one of 16 countries in Asia and Africa selected by the USSR to promote 'non-capitalist development'. The aim of the Soviets was to promote poorer countries without necessarily carrying out a radical socialist revolution. For this purpose, foreigners were invited to the USSR for training and further education. Moreover, training institutions were established, and

The aerial view shows the huge meandering hospital complex in the 1960s

medical and technological development was promoted abroad. The Khmer-Soviet Friendship Hospital was a gift from the Soviet Union to the people of Cambodia and the first of two major construction projects financed by the USSR after Cambodian independence. In 1956, while on a state visit to the Soviet Union, the then head of state Norodom Sihanouk signed an agreement on the construction of a hospital with Soviet funds, which was later supplemented by an agreement on medical equipment.

The Khmer-Soviet Friendship Hospital was inaugurated on 29 August 1960. It was, at the time, the largest hospital in Southeast Asia. The Soviet investment was highly welcome in Cambodia, as the young nation urgently needed to develop its healthcare system. In 1955, as Norodom Sihanouk explained in his opening speech, there were only nine Cambodian doctors. By 1960, there were 24 of them, and 41 more had just completed their training in France. Overall, the budget for healthcare almost quadrupled between 1955 and 1960, and this trend, which was also reflected in the number of healthcare buildings, continued. From 1955 to 1969, the number of hospitals and district clinics rose from 16 to 69, and the number of commune dispensaries also rose, from 103 to 587. Last but not least, the country began its own pharmaceutical production in 1963.

In the early years of its operation, the hospital had nine Soviet doctors and one Soviet pharmacist who supported the Cambodian workforce. The hospital quickly became known for its expertise in radiology, radiotherapy, pulmonology, and surgery, and it also published a medical journal between 1961 and 1971. During the Khmer Rouge era, it was the main hospital for higher party functionaries and the military. At present, the hospital has around 600 beds and 1,000 staff members and is financed by the government, user fees, health insurance policies, and the health voucher system under the Health Equity Fund designed for the poor. Nearly half of all the patients visiting the hospital each year are impoverished and receive health services free of charge. Each year, the hospital

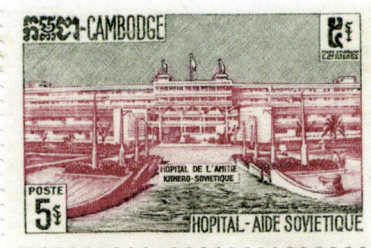

uses around 20 to 30 per cent of its revenue to subsidise care for its patients.

The hospital itself consists of a massive five-storey main building, which is set back from the road, and a series of pavilion-like bed wings with two floors. These structures are arranged on a spacious site located just inside the curved dyke road surrounding the inner city. The portal, with its undulating roof, has almost become a landmark on the way to the main building. The staircases to the left and right of the gate are clad with elegant, vaulted walls. These walls are playfully pierced with circular and rectangular openings.

In 2015, King Norodom Sihamoni and his mother, Queen-Mother Norodom Monineath Sihanouk, inaugurated the Preah Sihanouk Raja Geriatric Center on the hospital grounds to the right of the main entrance.

E

Pen Sereypagna
Architect
Director of the Vann Molyvann Project
Phnom Penh

Pen Sereypagna is the director of the Vann Molyvann Project and a freelance architect and urban researcher based in Phnom Penh. Pagna's works on the 'Genealogy of Urban Form Phnom Penh', the 'Genealogy of Bassac', and 'Phnom Penh Visions' have been the subject of several exhibitions and presentations in Cambodia and selected locations in Asia, Australia, and the US. He has contributed essays on urban transformation, with a focus on Phnom Penh, to books and journals such as: *Cité de l'Architecture & du Patrimoine* (2019), the National University of Singapore's *Urban Asias* (2018), Chulalongkorn University's *Nakhara* (2015), and *Parsons Journal* (2014).

What are the objectives of the Vann Molyvann Project?
The Vann Molyvann Project is carried out by an international team of architects and architectural students working in Phnom Penh. The aim of the project is to document the buildings of Vann Molyvann, Cambodia's foremost architect of the 1950s and 1960s. Our group includes participants from Cambodia, the United States, Russia, Australia, and New Zealand. The project started in June 2009. Over these past years, Cambodian and international students have worked together to measure and draw plans of Vann Molyvann's most important buildings. These extraordinary buildings are threatened by decay and development,

and Cambodia is losing them at an accelerating pace. In 2008, two of Vann's greatest works, the National Theatre and the Council of Ministers, were demolished. But demolition is not the only threat. Virtually all of Vann Molyvann's drawings were destroyed after he was forced to flee the country in 1971. As a result, no trace remains if a building is torn down. Our mission is thus threefold:
• To fill the gaps in historical records by surveying the remaining buildings and generating a database of drawings.
• To raise the profile of the work and improve the likelihood of its preservation through exhibitions and publications.
• To foster collaboration between Cambodian and foreign architects and students, connecting them to Vann Molyvann's works, which represent an extraordinary collection of Cambodia's modern heritage.

Why do you think the work of Vann Molyvann is still important today?
Vann Molyvann's works form one of the most important collections of postcolonial buildings in the developing world and are important for Cambodia's modern architectural heritage. Not only do his buildings demonstrate what sustainable architecture can look like in Cambodia's tropical climate, they also embody a kind of cultural engagement beyond architectural issues – an engagement that is related to human habits and

Cambodian tradition in general. His work is based on interdisciplinary knowledge and can be easily adapted by Cambodians for the future. As such, his work is also significant for the new generation of Cambodian architects.

Phnom Penh is changing its face again, as it did rapidly in the 1960s. What is your view on the city's contemporary urban development?
Phnom Penh's current urban development is not adequately planned for the long term. The development is based more on private interests than on the interests of the common good. Improper development forces people to live outside of the city due to high living costs, and there is a lack of public infrastructure, parks, sidewalks, and trees. Poor communities are not being integrated into the development. Instead, they are being driven out of the city in the name of beautification. In addition, most modern buildings have been demolished and replaced by contemporary commercial ones, and the city is losing its identity.

What makes Phnom Penh different from other cities in Southeast Asia?
Phnom Penh's order, architecture, and social and cultural lives in public spaces make the city different from others in Southeast Asia. The city's order refers to the urban grid layout – the system of blocks and streets in the city. The

architecture refers to the monumental, religious, and public buildings, and the distinct styles of the urban architecture in general. The activities on the streets and sidewalks and in public spaces are an expression of the culture of the people living in the city. All of this makes Phnom Penh unique.

What should architects visiting Phnom Penh pay particular attention to?
They should walk through the city and visit Cambodian vernacular and religious architecture, French colonial buildings, and works of modern architecture from the 1950s and 1960s. In addition, the activities on the streets and inside the urban blocks are also worth seeing.

What are your favourite buildings or places in the city, and why?
I like to walk through the urban blocks, to sit down and drink coffee while observing the local lifestyle in the city. There are a few places that are worth visiting, including the street café in front of the **National Museum** (073 C), and any street café shops inside the blocks or on the sidewalk around Kandal Market and the Old Market. My favourite buildings are the **National Sports Complex** (105 E), the **State Reception Hall** on the Chamkar Mon Compound, the **Institute for Foreign Languages** (121 F), and the **One Hundred Houses Project** (138 G), all of them designed by Vann Molyvann.

The Northwest

Interview: Antoine Meinnel

The urban axis along Russian Federation Boulevard was developed during the 1960s as part of the extension of Phnom Penh towards Pochentong Airport. The boulevard is lined with the newly independent country's institutions for higher education, among them the magnificent campus of the Royal University of Phnom Penh and the Institute of Foreign Languages by Vann Molyvann. Urbanisation of nearby Toul Kork started simultaneously in the 1960s. The booming district still has a couple of noteworthy 1960s structures as well as some interesting new architectures. A visit to the universities and Toul Kork can be easily combined with the northwestern outskirts (see Chapter G).

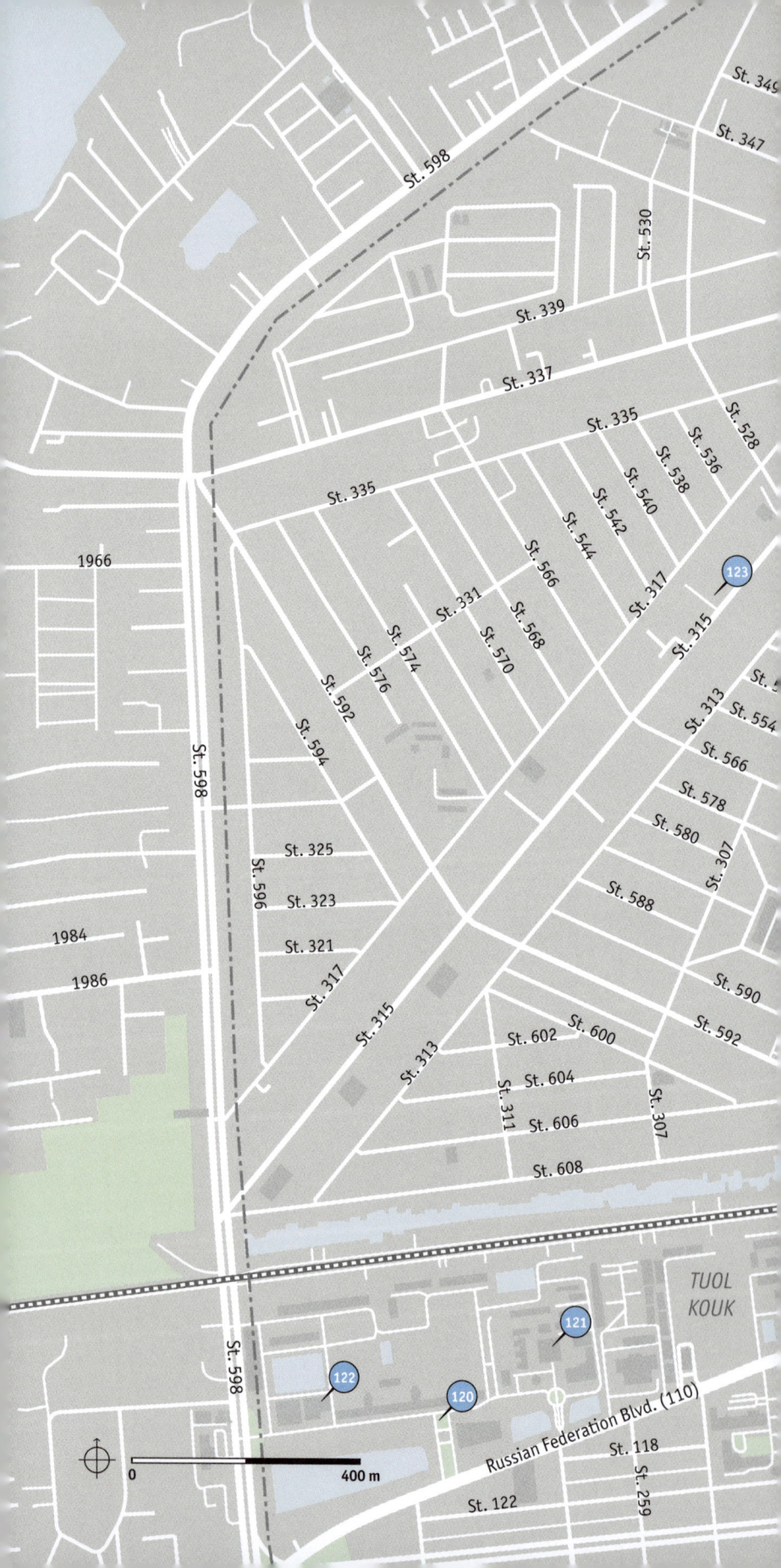

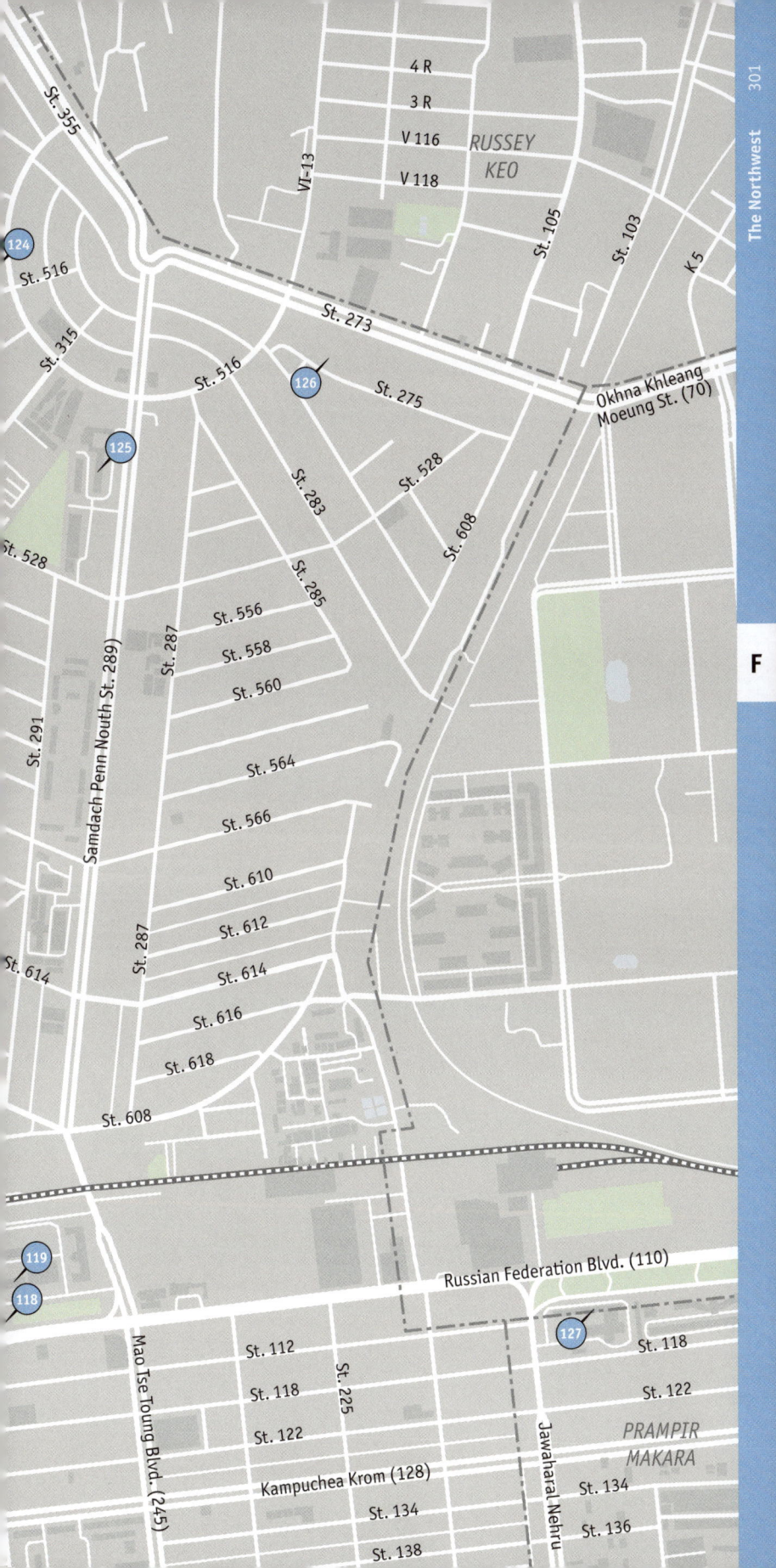

F

124

St. 355

St. 516

St. 315

St. 528

St. 291

St. 614

St. 608

Samdach Penn Nouth St. (289)

125

126

St. 516

St. 275

St. 273

St. 283

St. 285

St. 287

St. 556

St. 558

St. 560

St. 564

St. 566

St. 610

St. 612

St. 614

St. 616

St. 618

St. 287

St. 528

St. 608

4 R

3 R

V 116

V 118

RUSSEY KEO

VT-13

St. 105

St. 103

K 5

Okhna Khleang Moeung St. (70)

Mao Tse Toung Blvd. (245)

119

118

127

Russian Federation Blvd. (110)

St. 112

St. 118

St. 122

St. 225

Kampuchea Krom (128)

St. 134

St. 138

Jawaharal Nehru

St. 118

St. 122

St. 134

St. 136

PRAMPIR MAKARA

University Campus
Russian Federation Boulevard
Leroy & Mondet and others
1950s–1960s

 118 F

The development of the university campus was part of a massive educational programme launched by the then head of state Norodom Sihanouk after Cambodia's independence. Schools and universities were founded and built not only in Phnom Penh but everywhere across the country. Over 20 per cent of the annual government budget was invested in the expansion of the education system between 1955 and 1968. During these years, the number of pupils and students increased from 317,000 to 1,161,000, according to official figures. But the steady stream of university graduates also posed a problem, since the country's development did not keep pace with the development of the education system. The number of skilled jobs was still limited, and the lack of career opportunities led to growing dissatisfaction with Sihanouk's policies towards the end of the 1960s.

In the early 1950s, the architect duo Leroy & Mondet drew up the first version of the masterplan for the 45-hectare campus, situated between the railway line and Russian Federation Boulevard. This location was chosen in part in an effort to develop Phnom Penh towards the west. In the late 1950s, Vann Molyvann and Ung Krapum Phka, an engineer at the Ministry of Public Works, intervened to preserve around 25 per cent of the campus site as moats and basins. The campus was further developed over a period of 10 years, with the addition of new constructions. This led to an impressive

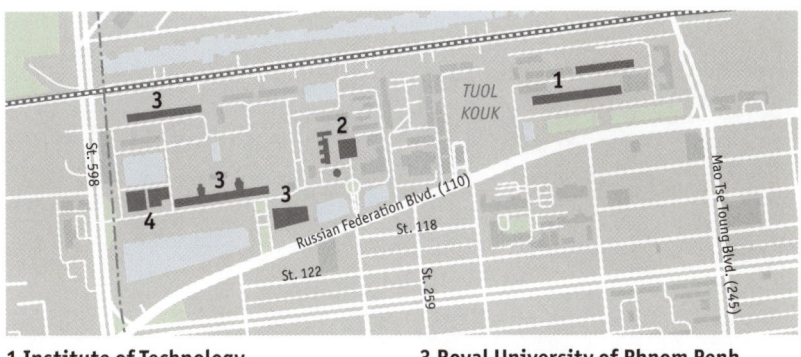

1 Institute of Technology
2 Institute for Foreign Languages

3 Royal University of Phnom Penh
4 Hun Sen Library

ensemble of buildings, loosely embedded in generous green spaces.

Many of the moats have since been filled in, despite the ecological benefits they offered, simply so that mediocre new buildings and car parks could be built in their place. Nevertheless, strolling around the campus makes for a wonderful experience. It is worth taking some time not only to explore the buildings, most of which are freely accessible, but also to sit down at one of the small coffee shops or restaurants and enjoy the relaxed student life pass by.

F

The buildings of the Royal University of Phnom Penh within the university campus, seen from one of the stairwells of Building A

University Campus: Institute of Technology of Cambodia (ITC)

119 F

Russian Federation Boulevard,
Campus of the Royal University
of Phnom Penh (RUPP)
Unknown Soviet architects
1964

The Institut Technique Supérieur de l'Amitié Khméro-Soviétique, today the Institute of Technology of Cambodia, was the second major project financed by the Soviet Union, after the donation of the **Khmer-Soviet Friendship Hospital** (117 E). In 1961, Norodom Sihanouk and Nikita Khruschchev signed a 'Khmer-Soviet technical and scientific cooperation agreement'. Three years later, on 20 September 1964, Norodom Sihanouk and representatives of the Soviet government certified the handover of the new university buildings. The new institute housed the departments of

architecture and civil engineering, electrical engineering, chemistry, textiles, geology and mining, and hydrology and agriculture on a 30,000 m² site. Administrative facilities, a swimming pool, and a sewage treatment plant were also part of the ensemble. In addition, two residential buildings with 28 apartments were built on a western part of the site. Until 1975, the Soviet Union financed the operations of the university, where up to 100 teachers from the Soviet Union trained Cambodian engineers. The Soviet Union once again began to provide funding in 1980, after the Soviet teachers had returned to their home country, and continued to do so until the dissolution of the USSR in 1991. The institute was used as a transition camp under the Khmer Rouge regime. From 1993 to 2004, the university was run with a French grant. During this time, it was renamed Institut de Technologie du Cambodge, with the name of the initial sponsor being erased. More buildings

The Institute of Technology in the 1960s

were built on the institute's premises in recent years, but none of them have the architectural quality of the original building. The two apartment buildings were demolished in 2006. The institute itself, like most university buildings on Russian Federation Boulevard, is set back from the street. It consists of two building blocks arranged slightly offset from each other and embedded in generous green spaces. Unless the security service denies access, it is worth going up the elegant stairs to the first floor through the open foyer, which is almost 1950s in its style. The rooms of the institute are cross-ventilated and accessed via corridors on the south side of the building. Screen walls along the building's southern side form an excellent buffer against the tropical sunlight and add to the elegant rhythm of the main façade. In particular, the public areas of the institute have the same cool lightness as the other tertiary educational facilities, such as Vann Molyvann's **Institute for Foreign Languages** (121 F), planned along the former Russian Federation Boulevard.

F

University Campus: Royal University of Phnom Penh (RUPP) (former Centre Universitaire du Sangkum Reastr Niyum)

120 F

Russian Federation Boulevard
Leroy & Mondet
1968

This remarkable ensemble was inaugurated as the Centre Universitaire du Sangkum Reastr Niyum in November 1968. It comprises three buildings: the main building (today Building A), two apartment buildings for teachers (Building B), and an auditorium. The ensemble also includes a swimming pool with a diving platform as well as tennis and basketball courts. The state-financed project cost an enormous sum, 210 million Riel, and its construction was a spectacular process. In the 1960s, when the trees on the site were little more than saplings, the university buildings formed an impressive entrance to the city along the Russian Federal Boulevard when coming from the airport. The enormous six-storey main building, which originally housed the Faculties of Arts, Science and Pharmacy, extends over a length of 200 m and has about 100 classrooms, a medical centre, and faculty rooms. The structure is elevated over its entire length on slender tapered pilotis. The small-scale façade is bordered by a huge concrete frame. Two towers with lecture halls are docked on the north side. The top floor forms a roof terrace of around 2,000 m² for open-air lessons. It seems impossible not to think of Le Corbusier's Unité d'Habitation in Marseille or his High Court Building in Chandigarh.

The ensemble, like many university buildings, ministries, and residential buildings of the 1960s, displays a wide range of tropical architectural elements: a double roof as a climate buffer against the harsh sunlight, deep arcades to shade the classrooms, cross-ventilation, and a building raised from the ground to allow air circulation. Though the buildings have been elaborately adapted to

F

the tropical climate, the classroom layouts are rather conventional. The auditorium reflects the technical possibilities that were available at the time. The building, which clearly alludes to Félix Candela's Bacardi Bottling Plant (1960) in Mexico, was designed to host events with up to 1,000 guests.

The parabolic geometry of the hall, however, makes it acoustically unsuitable for lectures or events, so it is seldom used. Nevertheless, extensive renovation measures have been carried out in the last few years, and so this beautiful building is in remarkably good condition. The residential building, with its original 30 apartments, is located along the northern perimeter of the compound and has also been carefully renovated. A number of other university buildings were added in recent years, but the new buildings do not tie in with the design qualities of the initial buildings, nor do they offer new perspectives for contemporary climate-friendly construction. Nevertheless, it is worth taking some time to stroll around, as the original urban vision of a green, landscaped campus can still be felt. Here and there small cafés and the large ponds provide pleasant opportunities for resting. It is worth going up one of the open stairwells of the main building to enjoy the spectacular view from the spacious roof terrace.

University Campus: Institute for Foreign Languages (former Teacher Training College)
Russian Federation Boulevard
Vann Molyvann
1972

Cambodia enjoyed only a short period of prosperity after attaining independence, and Vann Molyvann's productive phase in the country only lasted 14 years. In 1971, he fled to Switzerland, home of his wife Trudy, from the political situation in Cambodia, which was becoming increasingly complicated as a result of Lon Nol's coup d'état and seizure of power. Thus, the Teacher Training College, undoubtedly one of Vann Molyvann's masterpieces, was completed in his absence in

1972. The ensemble seems almost like an antithesis to the National Sports Complex, but shows equally clear references to European modernism as well as to Angkorian architecture.

The complex consists of three completely different components: a main building, a series of lecture halls, and a library. A small amphitheatre is placed on the north side of the main building.

Though the different components were each given an individual form based on their function, they are connected to one another through the use of the same materials – panels of red brick and reinforced concrete. The expressive, sculptural elaboration of the buildings and façades exemplifies Vann Molyvann's late, mature creative phase. A bridge flanked by *nagas*, snake-like creatures

originating from Hindu mythology, leads from Russian Federation Boulevard past water basins to the main building. All components of the complex are connected by this elevated path in the form of a ring. They are all raised from the ground, except for the library, which is placed directly in a water basin.

The main building contains the administrative office, accessed via a fantastic staircase, as well as seminar rooms, which are arranged around a huge atrium. Its shell has an exuberant, almost baroque composition of various elements: floor-to-floor wall panels, completely clad in red brick, almost seem to be floating, and they alternate with balconies and recessed windows. The roof, consisting of honeycomb-shaped tubes, gives the building an outline that directly contrasts with the towers of Angkor Wat, which dissolve upwards and become increasingly intricate towards the sky. The large surface of the roof, however, shades and thus cools the floors below, and the building shell thereby becomes a highly effective climate buffer. The building envelope is both aesthetically pleasing and well-adapted to the climate. The windows are set back deep behind concrete slats, and the cleverly designed roof is made of precast concrete elements, which protect against the sun while allowing pleasant light to shine in from above.

The small library appears somewhat bizarre. It is a circular building that seems to be very closely connected to the ground and whose shape, it is said, was modelled after a typical Cambodian farmer's hat.

The ensemble's third component entails the lecture halls, which are lined

up along one side of the bridge path like animals at the drinking trough. A stroll through the buildings reveals just how much careful adaptation to the climatic conditions can achieve. While the city's new shopping malls are often unbearably cold and lead to enormous consumption of energy, the rooms of the college are pleasantly cool without any air conditioning. This form of climate-adapted design indeed characterises many modernist buildings, particularly the works of Vann Molyvann. The Teacher Training College can be seen as an exemplary model for climate-adapted building in a tropical region – both in 1972 and today.

First floor

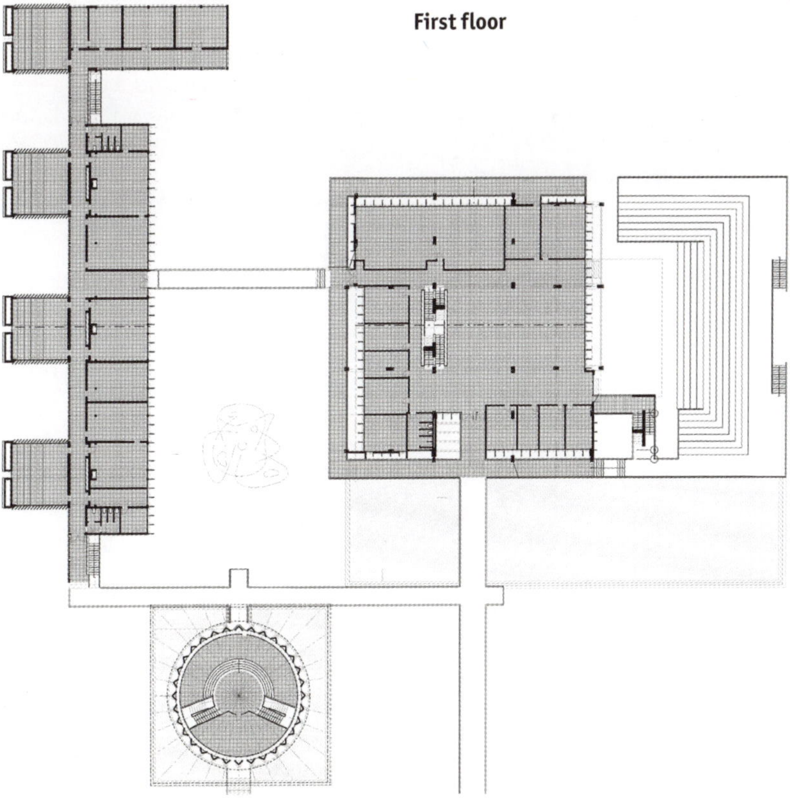

University Campus: Hun Sen Library and Extension

Russian Federation Boulevard
Mam Sophana/
Pyle Architects (Extension)
1997/2011 (Extension)

The library, together with its 2011 extension on the Royal University of Phnom Penh campus, is the largest in Cambodia. It was designed more as an academic library than a public one. With a floor area of around 4,100 m², it holds more than 100,000 books and offers 500 workstations. The building and its furnishings were financed by Prime Minister Hun Sen as well as by donors from Europe, the US, and Japan. Funding for the extension was provided by a World Bank grant as part of the Cambodia Education Sector Support Project. Mam Sophana's design for the library shares much in common with his projects from the 1960s and 1970s. Like he did with the **National Technical Training Institute (139 G)**, he gave the library monumental columns, which, however, are not as elegant as in the earlier building. Mam Sophana also made clever use of the height difference between the access road and the terrain. He ensured a certain amount of natural cooling by staggering the building, giving it a cantilevered roof, and keeping the basement open. The open basement can be used as a shaded workplace. Today, the building seems to be mainly used as an office space.

The extension building, by Pyle Architects, also represents successful adaptation to the tropical climate of Phnom Penh. The building is raised from the ground and has two levels: the entrance level and the upper level. These are connected by an elegant ramp, which ensures barrier-free access for trolleys and wheelchairs. The architects also added small work alcoves alongside the ramp, which traverses the entire building. The basement is, for the most part, kept free of fixtures; seating elements and informal workplaces are accommodated here. Architect Geoff Pyle, who ran his architecture studio in Phnom Penh from 2003 to 2011 and is now based in London, also founded Khmer Architecture Tours (see p. 160) in 2003. In an interview, he once explained his idea behind the building:
'The New Khmer Architecture of the 1960s represented a contemporary approach to design that considered the local culture and context. The design of the library aims to take a similar approach. It responds to the building site, to the climate, to the building methods, and particularly to the fact that students in Cambodia like to study both in groups and individually.'
The extension won the International Project of the Year Award by *Sustain* magazine in March 2012. It was also named winner of the International Property Awards 2013, in the 'Public Service Architecture Cambodia' category.

F

Brown Roastery Toul Kork

22–23 Street 315
Hok Kang Architects
2016

The history of the Brown café chain is a true Cambodian success story. At the end of the 2000s, good cafés and coffee were not easy to find in Phnom Penh. With its first branch, opened in 2010, Brown kicked off the invasion of more ambitiously designed cafés in the city. Nicely designed cafés opened everywhere in Phnom Penh, some of them obviously 'inspired' by the Brown cafés. Brown has steadily grown and now has 19 branches in Phnom Penh and Siem Reap. While the majority of the guests were expats in the early days, the ratio has reversed. The lion's share of the clientele seems to comprise younger Cambodians, some of whom spend hours with friends working or socialising in the cafés. Hok Kang, who co-founded the brand and is responsible for the design of all branches, sees Brown more as a public space than a purely commercial place. He is part of a young generation of Cambodian architects who studied abroad and returned to Cambodia to build up the country. After finishing secondary school in Singapore, Hok studied architecture and

entrepreneurship at Washington University. In 2009, he co-founded Brown Coffee Company together with his cousins. This also marked the launch of Hok Kang Architects, and the studio has designed all of the Brown cafés. In 2013 Hok founded Urbanland, 'Cambodia's award-winning boutique developer', which created a new kind of ambitious apartment tower, exemplified by the **Embassy Central** (**104 D**). Brown Roastery Toul Kork is Brown's second flagship store. The space is designed 'to be a modern interpretation of the traditional Khmer wooden country home, re-imagined as a gathering place', as the architect explains. The café has a sizable interior, along with a hipped, exposed-timber roof structure supported by concrete columns, all of which recall the barn typology. The glazed façade connects the interior with the surrounding greenery. Equally worth seeing is the small villa in the back of the property. Probably built in the 1960s, the former residential building now houses a flower shop. It has some wonderful 1960s features, including its quite unusual, irregular shape. Make sure to walk a few houses further to the southwest, to No. 35, Street 315, where you can see one of the few remaining 1960s villas by Mam Sophana.

F

Toul Kork Health Centre
22–23 Street 516
Architect unknown
1960s

The layout of Phnom Penh's Toul Kork district, one of the urban extension areas developed after the country's independence, is based on plans drawn during the time of the French Protectorate. However, the plan is not connected to the existing structure of the colonial city, with its uniform grid structure and urban axes. Rather, the plan forms its own system of fan-shaped boulevards and radial streets, a system that is only loosely connected to the surrounding urban fabric. The focal point of the plan was intended to be the building site for a new parliament building, designed by Vann Molyvann between 1958 and 1959 in collaboration with Japanese construction company Obayashi Corporation, as Masaaki Iwamoto recently discovered. But the project was shelved, and the original idea of a circular centre is no longer recognisable. Only a transmission mast marks what was once meant to become the centre of the district and of the country's political life.

The Toul Kork Health Centre is located on one of the radial streets. There are rumours that the villa was an early work by Vann Molyvann, though they have not yet been confirmed. The residence once belonged to one of Norodom Sihanouk's doctors, who was killed under the Khmer Rouge. Later, Vietnamese soldiers occupied the building, and in the 1980s, the Health Centre was opened, which today mainly serves garment workers and economically disadvantaged people. Some alterations have somewhat spoiled the appearance, but it is still worth looking inside during a walk through the area. The three-storey villa is accessed by an impressive staircase, which extends into an atrium with an interesting geometry. Many details are still preserved in their original condition. They thus give a good impression of what once must have been a stylish family home in the typical architectural style of the 1960s.

Police Headquarters Toul Kork
22–23 Street 289, between Streets 516 and 528
Vann Molyvann/Lu Ban Hap
1962/1967

Vann Molyvann's building for the police headquarters in Toul Kork, sometimes also called the Military Police Academy, is one of his lesser-known works. The huge building consists of a three-storey office building parallel to the street and a lower office tract built around a square inner courtyard with an attached auditorium. Lu Ban Hap designed an extension, which includes the bomb-shaped guard houses at the front. Though Lu Ban Hap originally proposed the two small structures as a joke, they were actually built, to his surprise. The police headquarters shows obvious similarities to Vann Molyvann's

Military Headquarters (127 F). As you can see in early photographs, most of the building was raised on pilotis, which kept the ground floor free of structures. Cantilevered corridors and large perforated screens shade the office spaces. There used to be a double-roof made of concrete half shells, which gave the building an appropriate top section and emphasised the three-tiered structure. However, it was replaced by a cheap tin structure in 2007.

F

Toul Kork Health Centre

Enfants du Mekong School

84 Street 275
Asma Architects
2009

126 **F**

This school, which belongs to the French organisation Enfants du Mékong, lies hidden in a small alleyway in the district of Toul Kork. The non-governmental organisation, founded in Laos in 1958, supports children who have no access to proper education. Today, it is active in Vietnam, Thailand, Laos, the Philippines, Myanmar, China, and Cambodia, where it arrived in 1991. The student centre in Phnom Penh has been set up to accommodate high school graduates aiming to study at university.

The school building itself is a successful example of cost-effective and climate-friendly design in an urban context. Two building tracts with classrooms, which are accessed via two stairwells and interior arcades, are arranged around an atrium. Like the traditional wooden houses in Cambodia, the building is placed on stilts. The open ground floor thus offers space for a dining room and a covered sports area. All classrooms are naturally lit and ventilated with ceiling fans. The entire building is wrapped in concrete slats, which protect against the sun and connect the two parts of the building. The side façades are further protected by climbing plants attached to the concrete slats by cables.

High Command Headquarters
Royal Cambodian Armed Forces
(former Ministry of Finance)

127 F

Jok Dimitrov Boulevard
Vann Molyvann
1967

It is not easy to get a view of this wonderful building, as it is surrounded by high walls. Things were different in the late 1960s, when the building was inaugurated as the Ministry of Finance, one of the new government buildings on Russian Federation Boulevard. Back then, the compound was surrounded by carefully maintained green spaces and enclosed only by a small fence. The ensemble originally consisted of an elevated two-storey wing facing the boulevard and a four-storey building behind it. Since then, the street-facing part has been extended, with two additional floors, and its design has been adapted to the rear building. The roof terraces have been enclosed to gain more office space. A transversal, five-storey wing, with almost the same design, has also been added. Despite all the alterations, the façade teaches several lessons on building in the tropics. The elevated construction enables air circulation; the cantilevered corridors shade the rooms; and floor-to-floor screens provide additional shading. Like in many of his other buildings, Vann Molyvann used the screens to introduce decorative elements, many of which resemble traditional motifs. Unlike many buildings of the New Khmer Architecture style, which have a folded roof, the former Ministry of Finance building has a wavy double-roof that shades the flat roof beneath. The fine detailing and the elegant, rhythmic structure of the façade made the building one of the most successful ones by the architect.

The Ministry of Finance in the 1960s

F

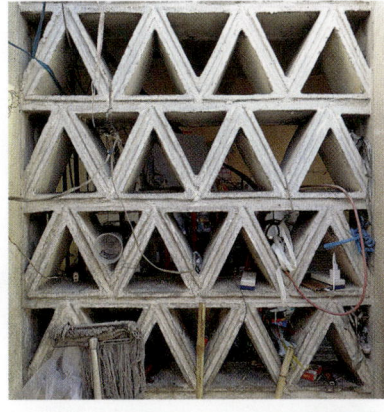

Antoine Meinnel
Architect, BLOOM Architecture

Antoine Meinnel studied architecture at the École Nationale Supérieure d'Architecture de Versailles, France. Son of a Khmer-French couple, he first came to Cambodia in 2011 on a family trip to find out more about the country and about his origins. For several years, he worked on a wide range of projects for prestigious architecture firms such as Herzog & de Meuron, OMA Office for Metropolitan Architecture, and Michel Desvigne Paysagiste. Antoine Meinnel then founded BLOOM Architecture together with Joko Tandijono in 2015. The duo seek to bring their experience to Cambodia and promote sustainable architecture. BLOOM is a boutique architecture studio based in Phnom Penh and Bangkok.

What is it that makes Phnom Penh special among other cities in Southeast Asia?
Phnom Penh is in a very unique situation at the moment. It is completely unpredictable. Phnom Penh's growth started later than in other capital cities in Southeast Asia such as Bangkok, Hanoi, Saigon, and Kuala Lumpur. But it has been catching up in the last couple of years – for the better and for the worse. The development is still very opportunistic and investment driven. It is at the same time very rough and very quick. It is fascinating to witness this change. No matter how small our role is, we are a part of it. Just two years ago, no experts could have predicted the way it is now, and today it is impossible to foresee how it will be in the next decade. We hope that developers will soon understand that it is in their own interest to think for the long term. They should consider quality public spaces, in part by studying the mistakes made in other capitals with very fast development.

You say your work is inspired by vernacular and New Khmer Architecture. What are the characteristics of these architectures and where do we find these in Phnom Penh?
Bloom's work is not directly inspired by the shapes or aesthetics of everyday Cambodian architecture or New Khmer Architecture, but more by the underlying concepts that lead to their production. Vernacular architecture and New Khmer Architecture responded to the Cambodian environment by adapting to its specific climate and culture. The works were the result of countless iterations and the trained application of western modern architectural concepts. We seek to work in that same spirit, but we acknowledge the gap between the glorious pre-Khmer Rouge era and the situation today. We believe that the production of exemplary and unique architecture requires an understanding of contemporary Cambodian behaviour and psyche. For instance, one cannot consider the advances of air conditioning and the comfort it brings to the domestic space without also considering the environmental crisis that the over-consumption of electricity can lead to. Bloom studies the urban fabric and tries to decipher the DNA behind each building. We think of buildings as cells,

each evolving from a previous one, with infinite variation. We try to define the correct design matrix for the future, one that can meet technical norms and raise the quality of the built environment. Khmer architecture is visible everywhere. Not only in masterpieces such as the Olympic Stadium or the temples and markets, but also in everyday architecture. It is expressed, for example, in the infinite variations of housing typologies around the market (which we see as the parallel to the infinite variations of the Hausmannian typology in Paris) as well as in the many typologies of wooden houses in the suburbs and the variations of colonial villas in the richer districts.

What challenges do you see for Phnom Penh's future development? And where do you see opportunities for positive development?
The first step to understanding Khmer architecture is to think about the reasons why the buildings were built the way they were. A society can be said to be mature when it produces its own vision, its own thinking. Architecture and art are the last step of that maturity. It is a beautiful thing to think that Cambodia is already at a point where it can produce a contemporary Khmer architecture. After all, we are talking about a country that lost almost everything during its recent dark times. The question is how long this Khmer architecture will need to take off, and whether it will be possible to avoid repeating the same mistakes that have

already been made – and solved – in other parts of the world. Our hope is that the new generation of Cambodian architects will be more exposed to global architecture, which can enrich their thinking. Yet they will need to maintain a critical mindset and use what they see only as a reference for their own creation.

What should architects visiting Phnom Penh pay particular attention to? What are your favourite buildings or places in the city, and why?
Architects visiting Phnom Penh should look at the passive design elements on buildings (such as louvres, shutters, overhangs, breeze blocks) that protect against the demanding Cambodian climate, especially the diluvial monsoon rains and the burning sun. These elements are used in many different interesting ways and often create a distinctive, strong aesthetic. I would recommend visiting the following places to understand what we call the DNA of Phnom Penh: the district around the **Central Market** (033 B) to see the typical housing block typology of Phnom Penh; the campus of the **Royal University of Phnom Penh** (118 F) to see the best examples of New Khmer Architecture still in use; the **Kantha Bopha Children's Hospital** (022 A) to see a contemporary building that clearly understands its context and function; and the **Factory** (141 G) to see a new kind of public space for the Cambodian youth made by preserving a former garment factory site.

F

Chrouy Changvar and the Outskirts

Interview: Tep Makathy

The peri-urban areas around the inner city of Phnom Penh, including the Chrouy Changvar peninsula across the Tonle Sap River, have undergone rapid development and transformation in recent years. The changes have entailed the conversion of former agricultural land into homogeneous residential communities and large-scale commercial developments. These urban-growth areas nevertheless have something to offer for architectural enthusiasts, from lesser-known modernist gems to interesting contemporary projects through to architectural masterpieces such as the 100 Houses by Vann Molyvann. For the Chrouy Changvar peninsula, allow half a day by bike or tuk-tuk, while the areas to the west can be combined with a tour of the Toul Kork district and the Royal University campus (see Chapter F).

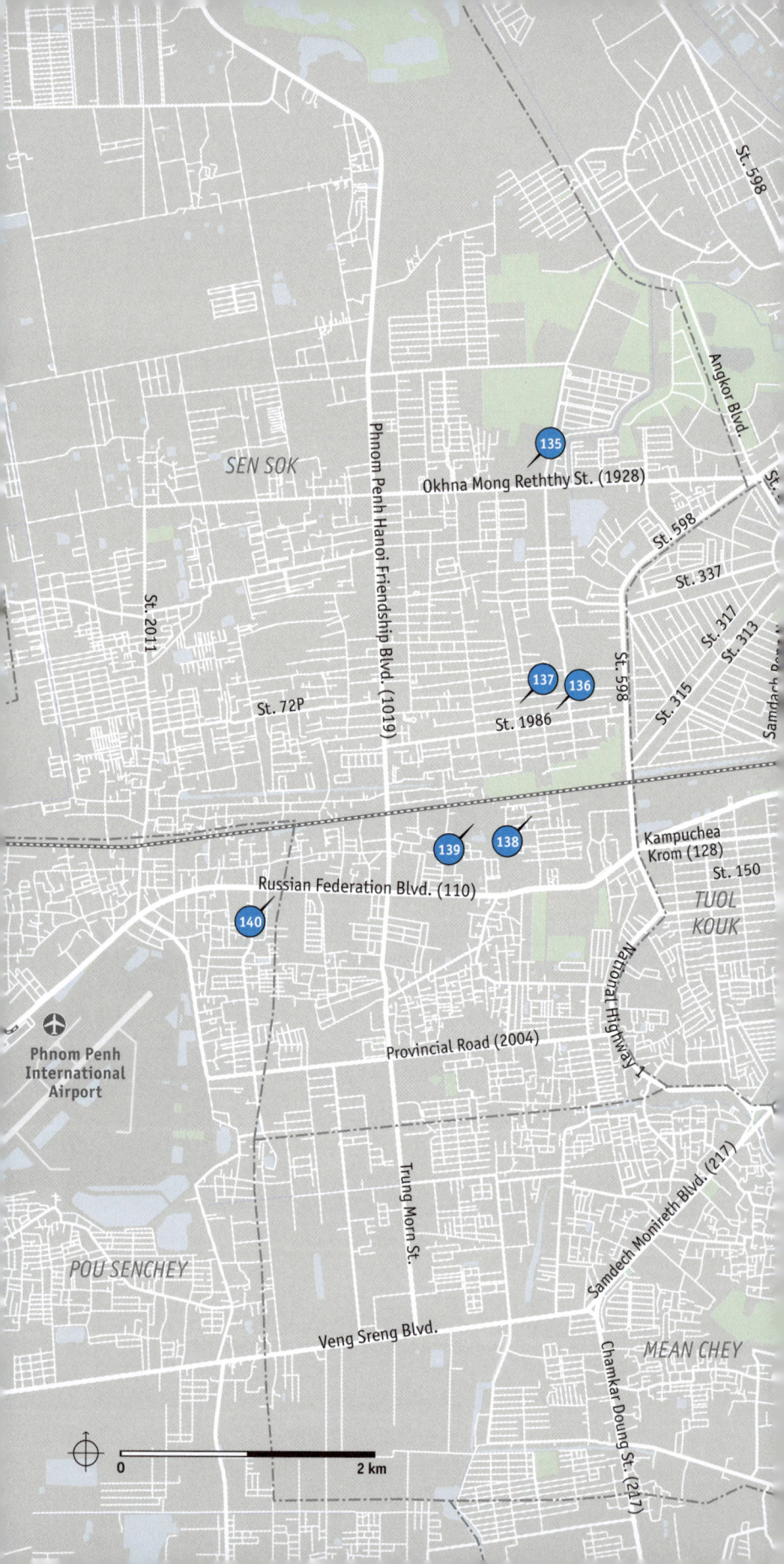

SEN SOK

St. 598

Angkor Blvd.

St.

135

Okhna Mong Reththy St. (1928)

St. 508

St. 337

St. 317

St. 313

St. 315

Samdech

Phnom Penh Hanoi Friendship Blvd. (1019)

St. 2011

St. 72P

137

136

St. 1986

St. 598

139

138

Russian Federation Blvd. (110)

Kampuchea Krom (128)

St. 150

TUOL KOUK

140

National Highway

Phnom Penh
International
Airport

Provincial Road (2004)

Trung Morn St.

Samdech Monireth Blvd. (217)

POU SENCHEY

Veng Sreng Blvd.

Chamkar Doung St. (217)

MEAN CHEY

0   2 km

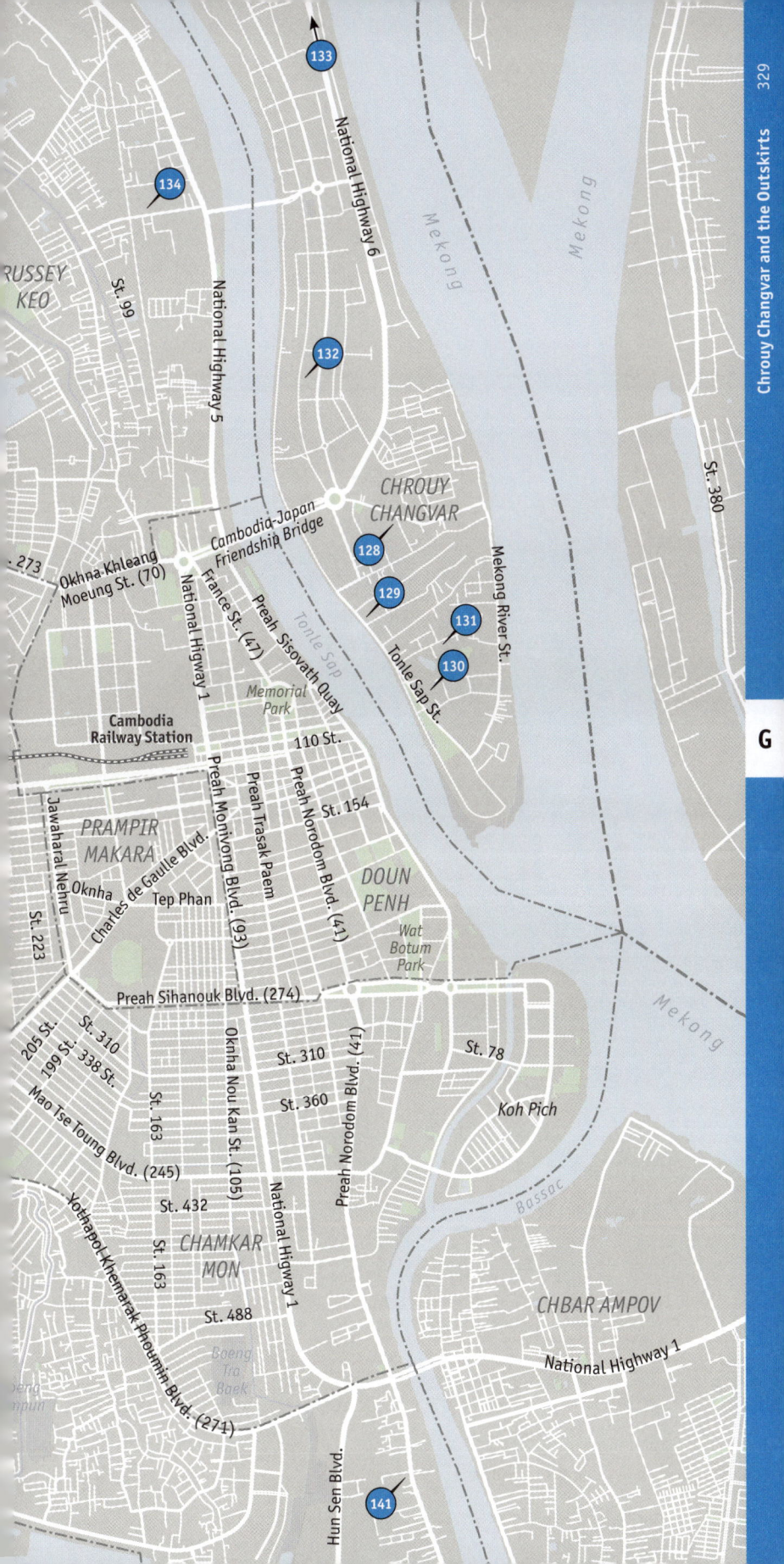

RUSSEY
KEO

St. 99

National Highway 5

National Highway 6

133

134

132

**CHROUY
CHANGVAR**

128

129

131

130

Mekong

Mekong

Mekong

St. 380

Cambodia-Japan
Friendship Bridge

Okhna-Khleang
Moeung St. (70)

.273

France St. (47)

National Highway 1

Preah Sisovath Quay

Tonle Sap

Mekong River St.

Tonle Sap St.

*Memorial
Park*

**Cambodia
Railway Station**

110 St.

Preah Monivong Blvd. (93)

Preah Trasak Paem

Preah Norodom Blvd. (41)

St. 154

Charles de Gaulle Blvd.

Oknha

Tep Phan

Jawaharal Nehru

St. 223

**PRAMPIR
MAKARA**

**DOUN
PENH**

*Wat
Botum
Park*

Preah Sihanouk Blvd. (274)

St. 310

205 St.

199 St.

338 St.

St. 163

Mao Tse Toung Blvd. (245)

Oknha Nou Kan St. (105)

St. 310

St. 360

Preah Norodom Blvd. (41)

St. 78

Koh Pich

Mekong

Bassac

St. 432

St. 163

Yothapol Khemarak Phoumin Blvd. (271)

**CHAMKAR
MON**

National Highway 1

St. 488

*Baeng
Tra
Baek*

Seng
mpun

Hun Sen Blvd.

141

CHBAR AMPOV

National Highway 1

Norton University
(Chrouy Changvar Campus)
Keo Chenda Boulevard
Lecturers of Architecture Faculty
2010

128 G

Norton University was the first private university in Cambodia, established in 1996 by Professor Chan Sok Khieng. Its city campus occupies the grounds of the former **École Miche** (047 B), and a new campus of Norton University was completed in 2010 near Chrouy Changvar Bridge. The bridge was first opened as the Sangkum Reastr Niyum Bridge on 15 March 1967. It traversed the Tonle Sap River in northern Phnom Penh and provided the city with direct access to the Chrouy Changvar peninsula for the first time. Built by a Japanese construction company and funded by the national budget, the bridge had a relatively short life. Explosions in October 1972 destroyed several spans, crippling access to and from the city for more than two decades. Prefabricated replacement spans from Japan were hoisted into place in the 1990s, which once more connected the city to the peninsula. Officially called Chrouy Changvar Bridge, it was given the moniker Japanese Bridge during the second inauguration in March 1994.

The university's five-storey flagship building has a floor space of almost 20,000 m². The ground floor houses offices and a library, while the upper floors house classrooms and laboratories. It is said that Chan Sok Khieng, the owner of Norton University, asked the architecture lecturers of the university to collaborate on the design. The architecture of the massive building tries to integrate elements of various styles. The central tower simulates the classical style of Preah Vihear, while the roof resembles the cloister of Angkor Wat. The main layout, with massive pilasters and cornices, recalls the styles of neo-classical temples. The rounded and glazed circulation cores of both wings round off the eclectic design. It seems obvious that combining various motifs, understood to characterise traditional Khmer architecture, took precedence over other aspects of design.

Bellevue Serviced Apartments 129 G

68–69 Tonle Sap Street
Ohira Tosimon / Arakawa
2010–2011

The Bellevue tower, inaugurated in 2011, was one of the first high-rise buildings on the Chrouy Changvar peninsula. It was constructed among humble residential homes and a school compound. The building footprint follows the L-shaped layout of the plot, perpendicular to the riverbank. Its volumes are divided into a rectilinear 10-storey tract (Block A) reaching out towards the river, and an almost square 17-storey tower (Block B) behind. Thanks to this arrangement, most apartments come with a panoramic view of the waterways and the city centre, while the lower building has a large communal roof garden overlooking the Tonle Sap River. On the building's façade, green vines cover much of the wraparound balconies, and plant containers and built-in irrigation systems are placed at an interval of six or ten metres. The building contains 147 spacious and contemporary furnished apartments, which are targeted principally at expats. There are various floor plans, from studios and one-bedroom units (62–95 m²), to two- and three-bedroom apartments (96–127 m² and 138–230 m² respectively).

At the time of its construction, the Bellevue tower was the first building in Phnom Penh with a partially green façade. Another pleasant feature is that the apartments are not only accessed via sterile, air-conditioned lobbies and corridors, but also via airy walkways. The floor plans are unusually well designed and clearly tailored to the needs of the target group. Each unit has its own spacious balcony. The ground floor of Bellevue Apartments has a gym, a children's playroom, a convenience store, and a swimming pool. With about 35,000 m² of usable space, the project was developed jointly between Oknha Ieng Sothera and Japanese investors.

G

Cham village on stilts along the banks of the Tonle Sap River

Cham Mosques

Alley off Tonle Sap Street/
Mekong River Street
Architects unknown
2012–2013

130 G

On Tonle Sap Street, around 150 m to the south of Wat Pothiyaram, there is an old gate and a small alley that lead to the **Masjide Deroesalam**. This is a mosque of the Muslim Cham community, which used to live in houses on stilts along the entire eastern bank of the Tonle Sap River. The Cham ethnic group first settled in Cambodia after the breakup of the Champa kingdom in today's central Vietnam. The people founded villages along the waterways, as their main livelihood was fishing. Here, regrettably, the old building from the 1930s was replaced by a new mosque in 2012. Another mosque, the **Masjide Arrahman**, is located on Mekong River Street. It was completed in 2013, with funding from Malaysia, and displays an international Islamic architectural style. The mosque stands on the site of a former 'Pagode Malaise', marked in the French map from the 1920s, which was levelled in 2012. The built religious heritage of the Cham in Cambodia is under eminent threat of being lost for good. In response, the Documentation Centre of Cambodia conducted a project between 2008 and 2012 to document the existing structures throughout the country.

Around the corner...

The **Chrouy Changvar Water Treatment Plant**, a work of colonial architecture, is situated further north on Mekong River Street. It stems from Phnom Penh's period of rapid modernisation and transformation in the late 19th century. Since 1895, water has been electrically pumped from the Mekong and sent to a filtration plant. From there, it is siphoned under the Tonle Sap River, and is transported through a 45-km network of pipes.

G

Former Pasteur Institute

131 G

Alley off Tonle Sap Street
Vann Molyvann
1965–1967

On Tonle Sap Street, if you turn into a nameless alley just before the Wat Pothiyaram pagoda, you will see on the right, after 500 m, a modern but dilapidated building that once housed the Institut Pasteur du Cambodge. The original Pasteur Institute was founded in France in 1887 by the chemist and microbiologist Louis Pasteur (1822–1895), famous for his work in pasteurisation and vaccines. Designed by Vann Molyvann, the building's history goes back to 1967, when it was constructed as a medical research facility on the site of a veterinary station. The institute was built in reinforced concrete, and its design was predominantly influenced by the extreme climate. The remaining building comprises two parts: a 60-m-long rectangular building tract, elevated on tapered square pilotis, with three floors; and an almost square tract,

with two floors, that is similarly raised from the ground. Open walkways connect the two tracts. Internal staircases on both ends of the central corridor also serve as lightwells, and a large atrium in the smaller building is illuminated by square ceiling lights. The double façade is designed to provide shading and cooling. The windows are recessed from the building's exterior concrete frame and further shielded from the weather by horizontal brise-soleils.

After the fall of the Khmer Rouge in 1979, the institute building was occupied by families returning from the countryside. It has been substantially modified by its occupants and is in a state of disrepair.

First floor

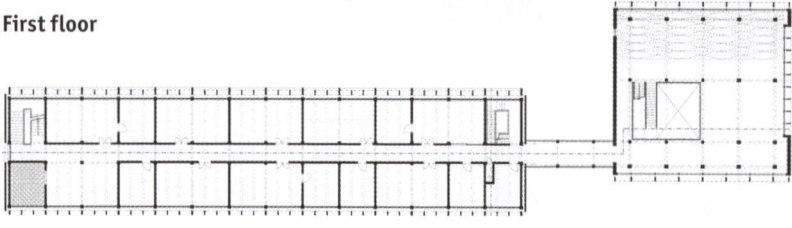

Former Roman Catholic Teaching Center

132 G

Boulevard north of Prohm Bayon
Roundabout
Henri Chatel
1966

G

In November 2017, Overseas Cambodian Investment Cooperation (OCIC), the developer behind the **Diamond Island (098 D)**, unveiled plans for its 'City of the Future' satellite city, in Chrouy Changvar, which will feature a commercial centre and mixed-use housing. Chrouy Changvar and the area along National Highway 6A have seen rapid development since the completion of the Chrouy Changvar Bridge, and most of the formerly quiet peninsula with its fishing villages and low-lying farmland has been completely transformed. Although these development areas today host a number of *boreys* (gated communities) and some entertainment facilities currently under construction, large tracts of land are still idle and are waiting for investment. If you take the new street leading north from the large roundabout at the east end of Chrouy Changvar Bridge, you will find on the left side, after around 800 m, a lonely building that stands out among the vast development sites. This is the former Roman Catholic Teaching Center, as it is named in the city

map from 1966. The 60-m-long rectilinear building was designed by Henri Chatel, the architect of the **Apartment Buildings for the National Bank of Cambodia (101 D)** and many other pioneering works in the 1950s and early 1960s. It was built for the seminary of the French Mission and was completed in 1966, some years after the architect had returned to France. The seminary was located right behind the Convent de la Presqu'île de Chroy Changvar (Convent of the Chrouy Changvar Peninsula). Jean-Claude Bouchut, a French Catholic missionary, was appointed Apostolic Vicar of Cambodia in 1902. In 1919, he founded the Carmelite convent Notre-Dame de l'Espérance on the east bank of the Tonle Sap River. The buildings of the convent were confiscated under the Khmer Rouge. Since the 1990s, the compound has been used as an orphanage operated by French NGO Association l'Eléphant Blanc. The old convent, with its cloister and church, braved the war and the passage of time, until the (new) owner of the compound completely levelled it in August 2018 to make room for the adjacent development frenzy. It thus seems like a miracle that the 1960s seminary building is still standing, among all this 'tabula rasa' urban development. The future will tell whether this modernist edifice can be preserved for future generations.

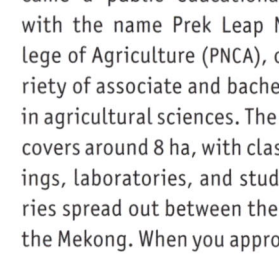

Prek Leap National College of Agriculture

National Highway 6A, ca. 6 km
north of Chrouy Changvar Bridge
Chinese architects
1998

133 G

Prek Leap National College of Agriculture (PNCA) is located somewhat outside the city, along National Highway 6A. An eccentric pylon greets the visitor at the main gate, with a signboard on the guardhouse reading: 'Prek Leap Agricultural School of Cambodia, aided by the Government of the People's Republic of China (partial facilities), May 1998.' The college was established as a research station for corn genetics in 1948 and became an agricultural training institute in 1951. In the 1960s, the institute developed a diploma programme in agricultural subjects with support from the US. The institute was closed in 1975, but

was reopened in 1984. In 2002, it became a public educational institution with the name Prek Leap National College of Agriculture (PNCA), offering a variety of associate and bachelor's degrees in agricultural sciences. The main campus covers around 8 ha, with classroom buildings, laboratories, and student dormitories spread out between the highway and the Mekong. When you approach the complex, the main buildings sit on the left side, perpendicular to the street. The group of three parallel buildings dates from the early 1990s and was probably designed by Chinese architects as part of the aid project. The three four-storey tracts further north were added in 2015. The buildings from the 1990s feature arched windows, semi-circular 'handles', and miniature hipped roofs, which create an almost playful appearance. However, behind the almost post-modern attitude lies a straightforward and climate-adapted design approach. The architects slightly raised the three wings, containing the classrooms, from the ground to protect the buildings against flooding. They placed the loggia-like corridors on the outside to accommodate the strong heat and torrential rainfalls during the monsoon season. It is worth further exploring the compound, as there is an interesting group of abandoned residential (duplex) houses located east of the classroom buildings. Next to the main entrance stands another administrative building from 1998, comprising two parallel wings connected by a joint staircase. The agricultural school is a fine example of tropical architecture in a style that is completely uncommon for Phnom Penh.

National Defense University 134 G

Street off National Highway 5,
opposite the OCIC Bridge
Dr. Lynn A. Emerson
1964–65

This somewhat remote building complex was completed in 1965 as part of a 'joint Cambodian-American aid project'. Originally designed to house the Faculté des Arts et Metiers (Faculty of Arts and Crafts) of the Royal Technical University, today it is used as a university for the Royal Cambodian Armed Forces. The project began in 1961, when Cambodia and the US signed an agreement to build a technical institute, dedicated to training engineers and technicians. The building was probably designed by Lynn Emerson, former assistant dean of the College of Engineering at Cornell University in New York, in collaboration with Cambodian technicians. In May 1965, the then head of state Norodom Sihanouk broke diplomatic ties with the US. As a result, only about half of the building was completed. The original design included eight 52-m-long structures, off-set from one another in a 'dancing' layout and connected at both ends by covered walkways. In 2017, an enormous Y-shaped building complex in the west of the compound was demolished. The four remaining wings containing the classrooms are in surprisingly good condition, having been renovated recently and painted in bright blue and white colours. Their façades, with loggia-like corridors and protruding brise-soleils, were designed to create shade and provide cooling. Expressive rounded external staircases, projecting from the western end of the buildings, add a formal dynamic to the composition. Its structural honesty and stylistic unity make this an exemplary public building complex from that period.

Borey developments in Phnom Penh Thmey

135 G

North of Street 1928 (Oknha Mong Rethy), Sen Sok District
Various architects
2010–2019

Several decades ago, Lon Nol's Khmer Republic government designated the commune of Phnom Penh Thmey ('New Phnom Penh') as a development zone. But its transformation only began to take place in the last few years, though at a rapid pace. Indeed, the (largely unplanned) urbanisation of Phnom Penh's periphery in general has been taking place at a breath-taking pace. In the early 2000s, real estate developers started to take an interest in this area and began to fill in the low-lying swampy land and Boeng Pumpeay lake. Just ten years later, municipal authorities relocated their offices to the commune, located in the Sen Sok district, and built major roads to access the large plots of land in the area. Local developers have built large-scale housing developments in the area to the north of Street 1928 (Oknha Mong Rethy Street) over the last decade. These include: the Peng Huoth Group's The Star Quateria and Star Emerald I (ca. 20 ha); the Chip Mong Group's The Park Land Sen Sok (ca. 20 ha); and the New World Group's La Sen Sok (ca. 25 ha). These developments represent

G

Streetscape inside borey The Star Emerald I

Entrance gate of borey The Park Land Sen Sok

a new type of neighbourhood, called *borey*. At first, they mainly comprised repetitive rows of shophouses or townhouses. But the range of housing typologies has recently become more diverse and now includes detached villas and semi-detached twin villas, often named 'King Villa' or 'Queen Villa'. Those in the growing upper-middle class still prefer to dwell in their own house rather than an apartment in a multi-storey tower, in part because of the increasing availability of other housing options and surging land and home prices. In present-day Phnom Penh, a *borey* is usually built by a local developer, mainly in a peripheral area, and it can be defined more or less as a 'gated community'. More than 100 *borey* developments have been built across Phnom Penh, and they are the real driving force of the city's urbanisation process. At the same time, the heightened activity in the land sector is intensifying urban sprawl and development of peri-central areas. The newly urbanised spaces in Phnom Penh's periphery appear to be increasingly fragmented. Each development is its own well-planned island – one that is poorly coordinated with its surroundings and with the city as a whole. This disjointed process, driven by massive private sector investments, rarely considers how the new developments will impact the city's infrastructure such as roads, public spaces, and drainage and wastewater systems. However, things may be about to change. More than 100,000 housing units have been completed (as of 2018), which means the market is running low on customers who can pay outright for a house.

G

As such, developers have started to target less affluent customers with tempting financing options. However, though property financing has become easier, a considerable amount of risk is built into the system. Financing options are coupled with high interest rates, and if buyers default on a payment to a developer, they can lose their home fairly quickly.

You can approach one of Phnom Penh Thmey's *boreys* from Street 1928. What is marketed as 'Cambodia's suburban future' announces itself with grand gateways. Yet the development's architecture and layout are so generic that it could be anywhere in the world, from California to suburban Shanghai. It contains pristine roads and driveways, manicured lawns, and quaint architectural clones, at best in a 'contemporary' style

and at worst wrapped in a mock-neoclassical façade. The construction quality of *boreys* is usually just average, due to the breakneck speed at which they are completed. Nevertheless, this suburban reality, as elsewhere in the world, is becoming a monument to a new mode of Cambodian middle-class living. It is likely that Phnom Penh's wealthy will continue to prefer to live in these gated communities, commuting to their jobs in the centre and requiring ever-greater infrastructural investments to accommodate the resulting flow of traffic.

Around the corner...
Once in the vicinity, have a look at nearby **Aeon Mall Sen Sok City**. Opened in 2018, this is the ultimate commercial complement to suburban living.

Villa For Four Families

5F Street 1982
Sambo Heang
2019

This impressive house was designed by architect Sambo Heang for her family. Born in 1990, she graduated from the Faculty of Architecture and Urbanism of the Royal University of Fine Arts in Phnom Penh. She then worked for Asma Architects from 2013 to 2016, when she became self-employed. The house shows clear influences from the architect's time working for Asma Architects.

The residential building is located a little outside the city centre in an area that is currently undergoing rapid urbanisation. It consists of a total of four units, each with a floor area of around 450 m², which are arranged into two separate structures. Each unit has its own living areas, kitchen, and bathrooms. However, they share a large garden between the two blocks, facing away from the street. According to Sambo Heang, the idea behind the house was to ensure that every single room receives enough light and ventilation – a seemingly self-evident requirement, though it is by no means standard in Phnom Penh. In order to give the street-facing balconies more privacy, she added plant tubs, climbing aids, and breeze blocks to the façade. These elements also protect against street noise, provide shading from sunlight, and ward off burglars.

Student Home Extension
554 Street 1982
Bloom Architecture
2018

137 G

Converting a nondescript building by adding one storey is certainly not a complex design task. However, this little project by Bloom Architecture shows that even small architectural interventions can be meaningful if carried out with sufficient care and empathy. The project was carried out for the French NGO Toutes à l'école. Founded by the former editorial director of *Marie Claire* magazine,

Tina Kittel, the organisation's mission is to provide girls living in the peri-urban areas of Phnom Penh with free education. Toutes à l'école runs various schools, a vocational training centre, as well as a health centre. The existing building was converted into a student house and extended by an additional storey to accommodate the common rooms as well as a kitchen. It was important for the architects to use inexpensive local materials and to ensure good craftsmanship. The extension is a modest volume with simple, rustic lime plaster, and bespoke wooden shutters.

One Hundred Houses

End of Street 10M
Vann Molyvann
1965

138 G

In 1965, around 100 detached houses were built for employees of the Cambodian National Bank on a 6.5 ha plot of land. They form an interesting contrast to the usual villas or apartment buildings of the 1960s. The present house has a floor area of 75 m². The columns, and the floors of the wet areas, were made with reinforced concrete; the walls were made with brick; and the floor of the living areas and the roof structure were made with wood. The house is raised above the ground and can be entered via two staircases. The floor plan allows the interior to be divided into rooms for male and female residents, as was the case in traditional Khmer dwellings. The rooms are equipped with floor-to-ceiling windows that enable better cross ventilation than in traditional houses. A military cap inspired the unique roof design, which allows air to flow freely through the house. Vann Molyvann once explained the project as follows:

'For the 100 houses project, I took the idea for those houses from the typical traditional Khmer house. But for the columns, I used cement so that the houses would last longer. When I made the moulds for the cement columns and posts, I used wooden boards so that the grain of the wood would be imprinted in the cement. This is one theory that I had studied. They taught us not to use architectural lies. If we used stone, then they should see stone. If we used cement, then they should see cement. I used a wooden mould and poured cement into it. What results is true to the nature of the two materials ... But in addition, there has to be 'fonctionalité': a building has to work and find a use, according to the habits and customs of the culture.' The experiment didn't find imitators. Today, most of the 100 houses have been altered or demolished.

First floor

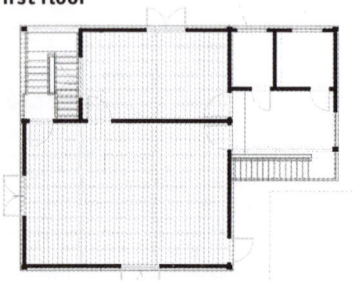

Section

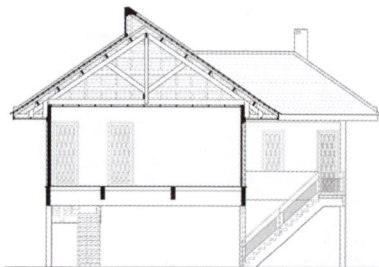

National Technical Training Institute

Russian Federation Boulevard
Mam Sophana
1969

The former Training Center for Electricité du Cambodge, or Preah Kossomak Centre, is one of the few remaining buildings designed by the architect Mam Sophana before his emigration to Singapore in 1974. Built on a plot of wetland during Phnom Penh's expansion towards Pochentong Airport in the 1960s, the building consists of several building blocks, beautifully embedded in a garden with lotus ponds and lush plants. The classrooms and offices are raised above the ground in a typical Khmer style, with the individual rooms being accessed via arcades. The impressive main façade gives the otherwise quite down-to-earth complex its distinctive character. It has 24 elegantly curved columns, an obvious reference to Oscar Niemeyer's Alvorada Palace (1958), the official residence of the president of Brazil, which are set in front of a finely articulated façade of deep brick pillars, plastered areas, and louvred doors. The cantilevered roof provides shade and cooling. The architect himself once said of his design:

'The columns are elegant and rhythmical, like dancers. This is like the Sangkum Reastr Niyum, representing the kingdom and its refined culture.'

He and his builders required nearly six months in order to create these columns. The then head of state Norodom Sihanouk himself inaugurated the building on 17 June 1969. The building then lay abandoned during the Khmer Rouge regime. After the war, it was used as a storehouse for Electricité du Cambodge, and in 1981, it was renovated with financial support from the Soviet Union. Later, the original flat roof, which is so important for the elegant lines of the building, was disfigured with the addition of an inappropriate tin roof.

G

Faculty of Social Sciences and Humanities

Faculty of Social Sciences and Humanities and Royal Academy of Cambodia (RUPP Campus II)

140 G

Russian Federation Boulevard
Trần Đức Nhuận, Nguyễn Văn Tiến, Đặng Kim Khôi, Nguyễn Thúc Hoàng, Nguyễn Tấn Vạn (Design Institute of Housing and Public Building, Ministry of Construction, Hanoi, Vietnam)
1990

Like the main campus of the **Royal University** (118 F), the smaller RUPP Campus II is located on the Russian Federation Boulevard, about 1 km further towards the airport. The ensemble is absolutely worth the trip.

Although Norodom Sihanouk's government vastly improved the country's educational system, all forms of schooling and university education came to a complete standstill under the Khmer Rouge. The motto was: 'Study is not important. What is important is work and revolution'. The consequences were devastating. Under the Khmer Rouge, 75 per cent of the country's university teachers and 96 per cent of the students were killed. Of the 21,000 secondary school teachers, only 3,000 survived. 90 per cent of the 5,270 primary schools, 146 secondary schools, and 9 colleges were destroyed. The reconstruction of the education system then began once more in the early 1980s under the Vietnamese occupation. From 1979 to 1989, a number of universities and technical educational institutions restarted their work using a mixture of teaching methods drawn from the Soviet Union, Vietnam, and other Eastern bloc countries. These countries also provided technical assistance, sending teachers and teaching materials, as the universities were attributed an important role in promoting socialism.

The institute, originally planned as the Cambodian Party School, was a gift from the Communist Party of Vietnam to the Kampuchean People's Revolutionary Party (KPRP). At the request of the KPRP, the Vietnamese government had decided to send architects and workers to Cambodia to build the institute. It was intended to teach Marxist-Leninist theories in accordance with the political agenda of the communist government and to show how society could be reorganised under the tenets of socialism. But that didn't happen: ten years after the invasion and victory over the Khmer Rouge, Vietnam withdrew from Cambodia, not only due to international pressure, but also due to its economic crisis and Moscow's refusal to continue funding the occupation. The buildings were handed over to Cambodia's Ministry of Education, and in 1994, the newly established Faculty of Social Sciences

opened here. Today, the buildings house the Departments of History and Sociology and the Royal Academy of Cambodia. The Research Centre of the Royal Academy of Cambodia is located in the former university dormitories; the former canteen is used as an office. At the time of writing, several other buildings were being erected in the rear of the campus.

The architecture of the institute reflects the design principles of the famous Angkorian temples, Cambodian vernacular architecture, and the New Khmer Architecture of the 1960s, but also, with a few years' delay, international design trends. Located on a 300 × 175 m plot of land, the main complex houses administrative offices, classrooms, two large lecture theatres for 100 people, and a large auditorium for 600 people. In addition, two four-storey buildings with dormitories for 300 people, a canteen with 300 seats, and a guest-house were constructed behind the main building. One enters the axially symmetric main complex via a generous central staircase crowned by a monumental roof, which alludes to both traditional Khmer roofs and buildings of the 1960s such as the **Hotel Cambodiana** (066 C). The classrooms, elevated above the ground, are grouped around two inner courtyards with large water basins and are accessed via open walkways. A bridge crossing the courtyards leads to the huge lecture hall complex at the back. The buildings are almost entirely made of reinforced concrete and masonry, although the black painted columns and beams simulate a wooden construction. It is also worth taking a look at the backside of the lecture hall and the former residential buildings located in the rear of the property.

G

The Factory

1159 National Road 2
Various architects
2018

Although The Factory is located a little outside the city centre of Phnom Penh, along the national highway to Ta Khmau, it is well worth a visit. In a city under constant transformation, where existing buildings are all too often demolished for quick gains, there are few projects that try to revitalise old industrial buildings. Therefore, it is quite surprising that on the 3.4-ha site of a former textile factory, a unique mixture of co-working and event spaces, traditional offices, gastronomy, an artistic hub, a skate park, and a wide range of other uses has been created since 2017. At the time of writing, not all of the 17 warehouse structures and eight smaller buildings on the site were ready for a new use. But Corbett Hix, lifestyle director at the young and ambitious developer Urban Living Solutions, has devised some impressive plans. He is responsible for the development and implementation of the concept. The plans entail the construction of a concert hall, a library, a building for artist-in-residence programmes, and much more.

Several architects are involved in the conversion. Bloom Architecture, the practice led by French-Khmer architect Antoine Meinnel, is responsible for the conversion of the large hall into co-working spaces. The architects retained as much of the shed roof's timber-and-steel structure as possible and used three local construction materials – cement tiles, concrete breeze blocks, and corrugated metal sheets – to emphasise the industrial style of the interior. Swiss architect Martin Aerne designed a multifunctional installation, for the hall's entrance area, that recalls the building's past as a textile factory. Atelier Cole, which has its office on the compound and also planned the conversion of the **Friends Futures Factory** (072 C), is responsible for the redesign of many outdoor spaces on the vast compound, which are to be given a cosiness and identity with furniture, seating groups, and textile sun sails. The Factory has hosted urban art festivals in the past, and walls all over the site display murals by local and international artists. It remains to be seen whether the concept will prevail at this location, as the competition is growing in Phnom Penh. Other providers of co-working spaces – which is by the way a fairly new concept in Cambodia – such as Impact Hub, Emerald Hub, Trybe, and Outpost, a Bali-based company, have also positioned themselves on the market. However, this wonderful project may only have a short lifespan anyway: according to the initial planning, the investments, including a return on investment of 10 to

G

20 per cent, should be recouped over five years. Then, the halls are to be demolished, and the entire site will be developed in several stages, as is already happening in the rear part of the site. Urban Village is a mixed-use development, designed by Harper Architects and Atelier Cole, that will provide over 4,000 apartments upon completion. The Factory would then have been little more than a clever instance of placemaking, but the unique concept at this exciting location is actually far too good for that. Phnom Penh needs far more than just upmarket apartments, designed mainly for a foreign clientele. It needs spaces where new concepts can be developed and tested, and where cultural activities can unfold.

Tep Makathy
Dean of School of Architecture and
Urban Planning, Pannasastra University
Cambodia (PUC); Founder of Cambodian
Institute for Urban Studies (CIUS)

Tep Makathy obtained his bachelor's degree in architecture at the Royal University of Fine Arts in Phnom Penh. He holds a master's degree in urban environmental management from the Asian Institute of Technology in Bangkok and a PhD in urban engineering from the Graduate School of Urban Engineering at the University of Tokyo. Makathy has worked on World Bank-financed infrastructure projects in Cambodia, Lao PDR, and Myanmar as an environmental safeguard specialist and was officially accredited by the World Bank Group in 2015. He has also been involved in developing important urban policies for Cambodia and GMS countries financed by the Asian Development Bank.

What makes Phnom Penh special among capitals in Southeast Asia?
Geographically, Phnom Penh is situated in the heart of Southeast Asia. The city was established in the 14th century on the 'four faces' (*Chaktomuk*), where four rivers meet in front of the Royal Palace, the centre of culture, politics, and trade. Cambodia has maintained a GDP growth of more than seven per cent over the last 10 years, with Phnom Penh as the major player in boosting the growth. During the 1960s, the city saw the development of the first modern Khmer architecture, introduced by architect Vann Molyvann, when several iconic structures such as the Olympic Stadium, public facilities, private villas, and housing were built. Most of the facilities are still in good shape today and remind young architects of the identity of Khmer architecture.

In 2018, Phnom Penh had 1.5 million registered residents and 2.5 million residents in a metropolitan area of 700 km². The administrative boundary has nearly doubled since 2004 to become an agglomeration area within a radius of 100 km surrounding Wat Phnom. The construction sector has seen rapid growth from 2016 onwards, primarily due to the contribution of China and other international investors. The city keeps on sprawling into the peri-urban areas and adjacent provinces, such as Kampong Speu, Kandal, and Takhmao City, primarily driven by road improvements and economic opportunities along the main axes.

What are the challenges for the future development of Phnom Penh?
Phnom Penh has developed a strategy for 2035. However, the plan is still vague. For instance, it presents future road networks and a classification of land use, but it does not guide and control density, building height, architectural aesthetics, and land use zoning at *Khan* (district) or *Sangkat* (subdistrict) levels. Several other sector-based plans – such as transport plans, wastewater treatment plans, solid-waste management plans – were developed with reliance on external resources.

Integration of sector-based infrastructure facilities is needed with a budget allocated for infrastructure improvement and development to cope with the growth. The city is vulnerable to rainwater flooding due to climate change and rapid urban development. Although parts of the current drainage system have been improved under the flood protection programme of the Japan International Cooperation Agency, it still largely remains ruined and dysfunctional. Existing water reservoirs and community water-retention elements such as ponds and canals have been gradually filled in for development. Human impact has led to even faster and more devastating consequences in the city. Strong enforcement of the laws and regulations is needed, especially regarding building height, building location, prevention of environmental pollution, and aesthetics. Phnom Penh needs its qualified planners, architects, environmental and social specialists, economists, and independent voices to help sharpen the future vision and make realistic plans to achieve sustainable development.

What is the role of the universities in urban development?
They are extremely important! But many people, including policy makers and even the universities themselves, are not aware of it. I have reached out to the World Bank and ADB, which are actively engaged in the urban agenda in Cambodia. PUC has stepped ahead: it incorporated urban sustainability courses in its revised curriculum and started implementing them in October 2017. Students and faculty members have been running summer schools and exchange programmes with universities in Southeast Asia, Europe, and the US since 2012. PUC plans to establish master's programmes in urban sustainability.

What should architects visiting Phnom Penh pay particular attention to?
One may look at the past achievements by the French such as the **Central Market** (033 B) and **Post Office** (004 A). Many of them face the threat of demolition and are being replaced by boxy glass-type buildings. I'd also recommend seeing the surviving works of modern Khmer architecture by Vann Molyvann, such as the former **Teacher Training College** (121 F) and the **Olympic Stadium** (105 E). It's a pity that the White Building is gone!

What are your favourite buildings or places in the city, and why?
I don't have preferences for specific buildings, but I have plenty of buildings that I don't like. For green space, I think Phnom Penh City Hall is doing a great job on Wat Phnom. I also like the public space along the riverside and onwards to the Independence Monument.

Index of buildings

Digits indicate the project number

Index of buildings

Digits indicate the project number

Bibliography

Atelier Parisien d'urbanisme (ed.), *Phnom Penh à l'aube de XXIe siècle* (Atelier Parisien d'urbanisme, 2003).

Atelier Parisien d'urbanisme (ed.), *Phnom Penh développement urbain et patrimoine* (Atelier Parisien d'urbanisme, 1997).

Becker, Elisabeth, *When the War Was Over* (Public Afffairs, 1986).

Blanchard, Michel, 'La disparition des fresques de Vat Chen Dâm Dek à Phnom Penh', in: *Arts Asiatiques*, 55, 1998.

Boswell, Steven, *King Norodom's Head* (Nias Press, 2016).

Brocheux, Pierre, and Henry, Daniel, *Indochina: An Ambiguous Colonization, 1858–1954* (University of California Press, 2009)

Chan, Vitharong, *Wat Phnom: Guide to Art & Architecture*, (Chan's Arts Edition, 2013).

Chandler, David P., *The Tragedy of Cambodian History* (Yale University Press, 1991).

Chandler, David P., *A History of Cambodia* (Westview Press, 1996).

Chandler, David P., *Brother Number One: A Political Biography of Pol Pot* (Westview Press, 1999).

Chandler, David P., *Voices from S-21. Terror and History in Pol Pot's Secret Prison* (University of California Press, 2000).

Clymer, Kenton, *Troubled Relations: The United States and Cambodia since 1870* (DeKalb: Northern Illinois University Press, 2007).

Coedes, Georges, *Articles sur le pays khmer* (Paris: EFEO, 1989)

Collins, Darryl, *Vann Molyvann: Situating the Work of Cambodia's Most Influential Architect* (Norton University, 2012)

Daravuth, Ly, and Muan, Ingrid, *Cultures of Independence*, (Reyum, 2003)

Delfosse, Thierry, *Saigon – Phnom Penh – Saigon: The Itinerary of Rene Nguyen Khac Scheou, a Modern Architect* (2019

Department of Conservation, The Ministry of the Royal Palace, *Preah Borom Reach Veang Chatomuk Mongkul: The Royal Palace* (2014)

Edwards, Penny, *Cambodge: The Cultivation of a Nation* (University of Hawaii Press, 2007)

Esposito, Adèle, and Fauveaud, Gabriel, 'The Atomization of Heritage Politics in Post-colonial Cities: The Case of Phnom Penh, Cambodia', in: *Environment and Planning C: Politics and Space*, Sage Journals 0(0) 2018

Filippi, Jean-Michel, *Strolling Around Phnom Penh* (KAM Editions, 2012).

Igout, Michel, *Phnom Penh Then and Now* (White Lotus, 1993).

Kolnberger, Thomas, *Zwischen Planung und spontaner Ordnung – Stadtentwicklung in Phnom Penh von 1860–2010* (Universität Wien, 2014).

L'Organisation des Nations Unies pour l'Éducation, la Science et la Culture, *Faculte de Genie Civil, Phnom-Penh: Rapport sur les Résultats du Projet, Conclusions et Recommandations* (1970)

Lamagat, Henri, *Souvenirs d'un vieux journaliste Indochinois*, (Hanoi: Imprimerie d'Extreme Orient, 1942)

Maugham, W. Somerset, *The Gentleman in the Parlour* (Penguin, 2001).

Mouhot, Henri, *Travels in the Central Parts of Indo-China: Siam, Cambodia, and Laos, during the Years 1858, 1859, and 1860* (Pacific Gates Press, 2016).

Muan, Ingrid, *Citing Angkor: The 'Cambodian Arts' in the Age of Restauration 1918–2000*. https://mccfulbrighthays2016.files.wordpress.com/2016/08/cambodian-arts-at-the-age-of-restoration-1918-200.pdf (15.03.2019)

Nelson, Roger, 'Locating the Domestic in Vann Molyvann's National Sports Complex', in: *ABE Journal* 11, 2017.

Osborne, Milton, *Before Kampuchea* (Orchid Press, 2004).

Osborne, Milton, *Phnom Penh: A Cultural History* (Oxford University Press, 2008)

Osborne, Milton, *Sihanouk: Prince of Light, Prince of darkness* (Silkworm Books, 1994).

Pierdet, Céline, *La cartographie de Phnom Penh depuis les années 1860: Bilan d'une recherche*, academia.edu/1117043/La_cartographie_de_Phnom_Penh_Cambodge_depuis_les_années_1860_bilan_d_une_recherche (01.04.2019).

Image Credits

Reeve, Paul, and Stuart-Fox, Martin, 'Symbolism in City Planning in Cambodia from Angkor to Phnom Penh', *Journal of the Siam Society*, vol. 99, 2011.

Ross, Helen Grant, and Collins, Darryl, *Building Cambodia: New Khmer Architecture 1953–1970* (The Key Publisher, 2006).

Ross, Russell R., *Cambodia: A Country Study* (1990)

Santini, Helen, 'Rebirth of the health-care system in Cambodia', *The Lancet Supplement*, vol 360, 2002.

Ser Sayana, So Farina, Eng Kok-Thay, *The Cham Identities Cambodia: Culture, Preservation and Education of the Cham* (Documentation Centre of Cambodia, 2011)

Uk, Someth, 'Phnom Penh and its Urban Growth', in: *Planification Information Housing*, no. 79, 1975

Yoshida, Nobuyuki/Iwamoto, Masaaki, 'Vann Molyvann', *Architecture and Urbanism*, no. 567, 2017.

Vann, Molyvann, *Modern Khmer Cities*, (Reyum, 2003).

Wright, Gwendolyn, *The Politics of French Colonial Urbanism* (The University of Chicago Press, 1991).

Yam, Sokly, and Ju, Seo Ryeung, 'Transformation of Shophouses in Phnom Penh, Cambodia: In the Aspect of Spatial Organization', *Fam. Environ. Res.* vol.54, no.1, February 2016: 13-26 (20.04.2019)

t=top
c=centre
b=bottom
l=left
r=right

All images by the authors, except:
Les archives de l'Aventure Peugeot Citroën DS: 93b, **Archives nationales d'outre-mer:** 83b, 38/39, 180b, 225b, **Asma Architects:** 227b, 240t, 240b, 259tl, **Atelier Parisien d'Urbanisme:** 121t, 127b, 128b, 199b, 215b, **bdv photography:** 84/85, 243, **Bloom:** 345t, 345b, 352b, 353b, **Bophana Audiovisual Resource Center/Paul Cummings:** 20/21, **Bophana Audiovisual Resource Center/Adolf Scherl Collection:** 293t, **Europe Asia, guide touristique et commercial, juin 1934:** 47b, **EFEO/Coedes:** 10, **Sambo Heang:** 344t, **Moritz Henning Collection:** 102b, 112, 139b, 168/169, 282, 279c, 295t, 306c, 308t, **Moritz Henning Collection/Historical postcards:** 11, 12, 13, 15t, 15b, 18, 19t, 19b, 32, 41b, 45t, 45b, 51b, 53t, 53b, 55b, 63b, 66b, 77b, 101, 126b, 154/155, 157t, 178b, 179b, 182b, 190t, 190b, 191t, 211b, **Stefanie Irmer:** 309t, **istockphoto:** 4, 6/7, **Hok Kang Architects:** 266, 267t, 267b, 291b, 316t, Library of Congress: 8/9, **Lu Ban Hap:** 187b, 188, 191b, **MAADS:** 86, 88b, 226t, 226b, 227t, 241t, 241b, 243b, **Mam Sophana:** 235t, 263b, **National Archives of Cambodia:** 14, 16, 182t, 227b, **National Archives of Cambodia, Charles Meyer Collection:** 17bl, 17br, 64/65t, 71b, 262c, 2810, 281, 283t, 283b, 294b, 307t, 336c, **Pinterest:** 137t, 184b, **Poum Measbandol:** 83t, **Raffles Le Royal:** 69t, 69b, **Roung Kon Project:** 137b, **Royal University of Fine Arts:** 321b, **Milena Schlösser:** 361tl, **Monika Täuber:** 361tr, **T3 Architects:** 292t, 292b, **Vann Molyvann Project:** 185c, 234b, 278b/279b, 313b, 336b, 346b, **Visa Sovannara:** 340, **wikimedia:** 61b

Acknowledgements

This book would not have been possible without the help of many people. Above all, the authors would like to express their deepest thanks to Din Somethearith and Chea Chanteborras from the Frangipani Hotel Group and Alexis de Suremain from MAADS, for believing in this project from the first day on, and for providing tremendous support in additional fundraising and logistics.

We would also like to express our gratitude to the many people who took the time to talk to us, share their expertise, and provide valuable insights. Ivan Tizianel, from Asma Architects, a great connoisseur of Phnom Penh, particularly encouraged us from the beginning, provided valuable feedback, and connected us with many other individuals. Hun Chansan, Hok Kang, Antoine Meinel, Pen Sereypagna, Hun Sokagna, Ester van der Laan, and Tep Makathy were always available for in-depth interviews and further questions. Many people helped us by providing valuable information about specific projects and topics, among them Phirun Noue, Loeung Sakona, David Cole, Martin Aerne, Seng Vannak, Sambo Heang, Thim Sophal, Sébastien Marot, Yvon Chalm, Dr. Denis Laurent, Dana Langlois, Willam-Norbert Munns, Vanessa Han, Corbett Hix, and Stefan Willimann. Poum Measbandol provided valuable help, answering some of our research-related questions about particular buildings.

Mr. Philippe Delanghe (UNESCO) and Ms. Men Chandevy (RUFA/Heritage Mission) deserve a special mention for their interest in this project and for their encouragement. Stefanie and Julien Sellon have been reliable friends, always interested in our work, even after leaving Cambodia. Som Songvasak has kindly helped with translating Khmer documents into English. Astrid Schulz was of invaluable assistance with her high-end Photoshop troubleshooting.

We would also like to thank the Atelier Parisien d'Urbanisme (APUR), the Archives Nationales d'Outre-Mer (ANOM) in Aix-en-Provence, the Bophana Audiovisual Resource Center (BARC), and the National Archives of Cambodia (NAC) in Phnom Penh for providing valuable information as well as historical photographs.

We are extremely thankful to the many corporate sponsors that were willing to provide additional funding for our project, namely: Jotun, Jumbo Gypsum, Botica, Phumi Phka Trokoun, Five Arc, Re-Edge Architecture and Design, HKA and Partners, Ray Building Group, Archi Cam, CamPain, the Build4People Project of the University of Hamburg, Tous Saphoeun, Yinkok, CBM, RS Residence, Zillennium, JM Asia, Lotus Green, Khmer 24, G.Gear, InBizNest, and Koki. A big thank you also to all the participants of our fundraising dinner.

And last but not least, a very special thanks goes to our publisher, Philipp Meuser at DOM publishers. With great patience, he has both accepted missed deadlines and allowed the book to end up being much more comprehensive than initially conceived.

The Authors

Moritz Henning is an architect, independent researcher, and writer based in Berlin, Germany. He studied at the Technische Universität Berlin and is a registered architect with the Berlin Chamber of Architects. Over the last 20 years, he has worked as a freelance project manager for a number of Berlin-based architectural firms on a wide range of projects, such as schools, hotels, and office buildings. Moritz Henning also develops symposia, workshops, discussions, books, and magazines and writes for architectural journals such as *Bauwelt*, *Modulor*, and *dbz*. He is particularly interested in the legacy of post-independence architecture in Cambodia. Since his first visit to the country in 2007, he has written numerous articles on Cambodia's post-colonial architecture and its planners, such as Vann Molyvann or Lu Ban Hap. Currently, he is one of the artistic directors of the international project Encounters with Southeast Asian Modernsim, which sheds light on the history, significance, and future of socially relevant design ideas of postcolonial modernism in Jakarta, Phnom Penh, Singapore, and Yangon. Moritz is a member of the board of stadtkultur international ev, which is dedicated to exchange between the major cities of the world. He is also a member of docomomo international and of Förderverein Baukultur.

Walter Koditek is an urban planner and urban development expert currently based in Hong Kong. After graduating from the Technische Universität Berlin, he worked as a chartered urban planner at urban consultancies on various design and planning tasks in German cities and regions. In 2000, he returned to academia as an assistant professor at the Brandenburg Technical University Cottbus, where he conceived and conducted design projects, seminars, and joint international studios in Europe and Asia. From 2007 to 2010, Walter lived in Cambodia to work as a technical advisor for urban planning in Battambang City, seconded by the German Development Service (DED). After three years in Cambodia and a four-year intermezzo working at the Ministry of Construction in Hanoi, Vietnam, Walter returned once more to Cambodia, where he worked as a freelance consultant for Gesellschaft für Internationale Zusammenarbeit (GIZ) from 2015 to 2016. He has conducted training sessions and provided support for land-use (master) planning and building regulations in several Cambodian provinces. He has also authored a handbook on municipal spatial planning in Cambodia. Walter Koditek has always been a strong advocate of cultural heritage conservation. In 2018 he published the photo book *Battambang Heritage*.

The *Deutsche Nationalbibliothek* lists this publication in the *Deutsche Nationalbibliografie;* detailed bibliographic data are available at http://dnb.d-nb.de abrufbar.

ISBN 978-3-86922-434-3

© 2020 by DOM publishers, Berlin
www.dom-publishers.com

Proofreading
Kyung Hun Oh

Design
Moritz Hening, Walter Koditek

Maps
Katrin Soschinski

QR-Codes
Christoph Gößmann

Printing
Tiger Printing (Hong Kong) Co., Ltd.
www.tigerprinting.hk